# KINGS
# WITHOUT
# THRONES

# KINGS WITHOUT THRONES

## European Monarchy
### in the Twentieth Century

*by* GEOFFREY BOCCA

THE DIAL PRESS 1959 NEW YORK

© 1959 by Geoffrey Bocca
Library of Congress Catalog Card Number: 59-9433

DESIGNED BY WILLIAM R. MEINHARDT
PRINTED IN THE UNITED STATES OF AMERICA
BY THE HADDON CRAFTSMEN, SCRANTON, PENNA.

# Contents

5

# *Illustrations*

7

10. And Samuel told all the words of the Lord unto the people that asked of him a king.

11. And he said. This will be the manner of the king that shall reign over you: He will take your sons, and appoint them for himself, for his chariots, and to be his horsemen; and some shall run before his chariots.

12. And he will appoint him captains over thousands, and captains over fifties; and will set them to ear his ground, and to reap his harvest, and to make his instruments of war, and instruments of his chariots.

13. And he will take your daughters to be confectionaries, and to be cooks and to be bakers.

14. And he will take your fields, and your vineyards, and your olive-yards, even the best of them, and give them to his servants.

15. And he will take the tenth of your seed, and of your vineyards, and give them to his officers, and to his servants.

16. And he will take your menservants, and your maidservants, and your goodliest young men, and your asses and put them to his work.

17. He will take the tenth of your sheep; and ye shall be his servants.

18. And ye shall cry out in that day because of your king which ye shall have chosen you; and the Lord will not hear you in that day.

19. Nevertheless the people refused to obey the voice of Samuel; and they said, Nay; but we will have a king over us;

20. That we also may be like all the nations; and that our king may judge us, and go out before us, and fight our battles.

21. And Samuel heard all the words of the people, and he rehearsed them in the ears of the LORD.

22. And the LORD said to Samuel, Hearken unto their voice, and make them a king.

—Samuel, Chapter 8.

# I

# *The Colony of Kings*

## Twilight or Dawn?

Old legitimate monarchies are everywhere declining and Demos stands ready to swallow them down its miry throat.

d'Annunzio.

*Il y a beaucoup de chomage dans mon metier—*

Albert I, King of the Belgians.

$\mathcal{M}$ay 20, 1910, marked the supreme moment of royal assembly in this century, and appropriately it assembled to honour a funeral. On that day an Emperor and eight Kings saw the coffin of Edward VII into the grave at Windsor. Beside the new King, George V, stood the Kaiser Wilhelm II of Germany, the "President of the princes' trade union." The Kings were Haakon VII of Norway, Frederick VIII of Denmark, Manoel II of Portugal, Alfonso XIII of Spain, George I of Greece, Ferdinand I of Bulgaria, and Albert I of Belgium. Also present were the Dowager Empress of Russia, (Marie Feodorovna, sister of Queen Alexandra of England); the Dowager Queen of Holland; the Crown Princes of Greece, Montenegro, Rumania and Serbia, and the Archduke Franz Ferdinand of Austria. Almost lost in this magnificent cortege were the delegates of the only two great republics in existence, ex-President Theodore Roosevelt of the United States and Stephan Pichon, the Foreign Minister of France.

There can have been little, other than due grief, to cloud the minds of the royal Danes and Germans as they watched their kinsman laid to his rest. War, the French Revolution and the Industrial Revolution had shaken them but their thrones remained. The last important overthrow had occurred far away and a long time ago when Dom Pedro was dethroned in Brazil in 1889. Kings really had little to worry about other than the occupational hazards of assassination, lunacy and an occasional tendency for blood not to clot.

Within five months of Edward's death the smooth canvas of European monarchy cracked. On October 6, 1910, King Manoel of Portugal was overthrown and his country declared itself a republic. Manoel escaped to Gibraltar and was then brought to England, where, following a nineteenth century fashion for ex-Kings he settled down and became a squire. In the nineteenth century ex-Kings sometimes received a second chance. But the twentieth century had already started, and it started as it was to continue.

By 1952 when George VI of England was buried, only a handful of European monarchs remained to mourn him. King Haakon VII of Norway was still there, unbent by the weight of history he had experienced in his eighty years, given precedence as the closest member of the family. There was strong representation from the royal Arab states, but the only other mourners from royal Europe were King Paul of Greece, Gustaf Adolf and Louise of Sweden, Frederick and Ingrid of Denmark, Juliana and Bernhard of the Netherlands and Archduchess Charlotte and Prince Felix of Luxembourg. King Baudoin, for reasons of his own, had refused to come and sulked in Brussels, sending his younger brother in his place.

The decline and fall of Kings has been one of the most extraordinary episodes of this century. A system of government that had sustained most of the world for a thousand years found itself all at once without roots. The first World

War accounted for four emperors and six kings. The second eliminated five more, if Albania and Egypt are included. True, in Greece they restored the monarchy after a civil war, and in Spain they talked about it, nevertheless it seemed to be an ineluctable fact of history that monarchy, unless something unimaginable occurred to change the structure of the world's politics, was on the point of extinction.

Even in England the value of monarchy had been called into question by responsible sources. The *Manchester Guardian*, Britain's most distinguished paper, was quite churlish when Queen Elizabeth II opened Parliament under the television cameras for the first time in November, 1958. "The Imperial State Crown" said the *Guardian*, "the Cap of Maintenance, the Sword of State, the Heralds, the Lord Great Chamberlain, the Earl Marshals make up a beautiful charade, but if all were swept away tomorrow it would not make the slightest difference to the government of the country. They are harmless relics—harmless, that is, so long as nobody mistakes them for anything significant . . . Abroad, Britain's reputation as an old curiosity shop will be enhanced and our tourist earnings may benefit".

If the trappings of the one unshakeable throne can be so casually laughed away by the nation's first editorialists, respect for the throne itself must clearly have sunk alarmingly since the days of the 1953 Coronation, in which case the end may come quickly and suddenly. Whether or not it will, depends on whether monarchy has any real function in modern Europe, whether or not a rôle has evolved to compensate for the loss of former powers. The early Christian Kings, deriving their inspiration from the Eastern Church, ruled their lands as the representatives of God. The medieval princes ruled for glory, aggrandisement and war. All the principles by which they existed were swept away but the Kings remained. Or rather they rose and fell in a series of double rhythms. Not many years after Charles I, in England, was beheaded, Louis XIV, in France, was able to say *"l'état, c'est moi"*. In 1789 the institution of monarchy was smashed by the French Revolution, and fifteen years later France possessed the most gorgeous empire in her gorgeous history.

The later nineteenth and early twentieth centuries saw monarchy and republicanism growing side by side. As new states emerged from the ebbing of old empires, the leaders of European monarchies and republics alike strove to provide those states with suitable and trustworthy princes. Bulgaria got Alexander of Battenberg in 1879. Carl of Hohenzollern-Sigmaringen was smuggled through the Turks into Bucharest in 1866 and became Carol I of Rumania in 1881. The United States and France joined the monarchies in persuading Prince Carl of Denmark to become Haakon VII of Norway in 1905, after Norway's secession from Sweden, and the major powers, France among them, made a gift of Albania in 1914 to Prince Wilhelm zu Wied.

It seemed such a logical system, and it worked. Cousins and uncles kept the peace on the thrones of nearly every capital in Europe. Then came the double holocaust and with it, after the dust had cleared, the bedraggled remnants of the monarchies, plumed like wet hens, scarcely daring to breathe let alone reign. In the place of the trade union of Princes the world found itself with a blue glass skyscraper in New York and the United Nations, with what happy results one can see by a perusal of the newspaper front pages any day of the week.

The end, then, of a system of government older than Christianity was surely in sight. As King Farouk said, shortly before being jacked off his own throne, "In ten years time there will be only five Kings left, the Kings of Hearts, Diamonds, Spades, Clubs and the King of England." Yet in the period following each great war it was not the monarchies but the republics which worried over internal and constitutional menaces. With the possible exception of Switzerland the best-run nations of Europe were the remaining monarchies. Germany, which scarcely knew a day of good government from the end of the monarchy to the election of Konrad Adenauer, measured with increasing nervousness its certain span of sanity on the heartbeat of a very old man. No one, German or non-German, could predict what fresh neuroses may afflict that incalculable people after Adenauer dies. France, torn by government which sometimes seemed positively demented, finally had to turn to a semi-monarchical figure to give it dignity. Democracy sat so easily in Italy that it could be all but overthrown by an incident like the Montesi affair which in the end proved to be no affair at all.

An investigation into contemporary monarchy may consequently show that the great collapse was not as inevitable as it seemed, or seems to this day. It may show that where absolute monarchy crumbled, without an interim period, into democratic republicanism the citizens went further than they intended, and found they had inherited a land and a constitution which they were able to acknowledge neither with joy nor pride. Anti-clericals and radicals thumbing their noses at the Church of Rome by toppling the thrones; newly half-educated, dirty-white-collar workers uniting against the privileges of a landed aristocracy, these succeeded in achieving greater successes throughout Europe than the majority of their fellow-citizens would have wished.

Where monarchy adjusted itself to the times, on the other hand, it fulfilled a rôle far beyond that of ornamental symbolism. Prime Ministers could legislate and Governments could fall, but the monarchy became the controlling force in the legislation of society, a guarantee of its stability and continuity. It saved the old ruling classes from feeling they were abandoned, softened antagonisms which in European republics, before the second war, resulted in a right-wing aristocracy and left-wing proletariat each indulging in treachery to defeat the other at the expense of the nation. Constitutional monarchy drew, by its honors, awards and accolades, men prepared to make sacrifices in its service, men who would otherwise have minded their own affairs and left the running of the country to the professional politicians and ambitious ward-heelers.

In almost every monarchy the Civil Service was able to call on a higher type of servant than the republics. Some Kings were pretty silly but few acted as ludicrously as some of the duly elected Presidents of France, for example, what with President Faure dying in *flagranti dilecti* with his mistress; and President Déschanel who, having fallen out of an express train at midnight in his nightshirt and bonnet, presented himself to the local *préfecture de police* with the words, "I am the President of France," the *agent* responding with the counter-claim to the Queendom of Sheba.

The dedicated man became footloose in the republics. The genuine patriot shrank in disgust before the excesses of the flag-waving rabble-rousers (it being always so much easier to wave a flag than wave a King). General de Gaulle was shunned for ten years until French politicians had ruined France almost beyond repair. Konrad Adenauer cultivated flowers in his garden throughout the Hitler régime. The hereditary aristocracy, having no one to bow the knee to, became clowns and buffoons of the worst order, a very easy process. Between the abdication of King Umberto of Italy in 1946 and the public frolicking of the Italian nobility with assorted showgirls in 1958, there is a closer link than is generally realized.

The cause of monarchy, however, which might have been

expected to prosper by its own example, and by the example of
the republics, continued to sag. This was a curious phenome-
non, but it is not difficult to trace the causes.

The trouble was that it happened too suddenly. All at once,
in the nineteen forties and fifties there were so many ex-Kings
around that their very numbers posed a problem to themselves, and all were new to the game of ex-Kingship. All the
major Pretenders, except one, the Count of Paris, had been
born to, or had experience of court life. One King without a
throne could command respect, sympathy, asylum and, where
necessary, a hand-out. A dozen would merely command a
housing shortage, and invite comparisons and laughs. Bit by
bit, after the war, they settled down. Each had a fixation about
his own position in the world, and by this fixation he could be
put into one of various groups. There was the group working
indefatigably for restoration, like the Count of Paris, and the
Archduke Otto of Hapsburg. There was the group which
hoped for restoration without working too hard at it, like
Umberto, Don Juan of Spain and Louis Ferdinand of Prussia.
There was the group which was simply sick and tired of the
whole royal farce, like King Michael who glowered if anyone
mentioned royalty, and his estranged aunt, Princess Ileana,
sister of Carol, who moved to America and called herself
"Mrs. Issarescu," the name of her husband. Albrecht of Bavaria, on the death of his legendary father Crown Prince
Rupprecht in 1955, dropped the *"Majestät"* by which Rupprecht was always addressed and went up into the mountains
to shoot.

Some of the ex-Kings, the more sterling, could see with
dismay what a King may become when he is no longer King.
They could see the preposterous King Carol, Michael's father,
assuming all the rights and privileges of his ex-position, pre-
ceding women through doors, conferring titles, insisting on

the curtsey, the deference, and the King's position at the head of the table at all times. There was Zog of Albania and the desperate, money-hungry Peter of Yugoslavia. They seemed an indifferent crowd, to put it nicely, these, the children of Charlemagne, Victoria and Louis XIV.

None was really destitute. Wise fathers had usually left a *cache* or two in Switzerland or England and most of them benefited from private philanthropists-royal. Before the war, for example, the first Lord Rothermere interested himself in the restoration of monarchies and arranged to pay the ex-Empress Zita of Austria the not inconsiderable allowance of £25,000 a year. He also made an offer to the ex-Kaiser Wilhelm which the old man refused. At worst the ex-Kings had enough to enable them to live in the sun and rot, and in an odd way their very energies seemed to slow down in comparison with their cousins in office, which leads to an insignificant but diverting point. It is noticeable that the sport of ex-Kings, as represented by the Duke of Windsor, Leopold and Don Juan, is golf, while princes in power tend to blow off by driving cars too fast, like Philip of England, Paul of Greece and Bernhard of the Netherlands. King Baudoin has even had a special banked track built at Laeken Palace for solitary racing.

It is the Riviera villa-Kings who always attract the publicity and damage the institution, not the hard-working monarchs. Publicity is their vicarious kingdom, and the gossip columns are their gazettes. But there are others who are well content that this should remain so, because it leaves them in the calm they prefer for contemplation. And without time for contemplation no philosophy can be solved.

"One is free when one can act, and, as power in the real world comes from money, one is not free when one has none."

This is the philosophy of His Royal Highness Henri of France, the Count of Paris, son of the Duke of Guise, and Pretender to the Throne of France. No King-in-exile would ever admit to another King being the spokesman for all, as that would imply inferiority; nevertheless the Count of Paris, by his brilliance, has made himself largely the mouthpiece and model for all aspiring monarchs. He has the advantage of not being plagued with the major curse of ex-Kings, a past. He has never known the comfort of a throne, but he hopes he will in his lifetime. Since his enforced exile was terminated after the second World War the Count has grown steadily more powerful in the political affairs of France. Knowing that he can always command the loyalty of the French Right he ignores them and has himself become a Socialist, and even performed official functions abroad for Guy Mollet's Socialist Government.

Nor is he alone in playing the royal game with astuteness. Leopold of the Belgians has made many mistakes but he has, with care, sought to restore his old status in his native land. After his abdication he effaced himself from the affairs of Belgium. His son's passionate loyalty to him, at first resented by the politicians and the people, is now accepted as something which cannot be changed, and Leopold has been to some extent absolved of blame for it. In 1957 the Belgian Government sent Leopold on an official tour of the atomic stations in the United States, and there was no hostile reaction in the country. Other men deserving of respect among the monarchs are Don Juan who has been half-promised his throne back, (but will probably die without one) and Crown Prince Louis Ferdinand of Prussia who until recently sold automobiles in Bremen.

If people wonder why these Pretenders work so hard in pursuit of something that they have not a hope of achieving, they might reply that monarchy itself has changed and in a way to give many Pretenders fresh hope. Before the war Charles Maurras, the French royalist rabble-rouser, was able to state that the great thing about monarchy was "it made republics impossible," and the philosopher could sigh, "*Que la Republique était belle sous le Royaume.*" That is no longer the point. Today one can say that the elimination of absolute monarchy everywhere in Europe (except in eccentric hold-outs like Monaco and Liechtenstein) has made it theoretically easy to re-impose a King as constitutional monarch over a re-public, and infinitely more appealing than electing a tame, superannuated politician as titular head of the state and calling him President. As the Count of Paris has seen, there is no longer any serious anomaly in a King becoming a symbol of the republican ideal.

The example of the European monarchies is profoundly envied by many people in every republic. Monarchists in a republic look to restoration to curb national passions which might otherwise get out of hand. Those who object that mon-archy has become a mere decoration, impotent to control the lusts of some demagogue misunderstand the modern concep-tion of monarchy as it is now practised. For the duty of a mon-arch in heady, dangerous times is to keep his ministers sane. The first characteristic of the politician, after all, is arrogance. He may be dedicated, and a man of vision, but arrogance is the first item in his makeup. Only an arrogant man would seek to put himself forward as a man better qualified than another to speak for his fellow-citizens in an assembly. And when a politician rises to the position that he is the effectual head of a country it is good, right and proper that he should have to account for his actions to some non-political figure higher than he. A European-style figurehead President like Coty of France, Heuss of Germany or Gronchi of Italy is not enough. They grew up in the same school as the Prime Ministers, the school of politics, and they talk the same language. The supreme figure must be remote and dynastic, so that the actual leader must make his account in terms of respect and deference. It is good for his own self-discipline. How graciously he does it is a more sure guide to the character of the man than his politics are. Clement Attlee, a constitutional Socialist, was more correct and respectful to King George VI than was Neville Chamberlain, a conceited Tory, who often treated the King high-handedly, and there is no question as to which of the two was the better Prime Minister. The basic principle of respect applies equally to the United States. American Presidents, good and bad, have always tended in moments of exuberance or irritation to treat their people contemptuously. One can lay at the door of Hoover, Roosevelt, Truman and Eisenhower innumerable examples of behaviour that was not only infuriating but also insulting to the intelligence of the electorate. This happens much more rarely in a monarchy, even in a monarchy like Canada. The fact of not having anyone higher to make obeisance to may explain why American Presidents pay their respects much more frequently than the leaders of other countries, to the Almighty.

The easier and the greatest mistake anyone can make in politics is to assume that temporary trends are an irrevocable and irresistible force. Socialism, Stalinism, Arab nationalism and New Dealism all stop and reverse themselves sooner or later. Because Kings have dwindled it is foolish to assume they will continue to dwindle. It all depends on whether those Kings in power are equipped to hold it in the event of new crises, and whether those out of power will know how to seize the opportunity if it comes. Thus each King, facing problems of his own, must overcome them by his own talents.

# II

# *Leopold—1*

## The Frustrated Idol

Royalty will be strong because it appeals to diffused feeling and Republics weak because they appeal to the understanding . . . Its mystery is its life. We must not let daylight upon magic.

—Bagehot.

$\mathcal{M}$ost men have their destinies chosen for them by events. Had England been occupied in the second World War or had France remained unoccupied, had Germany won the war or Russia lost it, the result would have yielded not only new figures for history but also the same figures in startling different roles. Between the traitor and the hero the difference is often merely one of opportunity.

Leopold of the Belgians is a rare example of a man who, at a critical moment of history, was in a position to choose. His moment was May 28, 1940, when the German Army was overrunning Beligium. Holland had already fallen, and the British and French allies were being swept aside. Although he was hard pressed, Leopold, unlike some of his ministers, kept his head and weighed his choice. He could have decided to follow his fellow-monarchs, Haakon of Norway and Wilhelmina of the Netherlands, to England. Or he could remain in his own country for so long as he was allowed to survive, as a symbol to his oppressed people. He chose the latter. It gave cold comfort to his allies, but when the fury and the fighting was over it might have put him on a pedestal with his people. But then he weakened, and married. The marriage cost him his throne and rocked the Belgian monarchy so hard that it is still shuddering.

Belgium is a curious country drawing its spiritual sustenance from three contrasting neighbours, from the Dutch to the north, from the French to the south, and from the English across the channel. As sometimes happens the squeeze of neighbouring cultures has yielded in the Belgians a temperament which seems to stem from none of them. Belgians are industrious like the Dutch but without serenity, democratic like the British but without dignity, sybaritic like the French but without self-confidence. Belgium is a country susceptible to riots and furies, volcanic and bad-tempered. What gives the story of Leopold its savage tragedy is that at the moment of crisis the Royal Family were left completely defenceless and alone. Politicians played their part, but fundamentally it was a story of personal duress. In the middle stood the obdurate King, his shy son and his beautiful wife, and around them the inflamed Belgian masses face to face with a dilemma they could neither explain to the outside world or rationalise among themselves. Between the two forces there was no shield, there were no significant spokesmen, there was nothing.

Unless one knows what emotions assailed Leopold on that morning in his headquarters, with the Battle of Belgium at its full pitch, speculation about the rights or wrongs of the matter are futile. Leopold has never revealed his thoughts, but the events of his life are such that in retrospect one can see that such a crisis as May 28, 1940, almost had to result in some cataclysmic explosion from an ego and a heart as weary as his.

Leopold was born on November 3rd, 1901, in Brussels. His father, King Albert I, was the third King of the Belgian dynasty of Saxe-Coburg and Gotha. His mother was the former Princess Elisabeth of Bavaria, a German with Portuguese and French blood, her grandmother being Louise Marie d'Orleans, daughter of Louis Philippe I, the last Bourbon to rule over France. Albert was a King out of the books of fables, a gigantic, golden-haired god of a man, good-looking enough to be called beautiful, and utterly without fear. On royal visits he towered over his cousins, George V and the Emperor Wilhelm, and crushed their hands in his huge paws.

When Germany invaded Belgium in 1914, Albert established himself at Belgian headquarters and stayed there from the beginning to the end of the war without leave or rest. More, even, than Lloyd George to the British or Clemenceau to the French, Albert was the symbol of resistance and victory to the Belgian people. When the Germans first invaded, his wife, Queen Elisabeth, escaped to England with her children. Young Leopold, titled the Duke of Brabant, begged to be allowed to return to Flanders and fight for his country. Eventually the King consented, and to Leopold's delight, allowed him to join the 12th Regiment as a private with specific instructions that he be shown no favouritism. This was what Leopold wanted, an opportunity to show what he could do on his own. He was too young for front-line fighting but served seriously and well for six months before the King sent him back to England to continue his royal studies. Leopold remained at Eton until the beginning of 1918 when he returned to the Front, old enough now to join in the killing.

He took part in the final offensive and was one of the first soldiers back in liberated Brussels. But he was beaten to it by his father. The screaming, delirious multitudes had eyes and voices only for the King and Queen. The prince in his sergeant's uniform was scarcely noticed. The war ended. In 1919 Leopold went with his parents on a trip to the United States and Brazil. In November, 1920, he enrolled in military school and was graduated, two years later, as a lieutenant.

Leopold was now a tall, exceptionally good looking young man in his mid-twenties, not without gaiety although his general mien was grave. He was travelling widely, gaining valuable experience and studying conscientiously for the time when he would become King. At the same time another prince was doing all these things except the last. England's Prince of Wales, seven years older than Leopold, with his shy smile, his excitement at new adventures and experiences, was attracting from the whole world a devotion that has rarely been equalled. No young man has ever been so much beloved by people so vastly different. The idolatry he attracted was greater than that which was soon to be bestowed on Lindbergh. Leopold, handsome though he was, and keen, was left in the shadows.

After returning from the Congo, Leopold went off again on a tour of the Scandinavian countries and there met Princess Astrid, the third daughter of Prince Charles, and niece of the King of Sweden. The meeting had been arranged by Queen Elisabeth of Belgium, whose indefatigable matchmaking had resulted, six years before, in the marriage of her daughter, Marie-José, to Crown Prince Umberto of Italy, a marriage which was already an unhappy one. Leopold and Astrid were married in Stockholm on November 4, 1926, and Leopold brought his bride with him to Belgium. They arrived in Antwerp in an all-white yacht, the *Flygia*, and began their married life living simply in the Pavillon Belle Vue in Brussels and at the Castle of Stuyvenberg, near Laeken. The Belgian people were prepared to cheer their new princess, but they were not prepared to have their hearts taken away, which was just what Princess Astrid proceeded to do. Her personality, her lack of affectation at all times, delighted them. They called her the "snow princess," and after Josephine Charlotte was born in October, 1927, she would wheel her baby carriage through the park and gossip with other mothers. On September 7, 1930, she gave birth to a son and heir to the throne, Baudoin, a huge child of 8 lbs and 14 ounces.

Leopold, once more, appeared to be left behind in the popularity stakes. The affection of the Belgian people seemed to be concentrated entirely on the Swedish princess he had married. In February, 1934, King Albert, climbing a mountain at Marche les Dames, slipped on a rock and fell to his death. He was only 58 years old, in excellent health and with many years' reign apparently ahead of him. On February 23, 1934, Leopold took his oath to the Constitution as Leopold III, inheriting not only a throne but also a tradition of dashing and imaginative monarchy. His three predecessors, Leopold I, Leopold II, and Albert were all men of vision who had built Belgium out of a French province into a country of importance out of all proportion to its size. It was triumphant in war, wealthy, and with a rich Empire. The name he bore, Saxe-Coburg and Gotha, was one of the proudest of all royal society. Famous families like the Hapsburgs and Bourbons had all but disappeared, but the Saxe-Coburg and Gotha Family reigned on two powerful, imperial thrones, the British and the Belgian. Belgian history and Belgian instinct were combined with Leopold III's personal background to make the future look auspicious. In international affairs Belgium turned for friendship chiefly to Great Britain who had helped her to independence from France a century before, and had rushed unselfishly to her assistance in 1914. Some of Leopold's most formative years had been spent in England, and when he was in civilian clothes he was rarely seen in any other tie than the black tie with the thin blue stripes of Eton. His family connections spread across Europe. His wife's family reigned in Sweden. His sister, Marie-José, was married to Prince Umberto of Italy. His sister-in-law, Umberto's sister,

was Queen Giovanna of Bulgaria. His Bavarian mother belonged to the richest royal House in Germany.

Leopold had been King for a year when Astrid gave birth
to her third child, Albert, Prince of Liege. In August, 1935,
the royal couple went on a motoring holiday to Switzerland,
near Lucerne, travelling incognito, as they preferred to do,
using the name of de Rethy which they had done so often that
it signalled hostel keepers for miles around to lay on their
most princely service. Astrid was pregnant for the fourth
time. One day when the sun shone on the mountains Leopold
suggested a drive. He took the wheel and they set out. Shortly
before reaching the little town of Kussnacht, Astrid took the
road map and asked her husband for a direction. Leopold
turned to her and, his control momentarily slackening, the
car skidded. It ricocheted off a tree, swerved off the road,
down a bank and through some rose bushes into the Lac des
Quatre-Cantons, where it rested, its nose under water as though
it were drinking. Astrid, her skull fractured, died shortly afterwards. Leopold was too grief-stricken to notice his own injuries,
and numbly allowed the doctors to treat him. It was a horrible,
shocking death, and Belgium, deprived after so short a time
of its fairy-tale Queen, was stunned into a heart-felt mourning. Leopold had not the heart to break the news to his three
motherless children, and he left it to a lady-in-waiting. Albert
was too young to understand but they say that Josephine
Charlotte and Baudoin sobbed themselves to sleep. Astrid
had been Queen for little more than a year. Leopold attended
the funeral with his arm in a sling and his face bandaged. He
prepared to shoulder a bitter burden alone.

Three years passed. One day in 1938, Henri Baels, an old
friend of the family was sitting by Leopold's side at the horse-

racing at Ostend, and was invited with his wife to tea. Baels, a controversial figure in the Leopold story, had had a distinguished career in Belgian public life. He was a lawyer and had served in the Government as Minister of Agriculture and of Public Works. He was now Governor of West Flanders, one of the nine provinces of Belgium. This was a position of great authority. The nine governors were, in effect, viceroys, the personal representatives of the King; and the residence of the Governor of West Flanders was the Palace of Bruges. M. and Mme. Baels asked their daughter, Liliane, to drive them to the King, and this marked the first meeting of the tall twenty-two-year-old girl, and the widowed monarch.

"What language do you speak, Mlle. Baels?" the King asked. "French or Flemish?"

"Both." said Liliane Baels. Leopold's pleasure increased when he discovered that she was an expert golfer, and he invited her to the links near Zoute. They played nine holes and then they did not meet again for another two years. Because, however, the story of Leopold III is also the story of Liliane Baels it is necessary to trace the story back to the beginning, to 1916,* and to London where Liliane was born.

London shaped most of her early life, although after World War I was over she was sent for a while to school in the provincial Palace of Bruges, and later to the College of the Sacred Heart in Ostend where in the course of *composition francaise* she had to write an essay on "The Man I Most Admire." The man she chose was "Prince Leopold."

* Officially Princess de Rethy was born in 1917. The fact that she is actually one year older than her record states is due to the fact that her birthday is mistakenly taken from her registration in Belgium and not her date of birth in London. It is not due to any feminine affectation on the part of the Princess and she has never hidden the fact, but it remains in the armoury of her many enemies.

In London she enrolled in a fashionable finishing school, the Holy Child, in Cavendish Square, and was a frequent guest of the Belgian Ambassador and his wife. It was clear even then, although Liliane was only sixteen, that she was on the way to a spectacular career. She took naturally to all sports. She was an expert golfer and swimmer. The moment her feet were long enough to touch the pedals she took the wheel of a car, and showed an instinct for unerring, fast driving. In appearance she was striking, almost six feet tall, with a Spanish profile and hair which gleamed blue-black in the sunlight. Her eyes were steady to the point of being disconcerting, and her chin was hard, but she laughed easily and possessed an energy that made her seem not so much to walk as to bound like a kangaroo.

In 1935 she made her debut and was introduced to the British Royal Family in Buckingham Palace. By the side of King George V and Queen Mary stood the Prince of Wales. He was even then secretly in love with Mrs. Wallis Simpson. Had he fallen in love instead with the eighteen-year-old girl who curtsied to him, the thrones of two nations would have been saved the most almighty shaking.

After the golf date at Zoute, Leopold devoted himself to Belgian affairs. Like all the small nations on Germany's borders Belgium had a craven but understandable fear of Hitler and Leopold's government followed a policy of independence from England and France, hoping that by not being too nice to their natural friends they would appease their natural enemy, the Germans. In March, 1940, Liliane, in Brussels, was invited to luncheon by the Belgian Queen Mother, Elisabeth. The Queen Mother was a woman of artistic taste and personality, with the nearest thing to a royal cultural salon that any monarch possessed in Europe. The only other guest was Leopold. The three of them enjoyed the meeting and another date was fixed. It was never kept, however, because on May 10, 1940, Germany invaded the Low Countries. As was expected, the British and French Armies rushed to their support and the Germans, attacking where the French were wheeling, broke through—as they had done in 1870—at Sedan and smashed a great gap in the French lines through which the armour poured. At the same time they attacked in terrific force in the north and knocked out the Dutch in four days. Leopold and Queen Wilhelmina had discussed what their duty should be in case this very thing happened and both agreed in principle that it would be more correct to remain with their people. Wilhelmina, however, changed her mind and decided that she would do better work for her countrymen free than as a prisoner. She remained until the last possible moment on Dutch soil and when a British destroyer finally took her away she was literally only minutes ahead of the Germans.

But while the Dutch Army had been annihilated the Belgians were still fighting. In the higher levels of the war councils there had been doubts expressed about Leopold's reliability and his attitude to the war, but the Allies, remembering the heroic resistance of Albert and his Belgians in the first war, could not visualise that Belgium would voluntarily remove herself from the fighting. The news everywhere was bad. General Weygand, the French Commander-in-Chief, hastened to Leopold and asked him to hold the Germans for as long as possible to give the French breathing space for a counter-offensive. On May 23, Leopold called his ministers to an emergency meeting, and told them to think over the possibilities of complete capitulation to the Germans. The suggestion brought the ministers to their feet in indignation, but Leopold sat silently before their protests. One said flatly that if Belgium were overrun it was the duty of the King and Government to continue the fight from Britain. The meeting broke up and Leopold was left alone with his thoughts.

Two days later he sent an ominous message to his soldiers, telling them to keep fighting, but that whatever happened he would share their fate. Everywhere the situation was deteriorating, the Allies were on the run, the Germans in the full flush of success. Leopold came to his decision. On the 26th he cabled Viscount Gort, the British commander, and informed General Weygand by radio. At 2300 hours, on that day, Leopold accepted German conditions and two hours later he notified the French. On May 28, at four a.m., the cease fire was ordered to all Belgian troops, and the King sent them this message: "I will not leave you in these tragic moments. I shall stay with you to protect you and your families and your fate will be mine."

It was a decision taken against the unanimous opposition of the Belgian Cabinet, when the Belgian soldiers still had as much fight in them as the British and French, which was not much, but which was more than could be expected.

The right and wrong of Leopold's action can be argued endlessly and without result. As General Weygand said in later years, when describing the agony of Pétainism and collaboration with the enemy: any man will do his duty. The tragedy comes when he must make a choice between two signposts each marked "duty" and pointing in opposite directions. Volumes of documentation have accumulated dealing with the incident, in Belgium, Britain and France, Defenders of Leopold point out that Leopold knew indirectly as early as May 20 that Lord Gort, the British commander, was planning to evacuate the British by sea from Dunkirk, and that Leopold foresaw Belgium being "sold" by the French in retreat and the British in the sea. On the other hand, there never was a war in which allies were not convinced that they were being "sold" everywhere and by every other ally all the time. Ten years later a group of Belgian generals wrote to Sir Winston Churchill asking him formally to clear Leopold's reputation and declare the rightness of his action. Sir Winston saw no reason to change the unfavourable judgment he formed at the time and sustained in his subsequent memoirs, and ignored the petition. It remains today an argument which neither side wins. Leopold's decision was a stunning blow to the Allies, on the other hand it was a gesture inspiring to many Belgians stricken for the second time by German occupation. Most of the Belgians loved him for it, and most of the Allies hated him. In the end it made no difference to the Allied war effort except to drive the British a little sooner into the undignified glory of Dunkirk.

What was incontestable was that at the climax of the fighting Belgians, British, French and civilian refugees had been driven into a corner of Belgium so tiny that there was scarcely room to move, let alone maneuver. Belgian soldiers dug their foxholes and gun emplacements among their women and children. An officer, after one engagement, counted forty military dead and 160 civilians, these being casualties not from artillery or bombing, which would have been understandable, but from infantry and tank fire.

The Belgians laid down their arms. The King surrendered. The British Army escaped and the shooting died away. Those who have never lived under enemy occupation must be wary of judging those who have. Judgment on Leopold in Britain was harsh. Had Britain been occupied, however, as she might have been, most Britons, I think, would have been happier knowing that their Royal Family was safe to continue the war in Canada, rather than kept hostage in Buckingham Palace under Nazi patronage.

While all these events were taking place Liliane Baels had

been lost among the helpless millions uprooted by the war. She was at the wheel of an ambulance trying to struggle through the panic-stricken mobs of Belgium and Northern France. The roads were choked with refugees in cars, carts or on foot. Every now and then the Germans added to the terror by dive-bombing, strafing the civilians. Liliane's orders were to evacuate the aged from the battle areas. Liliane, all her life, had lived a sheltered upper middle-class existence, and this was her first experience of hardship and the ugliness of war. Where her mother and father were she did not know. Nor did she know the fate of her invalid sister.

The dawn of the 28th found her near the French border. She had not heard the news for days, but only knew that disaster was blending with disaster in a prolonged roar. She stopped the ambulance in a village crowded with troops and went into a *bistro* for some coffee, pushing a path through crowds of exhausted, sprawling French soldiers.

She was dressed in her Belgian Red Cross uniform and ordered her coffee as the wireless broadcast the latest news, the news of Leopold's decision to surrender. For a moment a stunned hush fell on the café and outside the noise of soldiers and traffic died away. Then one soldier hurled his coffee cup against the wall, and Liliane was deafened by the torrent of curses. She found herself with her back to the counter arguing furiously with French soldiers savage with rage, who shouted of treachery and sabotage.

"How dare you?" Liliane cried through angry tears. "You should be ashamed to speak in such manner of a man who fought to the end. You should be ashamed to insult him like this." Blindly she pushed her way out and drove off in her ambulance until she was out of the village and able to find a quiet lane. She took out some paper and impulsively wrote the King a letter. Once it was written she scarcely knew what to do with it. She put it in a mail box at Bernay, near Rouen, and forgot all about it.

Some time later, she caught up with her mother and they set out to cover the swarming refugee centres in search of Henri Baels. In the town hall of Le Havre she finally saw him, unshaven and asleep on a straw mattress on the floor. Meanwhile the English khaki and the French skyblue were thinning from the crowds. One day they disappeared altogether and were replaced by German field-grey. The war swept over them and left them behind. As far as Liliane was concerned it was over. She and her family gathered their possessions and drove with difficulty back to Brussels. The first appointment of Baels and his daughter was with King Leopold. Liliane found him tense, pre-occupied and looking much older.

"Liliane," he said, "did you have any doubt about my conduct here?"

"Never," said Liliane simply, but she knew that he only half believed what she had said. By a romantic coincidence confirmation came next morning. The letter which Liliane had written weeks before in Normandy had finally made its way to the palace and the King was on the telephone to her about it.

France surrendered. Britain prepared for invasion and Europe settled down to make of German occupation what its various national temperaments allowed it. For a Flemish girl of breeding, not herself emotionally committed to the struggle, the war had a certain sense of unreality. A year after the fall of France, in July, 1941, when the Germany Army was in hot pursuit of the Russians, Liliane was down in the French *pays basque* where her parents had decided to settle for the the duration. She would have been surprised to know that her name was already being studied in secret files by the Belgian

Government-in-exile in London. A Belgian resistance fighter
smuggling out intelligence had reported that "the King is
seeing too much of a Mlle. Baels." Nevertheless, she was
astonished to receive, while she was sitting in the sun, a letter
from King Leopold written in strange and circumlocutory
phrases asking her to return to Brussels urgently to discuss
an important matter. Liliane showed the letter to her mother
who read it in perplexity.

"I don't know what it means," she said. "I don't know
what to advise." Next day another letter addressed to Mme.
Baels arrived from the Queen Mother Elisabeth asking that
Liliane come to Brussels for a few days. It is probable that
Liliane had a better idea of what was in the King's mind than
her mother had. She took the train back to Brussels alone and
was taken to the Bungalow, a little wooden house in the park
at Laeken. Leopold said without preamble, "Liliane, would
you marry me?"

Liliane, her natural ebullience deserting her for once, said
uncertainly, "I don't think you can. Kings marry princesses."
The King insisted and Liliane accepted. When Henri Baels
heard about it he was furious and set himself completely
against the match. Baels had spent most of his life in politics.
He could see as neither the exhausted King nor his daughter,
the trail of disaster, of calumny and misrepresentation the
marriage would bring. He loved both his King and his daughter as only a profound monarchist and a father can. The people,
Baels knew, would not see Leopold any more as a solitary hero
tormented by doubt and by patriotism, but as a man who put
his happiness first and married a woman while the country was
flat on its face with a German boot on its neck. His daughter,
an innocent apolitical girl, was being condemned to an in-
tolerable fate; she would be compared every day to Astrid,
whose death had turned her memory into something legendary

and almost holy. Baels argued day after day for ten days. Those ten nights he passed sleeplessly turning and often in tears.

Seeing his arguments had made not even a dent in the couple's mind he yielded, but on conditions. One of the conditions was that the Dowager Queen Elisabeth must be present to give her approval and blessing, and the second was that Cardinal van Roey, the primate of Belgium and none other, was to perform the ceremony. These were the most eminent authorities that Baels could think of to muster at the time. He also insisted that Mme. Baels not be informed until afterwards. He knew that the shock to his sensitive and intelligent wife would be as great as it was to him, and he wished to tell her in his own way.

So, on September 11, 1941, was contracted one of the queerest royal marriages of the century. Within the Palace at Laeken, half of it occupied by German soldiers, in the private chapel, Leopold, aged 40, married Liliane Baels, aged 25. Cardinal van Roey who had married Leopold and Astrid, performed the ceremony, assisted by one priest who had been a friend of Leopold's at military school. Only two witnesses attended, Henri Baels and the Queen Mother. Liliane wore a wedding dress and a tulle veil loaned to her by Queen Elisabeth. The church was decorated with pink and white flowers picked in the castle grounds. The ceremony over, the King gave his bride the title of Princess Liliane de Rethy, the name which he and Astrid had always used when they travelled incognito.

Liliane could not move into the Palace because of the presence of the Germans. She was accommodated in the Bungalow where she would not be so quickly suspected. The day after the wedding Liliane heard that her mother, puzzled by her daughter's silence, was on her way back to Brussels.

Henri Baels and the new princess, using her old passport, hastily took the train to Paris to intercept her. They found Mme. Baels at the Hotel Bristol and they confided what Liliane had done. Mme. Baels, as Henri Baels had feared, saw as quickly as he what catastrophe this act would bring in its wake, and broke down.

There were a few days and weeks of peace ahead of them. Neither the bride nor her husband deceived themselves into thinking they could keep their marriage secret for long, but they decided to let events take their course. Liliane went on to see the children who threw themselves into her arms. Josephine Charlotte was thirteen years old, Baudoin eleven, and Charles six. For the first time in six years Laeken heard the sound of a woman's laughter. The children's laughter too had a different sound to it. It took no more than a few minutes for these largely loveless children to be captured by the merry Liliane whose charm was irresistible. The love which had been starved inside them was poured on to her. She told them to go away and think up a special name for her. They insisted on "maman." Liliane protested that only their real mother could be thought of as "maman."

This argument baffled the two older children with its logic, and it was the smallest, Charles, who was obliged to find a constitutional way around it. "Well," he said, "once we had one 'maman.' Now we have two." And "maman" it remained.

Had the world of King Leopold III stopped at the gates of Laeken Palace there would have been nothing more to add to the story. But Leopold was a King, the compromised ruler of a divided country occupied by a ruthless enemy, a King, therefore, whose reputation was in multiple jeopardy. The tragedy of the situation was that outside of Belgium, in the Allied camp, his stature was growing. Those who had condemned him in immoderate language were now somewhat ashamed of themselves. The Belgian Government in London and the directors of the Allied war effort knew that Leopold was finding consolation with "Mlle. Baels," but they were worldly men and it did not worry them. Leopold had thought of himself as utterly alone and universally condemned. If only he had known how highly his countrymen in exile esteemed him, many of his doubts and torments would have fallen away from him and it could well be that it would have given him sufficient strength to carry on alone.

As it was, a letter was on the way to him which would have changed his entire attitude toward himself and the war, but ironically it came just too late to prevent the marriage. In London, Paul-Henri Spaak, Foreign Secretary of the Belgian Government-in-exile, and emerging then as one of Europe's great statesmen, was told by a secret courier that if he wished to write a note to the King in Brussels a channel existed for smuggling it through the Nazis to Laeken Palace. It was November 21, 1941. Leopold and Liliane had been married for two and a half months but the secret was still closely kept, and Spaak, of course, had no inkling of it.

"Sire," Spaak wrote, "A chance of writing a few words to Your Majesty being offered to me, I am seizing it with dispatch. I have just returned from a trip to the United States where I represented Belgium at the International Labour Conference. With compatriots I met everywhere I developed the following ideas which are forming the basic policy being followed by the Government. Only the victory of England and her allies can assure the independence of Belgium, and secondly that victory is becoming more certain every day." After listing other points of policy Spaak went on to say:

"The King, by his obstinate refusal to collaborate with the enemy is not only the symbol of the passive resistance of occupied Belgium. He has become also an element in the active resistance (that is the resistance carried on from London). Although every day we regret the absence of the King, which makes our task so much heavier and more difficult, we admire his attitude in the occupied country and we know what comfort it gives to our countrymen. We think often of Your Majesty, of his troubles and trials, of his so severe isolation; and I am convinced that my colleagues are in accord with me when I say have confidence in a better future. *Que Votre Majeste ait confiance en nous*. Signed, "P-H Spaak."

We do not know, and we may never know, with what mixed emotions Leopold read this letter. Now, too late, the grim warnings of Henri Baels must have flooded his mind like a torrent. Spaak did not know of his marriage. If he had, it is unlikely he would have delivered himself of sentiments so admiring and loyal.

Spaak's letter represented the high water mark of Leopold's wartime standing. Shortly after it was written his position disintegrated. Liliane became pregnant and it was impossible to keep the marriage secret any longer. Three months after the ceremony Leopold was obliged to authorise the Cardinal to announce to the Belgian people, by a pastoral letter read in every church, that he was married. This began the first of many self-perpetuating slanders, that Liliane was pregnant before marriage.

The Germans, of course, were delighted, if only for the painful impact the news had upon the Belgian people. They calculated that this would knock some of the fight out of the increasing resistance movement inside the country, and they were right. A Brussels newspaper wrote: "Sire! We thought you had your face turned towards us in misery; instead, you had it hidden on the shoulder of a woman."

From the start Liliane made Leopold and his three children so happy that their very happiness defeated its own ends.

Some of the sharpness went out of his approach to the war. As a symbol of resistance his silhouette faded.

In June, 1944, the Allies landed in France, and the liberation of Europe from the West began. Twenty-four hours after the first landings, a German officer entered the Bungalow and told the King politely but firmly to come with him, and bring with him not more than a small suitcase. Leopold looked outside and found a large staff car drawn up outside the house, flanked by motorcyclists of the S.S. Leopold concurred.

Later the same evening, they came for Liliane. The princess protested vigorously. Her two boys, Baudoin and Charles, were ill, but the Germans insisted, and Liliane departed with her whole family under a heavy escort of the S.S. Three days later, after days and nights of exhausting driving, they were reunited, to their relief and delight, at the Castle of Hirschstein, near Dresden. Then followed almost a year of captivity, life becoming more and more severe. Their gaoler, Lüker, terrified that they might escape, deprived them of all news and contact with the outside world. Food grew scarcer. The children were constantly hungry and there was often no milk for the baby, Alexander.

Every day, however, Leopold and the small staff allowed to accompany him, appeared, in full uniform. All of them laughed and joked, determined not to allow their captives the comfort of seeing them depressed, even when the Runstedt offensive began in the winter of 1944 and seemed at one point likely to make all Belgium a battleground yet again—and would have done so, but for the heroism of the United States soldiers holding out in the Bastogne hedgehog.

In March, 1945, they were moved once more. In Munich they were caught in the middle of one of the obliterating air attacks which had to be experienced to be believed. Unlike the all-night German raids of earlier in the war, the Allies managed a much more deadly effect in raids which lasted minutes or even seconds. Lüker would not allow the Royal Family to take shelter and the cars were pulled up under a railway arch. The children were crying and terrified and for the first time Leopold lost his attitude of contemptuous self-control and turned on his German guards in a fury, telling them what he thought of men who made a woman and children stay out in the open during a bombing raid when there were shelters only a few metres away. When the raid was over they spent the rest of the night in a dirty hotel of doubtful reputation. Two months later, at St. Wolfgang in Austria, they were liberated by the Seventh American Army.

Dizzy with the joy of freedom, Leopold made plans for return, and then received his greatest shock, a tactful but unmistakable message from his brother Charles to stay out of Belgium for the time being. The interesting factor of the situation was Leopold's obvious surprise, which showed how completely he had lost touch with events and his own relation to them. He had been incarcerated in Belgium when the important decisions concerning his country were being made by his legal ministers in London. He had been held a prisoner in Germany when the government was back in Brussels trying to put things in order. Leopold had never been in the right place at the right time, and with the war over and won he symbolised not the most unyielding in the Belgian war effort as his father had done in 1914-1918, but rather the doubts and anxieties of a nation that had faced long occupation and was unsure of its own place in the picture of the war.

Nor was the progress of events reassuring. On May 4, 1945, while the King's whereabouts were still unknown the Socialist Party called on Leopold to resign. Leopold's brother Charles was made Regent. In view of the relations between the two men over the years this act, logical though it was, did not augur well for Leopold. Charles, a bachelor, had lived his life as the younger brother of the heir to a dynasty, an agreeable enough existence to a prince lacking ambition, but galling to a prince who enjoyed responsibility and power as Charles did. Charles, with the Government, travelled to St. Wolfgang to pay their respects to the King, and put up at the White Horse Inn there. Leopold, entering the inn to see his brother, was told that the Prince had retired for the night and would see him tomorrow. It was a bad start, and it gave Leopold a new and strictly personal reason for winning his throne back —to deprive Charles of it.

Belgian critics called Leopold a "bitter, stubborn man," but he had cause for bitterness. As a young man he had followed his quest, like any other, for his place in the sun. Handsome, high-principled, courageous, intelligent, an exceptionally fine sportsman, he had everything a youth could wish for, and what had happened? He had been overshadowed by his father, the *roi chevalier*. The intellectuals sat at the feet of his mother. In the outer world he was eclipsed by Britain's Prince of Wales. When he married, it was his wife who dazzled the public; and when she died the people went into mourning and looked at him in reproach. Finally he had been left alone, with the stage to himself. He had uttered his agonised soliloquy, and the end was not applause, but exile.

Leopold and his family moved to the Villa du Reposoir, near Geneva, and he told the press, "I deny all the accusations and ask for a plebiscite. I will only accept the verdict of the Belgian people."

Under the Regency of the tall, ungainly Prince Charles, Belgium began, more quickly than most nations, to recover from the war. She put her great imperial wealth to use and it was not long before she streamed into a sustained period of great prosperity. Leopold remained in Switzerland, and the problem of the monarchy grew more and more acute. Any alternative to the monarchy was unthinkable to the mass of the Belgian people. The Communists and Socialists declared themselves for a republic, but this meant a degrading squabble every four or five years for a figurehead President, with Flemings and Walloons alternating in power and the old race differences between the Flemish and French-speaking Belgians constantly exacerbated. Charles reigned as Regent quietly but confidently and some political circles in the country looked to him as the answer to the royal problem. There is no doubt that Charles would have enjoyed being King, but the Legitimists realised that it could not be. That was the essence of monarchy. Leopold might be unpopular and his son an unknown quantity, but if you have a monarchy you cannot monkey about with the legitimate descent. Some Belgians certainly toyed with the idea of re-directing the crown towards Charles, but such an act would have resulted in consequences to succeeding generations that would destroy the monarchy and perhaps the nation. Baudoin or Baudoin's heirs would become Pretenders, and Pretenders with a more legitimate right to the throne than the children of Charles. And Charles as a "usurper" was hated by the Belgian royalists. No, it was Leopold or Baudoin or a republic, and as Leopold remained determined not to abdicate, the Belgian people with tempers wearing thinner and thinner, found a plebiscite on their hands. Leopold would not or could not see that it was only his own person that was objected to, that the country, even including his supporters, would accept his abdication in favour of Baudoin with relief. Leopold made the mistake no King should ever make. He made himself an issue to his people. The man whose job it was to symbolise the unity of the country declared he would regard a vote of 55% in his favour as a sign of confidence in his return. It was an unfor-

givable announcement to make. It showed that he was banking
on the Flemish vote against the Walloon vote. Max Busset,
the Socialist leader, cried out: "We have a monarchy in Belgium because we want to remove the Flemish-Walloon question from politics. This King, whether he willed it or not, has
become a Fleming. His presence here would destroy the
purpose of the monarchy." The plebiscite was carried out in
May, 1950, in an atmosphere of furious politicking and im-
pending revolution. The anti-Leopold campaign was headed
by Paul-Henri Spaak, regretting bitterly the letter of praise
he had sent to the King in 1941.

The vote revealed 57.68% in favour of the King's return.
It was technically a victory for the King, but it was implicitly
Pyrrhic. The Royal Family returned in silence, the streets
under heavy guard. Leopold went to the microphone and
made a speech urging unity. It was the signal for the riots,
the ugly scenes which make Brussels so notorious periodically.
Leading the rioters was Paul-Henri Spaak himself. This was
not the most noble act of Belgium's most eminent statesman,
but that a constitutionalist of Spaak's stature should be driven
to such anti-democratic measures revealed the passion of the
country. Leopold was not a wicked man. When he realised
that the price he must pay for a return to the throne was the
bloodshed of his countrymen, he yielded at once. He telephoned Socialist headquarters and asked Max Busset to come
over and advise him what to do. For more than an hour the
Socialist and the King were alone together. "I got the impression," Busset said later, "of a broken man who knew he
had been ill advised, if not betrayed."*

Busset expected him to open the talk with some kind of
statement justifying his action. Instead the King said nothing,
but with a gesture invited Busset to speak. For some reason

* Ernest O. Hauser in the *Saturday Evening Post*, December 2, 1950.

Busset found himself inarticulate and the words came awk-
wardly. All the things he had come prepared to say were
forgotten.

"I too have a son," he said at last, "and I understand what
all this must mean to you." From that moment it was simply
a question of how Leopold could withdraw and still keep his
self-respect. Always stubborn, he was stubborn now with those
advisers who pleaded with him to stay and ride out the storm.
He agreed he would live in Belgium as King in name only.
Baudoin would take the title of Prince Royal and when he
came of age, a year hence, Leopold would abdicate.

Baudoin's oath-taking as Prince Royal was on August 11,
1950. The day before, he was created a Lieutenant General,
the highest rank in the Belgian Army, and he put on the uniform for the ceremony. Baudoin had never worn a uniform
before and he carried it with touching lack of assurance. As
he raised his hand in the Palace of the Nation to take his
Oath, a Communist deputy shouted "*Vive la Republique*" and
the cry was taken up by other Communists. After a second's
shocked silence the Communists were drowned out by cries
from the rest of the company of "*Vive le Prince.*" Baudoin
waited for silence to be restored and then he said, quietly,
in French and in Flemish, "I swear to observe the Constitution and the laws of the Belgian people, to maintain the independence of the Nation and the integrity of its territory."

Baudoin's youth and awkwardness was not necessarily a
disadvantage in itself. The Belgian people had had their fill
of over-confident Kings. They were hurt, weary of royal controversy and anxious only for a figure that they could rally
round in good conscience. But if the Belgians thought that
their royal troubles were over they were mistaken. Old statesmen had noticed with approval that Baudoin had not flinched
at the unexpected shout of the Communists and had made

his declaration in an unwavering voice. From his father, Baudoin had inherited stubbornness. In the boy's heart blazed a resentment of England. Baudoin loved his father and his stepmother equally. If he willed anything from the throne it was to reconstitute the good name of his parents. Meanwhile the plebiscite posters clung, flaking, to the walls of the Brussels buildings. Across portraits of Leopold, put up by Legitimists, were slapped the slogan, "Stop Baels." Other posters showed Leopold shaking hands with Hitler. Baudoin had a hard task ahead of him.

# III

# *Leopold—2*

## Half Way to a Happy Ending

In as much as the (hereditary) prince has less cause and less necessity to give offence, it is only natural that he should be more loved; and if no extraordinary vices make him hated, it is only reasonable for his subjects to be naturally attached to him, the memories and causes of innovation being forgotten in the long period over which his rule has extended; whereas one change always leaves the way prepared for the introduction of another.

—Machiavelli.

$\mathcal{B}$y the time Leopold's abdication was made final on July 16th, 1951, the tensions had eased. The King had called to the Great Throne Room members of the Government, representatives from the nine provinces of Belgium, the Universities, the Arts and Sciences, the Empire, the Church, the Armed Forces and the Press.

Baudoin, his hands behind his back, his eyes down, stood by the side of his father and the King spoke a few words to the gathering. "I have brought you here," he said, "because the nation's interest requires, as also does the stability of the Royal House, that my decision to put an end to my reign be accompanied by a solemn public expression of concord."

He turned to the Prince and spoke to him so that all could hear. "My dear Baudoin, I am proud to hand on to you the noble and onerous mission by which, from henceforth, it will be you who shall wear the Crown of a Belgium, which, despite the most terrible of wars and the upheavals which come in its train, has remained intact in its territory, free and faithful to its traditions. You will discharge this mission with the will to serve your country and to continue the works of the Dynasty in conformity with the principles I have taught you. These principles I learned from my father, King Albert, and they have always determined my attitude during the difficult years of a reign, the judgment on which I leave to history. The sympathy and confidence with which the entire population has acclaimed you permit me finally to lay down the royal powers without fear for the future and with the consciousness of duty done."

Leopold turned back to the assembly. "At the moment of laying down my charge," he concluded, "my thoughts can but run upon the years I have passed in your midst. I have shared your joys and your sorrows . . . My last words as King of the Belgians are a forcible reminder, my dear countrymen, that the future of our country depends on your national solidarity; and a request that you unite with fervent loyalty behind my son, King Baudoin. . . ."

Baudoin looked his father in the eyes and spoke two short sentences. "My dear father, I am deeply moved by the noble words you have spoken. I promise you I will do all in my power to show myself worthy to be your son." Not a word about Belgium or the justice of the public will.

Baudoin Albert Charles Leopold Axel Marie Gustave, Duke of Brabant, Count of Hainaut, then became Belgium's fifth King. He was a boy of uncertain education and confidence. His progress to the age of twenty had been marked by the violent death of his grand-father and his mother, by the German occupation of Belgium and by the imprisonment of his family and himself, by exile, and finally by the fiasco of Leopold's return to the throne. All the traditional channels of education and growing up had been dammed up against him. He had had to change school too often to be able to plant childhood roots or make childhood friends and he had had to rely on private tutors. He knew nothing about girls. He was, withal, a boy of excellent heart, as one story from his youth reveals. Handing round candy to his fellow-pupils and tutors, he noticed that one of the tutors put his own caramel in his pocket to keep until after he had finished his cigar. Baudoin interpreted the action to himself and next day sent the tutor a large bag of caramels, with a note saying, "These are for your little girl. I noticed yesterday how you put your caramel aside." Later, when the tutor's daughter fell ill, Baudoin sent him a small image of St. Joseph with a note: "To help Josette get better quickly."

It was not long before the young King Baudoin was in trouble. Alone among the crowned heads of Europe he failed to attend the funeral of King George VI, and delegated his younger brother, Albert, to represent Belgium. The King's ministers were appalled at this discourtesy, and the Prime Minister, Jean van Houtte tried to persuade him to change his mind. But Baudoin was the son of Leopold. He had made his decision and he stuck to it. Constitutionally the Prime Minister of Belgium accepts reponsibilities for the King's decisions, and the Parliamentary Opposition insisted on a vote of censure. Belgium, after all, felt deep bonds towards Britain. The King's ministers stalled on the request for a debate, hoping to change the King's mind. They failed and then lost the vote by 91 to 84. Nevertheless Albert went to London and Baudoin stayed home.

The following year indignation in the country burst into fury. From the Belgian Royal Family's point of view it was the most miserable luck. In February, 1953, the worst storm in living memory sent the North Sea rolling over low-lying areas of Britain, Holland and Belgium. In Britain the new Queen Elizabeth and Prince Philip arrived with the rescue parties. In Holland Prince Bernhard and Queen Juliana remained on the spot without sleep for days and nights together.

Baudoin had left Brussels with his father and stepmother for a holiday on the Riviera. It was hardly the King's fault that he did not know the floods were coming. Photographs in the Belgian papers showed the King sunning himself, side by side with catastrophe photos. He hurried back and promptly went down with influenza. He then arranged to return to the Riviera to recuperate but vented his resentment on a French reporter from the extremely alert Paris evening paper, *France-Soir*. "It is Belgian unity itself that is being attacked through the attacks on the Royal Family," he said.

In the Chamber of Deputies Jean van Houtte wearily accepted responsibility for the King's action, insisted that Baudoin was seriously ill and that he never talked to the French journalist anyway. *France-Soir* promptly produced photographs of the King doing just that. These successive crises had an important effect on the Belgians. It is an important fact of monarchy that people hate to criticise their sovereigns. Scandals and gossip are one thing. Sustained criticism is quite different. If the King is caught in an invidious position a scapegoat must be found. If Queen Elizabeth of England surrounds herself with a panoply of ceremony that appears too old-fashioned for modern times, it is not the Queen but her advisers who are attacked, although it is obvious that the Queen herself would do something about it if she really objected to it. Even the most controversial of ex-Kings, the Duke of Windsor, is criticised only reluctantly. It is easier to blame the Duchess of Windsor for everything.

So it was in Belgium. Baudoin and Leopold did things that offended their subjects. Rather than attack their Kings the Belgians preferred to vent their anger on others. Sometimes they fired on the ministers but usually they preferred their easiest and choicest target—the Princess de Rethy. The Belgian press, one of the most sensational in Europe, turned on Liliane with a venom that has scarcely been equalled in print, except perhaps by some of the extreme right-wing attacks made on President Roosevelt in the United States. Some of the attacks were unprintable. Liliane was called "the Shrimp Queen," based on the fact that Henri Baels was once in the fish business. The responsible Socialist newspaper *Le Peuple*, wrote at the time of the floods, "Madame de Rethy, we are sure, was primarily responsible for this detestable incident. She is exercising a palace influence to which she has no right." The newspaper continued irrelevantly: "Her open-necked blouses and slacks are provocative, and her behaviour indiscreet and boisterous. The Government must regulate her status."

Baudoin, like his father, Leopold, and his brother, Albert, adored Liliane and took every attack on her as a personal mortification. A friend of the Royal Family told the able English journalist, Sam White, in 1953, "I don't know how that boy can carry on. He read one slanderous attack on Princess de Rethy, dropped the paper and left the room. He returned a few minutes later and was under control but he cancelled all official duties for the day."

In 1952, 1953 and 1954 the cult of Rethy hatred was so widespread and noisy as to sound like a continuous roar. Liliane's special beauty in some way seemed to add a sadistic note to the attack. Pictures of Queen Astrid continued to hang in the Brussels stores as a mute reproach to Leopold. Liliane was accused of being pro-Nazi. The story that she was married after becoming pregnant had become so firmly implanted that one member of Belgian society, feeling it necessary to settle the matter, asked for an audience with Cardinal van Roey, with the sole purpose of cornering him into a confession.

"I swear before God," said the prelate, "that I married the King and Liliane Baels on September 11, 1941, as announced."

But luck continued to run cruelly against Liliane. Her

brother was arrested on a charge of attempting to evade military service, and deprived of his civil rights for a while. To make matters worse, it could be seen that there were serious tensions within the family, for which—inevitably—Liliane was blamed. Charles who had enjoyed his years as Regent, locked himself inside his seaside villa at Ostend and became a recluse, spending his days gloomily playing the organ or painting. He never visited either his brother or his mother, not even for family celebrations.

The Dowager Queen Elisabeth who had once supported Liliane now saw little of her. Unpopularity needs its complement. If Liliane was compelled to be the villain of the Belgian scene, there had to be a heroine and the role fell on the Dowager Queen whose magnificent eccentricities delighted the Belgians. Her passion for music and the arts had had an important influence on Brussels cultural life. She travelled to Communist Poland for the Chopin Festival when she was 79, and in 1958 when she was 82 she scampered up the steps to a Russian airliner which the Soviet Government had put at her service to fly her to the Moscow Music Festival. Elisabeth loved people and her circle was disconcertingly wide. Some of the friends she invited to her palace at Stuyvenberg startled not only her family but even the police. The Dowager Queen acted always on impulse. One morning at six o'clock, at the end of the war, she was seen playing the violin in a bomb crater in her garden. "It's such a lovely morning," she said, "and the accoustics in this crater are perfect."

Queen Elisabeth's antics on the one hand, and Prince Charles's undisguised hostility on the other, all seemed to make the withdrawn little family group at Laeken more isolated and alone than ever.

One of the blessings to the oppressed of the world, however, is in the circumstance of change. Passions wither. Enthusiasms die and new sets of principles emerge to replace the old. Had Leopold been able to ride out the storm of 1950 he would undoubtedly be a respected King today. The Belgian people just could not go on hating Liliane that much, or resenting Leopold. The first to benefit from the softening attitude was Baudoin himself. As a King he gained in both confidence and authority. He no longer stammered in front of his father. His salute became less awkward and he wore his uniform with more assurance. He could snap and make ministers tremble. He could apply himself with single-minded intensity to his papers. He began to enjoy his job.

At the palace at Laeken he built for himself a closed motor track several kilometers in diameter; and when he wanted to relax he would take out his Lancia and go roaring round the track. His driving on the public roads gave his ministers cause for anxiety. People who had known Baudoin over the years became increasingly impressed with the strength of his character and the extreme respect which aides and ministers gave to him. Robert Delmarcelle, the distinguished royalist journalist, who had been received by the King on numerous occasions gave a picture of Baudoin at work. His eyes had a bright and amused look, and he would ask questions as skilful and as searching as a lawyer. His own conversation was clear, well-expressed and stripped of unnecessary frills. One felt in his talk a certain undercurrent of impatience, as one did with both his father and grandfather, giving the idea that, for so long as the talk was constructive, interesting and to the point, the visitor was welcome, but that he would be wiser not to waste time with small-talk. Consequently, dialogue between the King and his visitor tended to take on a summary form with quick entrances and exits. The King's smile was purposeful, making the visitor feel as though he earned it, as though

Baudoin did not smile for everyone. When the King laughed it was a hearty, robust and sincere laugh.

Baudoin, seen in a new and more impressive light, began to influence the people by his own example. Respecting Baudoin—and even slightly nervous of Baudoin—the Belgian people inevitably had to respect his unswerving loyalty to his father and stepmother. Once the perspective changed, the whole picture took on a new dimension. Liliane had, after all, not only proved a splendid mother to the children of Astrid but had given to Leopold three children of her own, Alexander in 1942, Marie-Christina in 1951, and Marie-Esmeralda in 1956. There were no rivalries or distinctions among them. Only a mother of genius could have created such family harmony. And only the most prejudiced eye could fail to see that there was no family influence being exerted by Leopold or Liliane on the tough young King who, even if he wished it otherwise, was too busy at his royal duties to see them more than once or twice a month. Occasionally, still, the bad luck that pursued Liliane kept up with her. In 1957, after her son Prince Alexander had been cured of a serious heart disease in Boston, Massachusetts, she arranged to have other children with the same condition sent to Boston for treatment at her expense. Two who accepted her offer died and the plan was discontinued. Once again the old hatred glowed red, but the fire died quickly because there was not so much to feed it as there had been in the old days.

Through all her ordeal Liliane de Rethy behaved with dignity. A gay, gregarious person, she accepted without question the cloistered existence which her marriage imposed on her. It is a remarkable fact that from the time of her marriage to the ceremonies of the World Fair in 1958, in which she was pushed into the foreground by Baudoin, not two hundred

WIDE WORLD PHOTOS

The funeral procession of Edward VII of England. European monarchs in the ranks of marchers ~e the Kings of England, Germany, Spain, Greece, Norway, Portugal, Denmark, Bulgaria and ~elgium.

eopold III, King of Belgium from 1934 ~ 1951, and his first wife, Queen Astrid.

King Baudouin of Belgium who replaced his father, Leopold III, as ruler.

ROWN BROTHERS

BROWN BROTHERS

The Comte de Paris, Pretender to the throne of France, with his wife, surrounded by their 11 children. Ironically, if one more child is born to the Comte, the President of the Republic of France will become its godfather according to French custom. At the extreme right is Prince Henri, eldest son of the Pretender.

Prince Henry of France, eldest son of the Comte de Paris, Pretender to the French throne, at his marriage to Princess Theresa of Wurtemberg, July 5, 1957, the greatest gathering of royalty since the turn of the century. At his left is King Paul of Greece who served as the Prince's witness.

At a reception given in their honor are King Paul (center) and Queen Frederica (to the right) of Greece with their daughter Princess Sophia (left of the King) and their host, M. Christian Pineau (extreme left).

Belgians had so much as set eyes on her. Hardly a score had heard her voice. She had appeared in public only once, at a birthday party for Queen Elisabeth in 1942. She laughed away the attacks on her and did not let even her husband see what distress she had suffered. She confided one thing to friends: that she would like to leave the Belgian scene with her reputation higher than it is at present; this, with the progress of time and the re-weaving of attitudes, is most likely, providing her own deadly luck changes. After all no one would have thought, five years ago, that the prospects for the Belgian Royal Family would so suddenly improve or could look so bright as they do now.

Perhaps nothing pleased Belgians more than Leopold's meeting with Queen Elizabeth of England. On May 15, 1956, for the first time in nineteen years, a King of Belgium was received at the English Court and a heartbreaking split was healed. Leopold was in Britain to attend the celebration of the Inniskilling Dragoon Guards, of which he was Colonel-in-Chief. Afterwards he saw Sir Anthony Eden, then the Prime Minister, and stopped off for tea at Buckingham Palace. From that time on Leopold quietly worked at renewing his old British contacts. He invited a party of former classmates at Eton to stay with him. He added a charming touch. He also invited his old housemaster, Mr. Samuel Gorney Lubbock, an octogenarian. In 1957, Leopold, Baudoin and Liliane entertained the Duke of Gloucester at dinner and some weeks later Leopold and Liliane were dinner guests of the British Ambassador.

Early in 1958, Leopold and his children had a frightening escape when the door of a Sabena Convair flew open ten minutes after taking off from Nice. Leopold and Prince Albert threw themselves on the smallest children, Marie-Christina, aged six, and Marie-Esmeralda, fifteen months, to save them from being sucked out. The pilot, an Englishman, Charles Bryant, flew the plane back to Nice Airport and landed safely. Afterwards, Leopold sent the pilot a telegram worded in an interesting and significant way. It read: "Congratulations on your flying skill and on your British pluck. Leopold." The coupling of the word "British" to "pluck" suffused the note with a special kind of intensity and warmth.

It is a sign of the change in the temper of the Belgians that the most pressing problem of the Royal Family today is the problem of the succession. No personal difference remains between the Belgians and the Royal Family that cannot be solved by Baudoin's finding a wife. Once he is married, Leopold and Liliane could retire to the south of France as they want to do. Baudoin, in his public appearances, has given an appealing picture of sensitivity, strength and loneliness all in one, that has turned all royal Europe into matchmakers. The Dowager Queen Elisabeth told him that not until he married would he become Baudoin I. Until then he would remain "the son of Leopold III." Even *Le Soir*, the most dignified and deferential of Belgian newspapers felt obliged to have its say. "It is well known," the paper stated flatly, "that the prayer of every Belgian is that the King will soon give a Queen to Belgium. The announcement of a royal marriage will be received with an inexpressible joy."

The field is deceptively large. Europe teems with eligible princesses. At various times Baudoin has been reported engaged to Princess Margaret, and Princess Alexandra of England; Princess Isabelle of France; Princess Astrid of Norway; Princess Maria-Pia and Princess Maria Gabriella of Italy; Princess Margarita of Aosta-Savoy; Princess Sandra Torlonia of Italy; Princess Marie Therese of Bourbon-Parma; Princess

Elizabeth and Princess Marie-Adelaide of Luxembourg; Princess Margaretha and Princess Birgitta of Sweden; Princess Elizabeth of Liechtenstein; Princess Cecile of Bourbon-Parma, Princess Beatrix and Princess Irene of the Netherlands and even a Belgian Princess, Elisabeth de Merode.

The matchmakers ignore an intense human factor. Baudoin, having been deprived of everything a boy can expect to enjoy: school, friends, girl-friends, parties; who was made the head of the state when he should have been having his sophomore year at the University, and was King before he was twenty-one, claims the last human right open to him, the right to fall in love.

And how does a King fall in love? He works seven days a week with only a few hours left for driving his car, listening to records, catching up with his reading. When vacations come, he sees his family whom he has neglected. When he meets a girl he asks himself. "Is this all arranged? Has it been discussed and planned? Does the Dynasty demand it?" Several princesses have already received startlingly brusque rebuffs from Baudoin, who is nervous in their presence and finds himself caught with a dilemma that only an unexpected attack of love can solve.

So the Brussels World Fair of 1958 came and went. Liliane de Rethy emerged from her long seclusion, and Baudoin remained where he was. The value of a constitutional monarch, as Bagehot says, lies in the increasing repository of wisdom he acquires over the years. Governments come and Governments go, but the King remains, enriched equally by witnessing the folly that brings a Government down and by the intelligence that keeps a Government up. He is the confidante of all. Young monarchs can be ignored. So can old monarchs who have learned nothing. Baudoin possesses strong cards, is a young monarch who has suffered much and is learning conscientiously. He could, one day, become the most dominating monarch in Europe, the model and ideal to others; but not so long as he remains a bachelor, obsessed by his private resentments. The patience of people who live in monarchies is long, but it tends to exhaust itself overnight.

# IV

# *The Count of Paris*

## Left from the Start

*O couronne de France que tu es précieuse et très vile tout à la fois! Précieuse et d'in-estimable prix si l'on considère le mystère de justice qui, en toi virtuellement est inclus et réside. Mais vile et plus vile que tout au monde, si l'on considère le fardeau, les fatigues, les angoisses, les tourments, les peines de coeur, de corps et de conscience dont tu accables ceux qui te portent, les périls d'âme ou tu les exposes.*

—Charles V, on his deathbed.

"My colleagues think I am mad," said the Count of Paris complacently to a journalist in 1957. "By 'my colleagues', I mean the other Kings without crowns. They think I am mad because I am convinced that an economy which has favoured the hatred between classes, which has tolerated work in conditions which make the workers not workers but slaves, and has favoured the complete power of money, is a miserable system surely condemned to perish. The high clergy think I am mad because I am convinced that it is the break between Christian and Socialist thought which has opened the gates to Marxism. I am a Capet," the Count concluded, "and the Capets have always been on the people's side against feudalism."

Two words explain this buoyancy of the Count of Paris, Pretender to the throne of a nation whose very name symbolises republicanism. Change and time. The inevitability of change is the consolation of Pretenders. But for the Count of Paris alone, among the royal aspirants, time is on his side. Not since 1870 has France been so close to monarchy.

In one of his judgments the Count of Paris is wrong. His

colleagues do not think he is mad. They do not love him, it is true. He is not the most popular of Pretenders. Some think he is a busybody, and others a renegade, but nobody considers him mad. Rather do they try to imitate his lucidity. No living Pretender sees his own position more clearly, nor has any prince expressed the dilemma of monarchy better. He has, after all, devoted a lifetime to its study, as the heir to a dynasty that has known no power for more than one hundred years. The Count's career has been a delicate weighing of political balance, not merely of the political support he could command but the value of that support and of the outside support worth cultivating, of the conflicting republican and right-wing ideals which traditionally move France, and of which lessons history has taught him to accept and which to shun.

The basic principle of his life has been to ignore the Right which will always vote for him anyway, and woo the Left which, as a point of principle, would rather go to the barricades than support a King. The Count has not succeeded in converting the French Socialists to the monarchy, but he has earned their respect as a person, which is just as difficult, perhaps more so. In 1945 Leon Blum said to him, "I wonder if, at the Chamber, even we, the Socialists, could vote for your revolutionary programme of reforms." The Socialist Government of Guy Mollet, which served in 1956 and 1957, actually sent the Count as its official delegate on a mission abroad. Among his left-wing supporters he has been called *le Dauphin de la Republique*.

This paradoxical philosophy of the Count's would seem to be political opportunism at its most cynical if it were not taken in context with the history of the House which devolves upon him, or upon the unsavory course of royalist feeling in 20th century France as expressed by the royalist spokesmen, Charles Maurras and Léon Daudet. Maurras, a brilliant, ruthless writer, elevated to the Academy in 1938, was editor of *Action Francaise*. For fifty years Maurras wrote of what the French Right wanted to read, of a Fascistic, anti-republican, Jew-hating chauvinism, made more dangerous because expressed in splendid words. This "blind misanthrope and brawling litterateur," as Luethy called him, was stripped of his glamour in 1945, when he was condemned and imprisoned as a collaborator of the Germans, and he was never a fit spokesman for a respectable Royal Family, nor were Maurras's followers, his spiritual heirs, the *camelots du roi* (the King's travelling salesmen) the young thugs who tend to cluster round the monarchist movement of France, a desirable core of supporters. The Count of Paris today is obliged to tolerate them, as a Republican President of the United States must tolerate the various American First associations, but he has been careful not to embrace them.

The Count of Paris's leaning towards Socialism rests on deeper foundations than opportunism or on simple revulsion against the primitivism of a few right-wing royalist *vauriens*. The history of his family has not only guided him towards the Left, but has, in effect, dictated it.

The Fourth House of Orleans had for its first head, Philippe (1640-1701), brother of Louis XIV. His son, Phillipe, governed France during the Regency of Louis XV. The line, as is the wont of royal lines, went on to produce its share of clever men and nincompoops, but two men in particular have influenced the thinking of the Count of Paris. The first was Louis Philippe Joseph (1747-1794), who took an active part in the Revolution. He joined the moderate Jacobins, de-royalized himself and renamed himself Philippe Egalité. He became one of the deputies to the Convention and even voted for the execution of his cousin, Louis XVI. It did him little good. Shortly afterwards he was guillotined too. The moral of that was, keep Left but not so far as to lose one's head.

Louis Philippe I, the son of Philippe Egalité, was King of the French for eighteen years. His presence on the throne was a testimony to the continuing strength of monarchical feeling in France, but it would be a foolish man who, with such a distinguished background of guillotined ancestors, would underrate republican feeling. Louis Philippe was no fool. The doors of the Palais Royal were thrown open for any citizen to enter and shake his hand. The royal crests were removed from the carriages. The King was given, and encouraged, the title of "King of the Bourgeois." Once he felt he had consolidated his position, however, he changed, became more royal, and was kicked out. The man who came to the throne by revolution in 1830 was removed by revolution in 1848, and died two years later in England where he was living under the modest name of "Mr. Smith." The moral of all that was: if you can't fight them join them, but if you have to join them, join them properly.

Louis Philippe I was the last Bourbon to rule in France, the last King but one that France was to know to this day. If the record shows nothing else, at least the Count of Paris can say that few other royal families have histories which so clearly point the way he ought to go. The years following the overthrow of Louis Philippe up to the emergence of the present Pretender, were aimless ones for the House of Orleans. One of the few incidents of note was a love affair which might have resulted in a most unusual union between the Houses of Britain and France, something which has not happened since Charles I married Henrietta Maria, daughter of Henri IV. Louis Philippe Albert d'Orleans, the Count of Paris (1838-1894) settled in England in 1886. His elder daughter, Amélie, married Dom Carlos of Portugal who was assassinated in 1908. His second daughter Hélène (born 1871) fell in love with the Duke of Clarence, eldest son of the subsequent Edward VII and Queen Alexandra. Queen Victoria did not oppose the engagement, but the Pope refused to grant Hélène a dispensation to change her religion, and the suit was dropped. The Duke of Clarence became engaged to Princess Mary of Teck, but he died and Mary married his younger brother George (subsequently King George V) instead. George having been pliant to his family wishes, would presumably have married Princess Hélène instead, and a very different British Royal Family would have existed today.

The present Count of Paris was born on July 5, 1908, at the Chateau Nouvion-en-Thierarche (Aisne). His parents, in the Bourbon tradition, were first cousins, his mother being Isabelle of France, sister of the Duke of Orleans, grandson of Louis Philippe. In World War I, Henri's father the Duke of Guise, left Morocco, where he was living with his family, and enlisted in the French Army under the name of Orliac; the Duchess remained with her four children, Henri, and three daughters older than he, Isabelle, Francoise and Anne. Henri grew up a sensitive, intelligent boy with the serious, small-faced good looks of the French aristocrat. He rode on his father's estates and played games with the sons of Arab pashas and Caids. One of his tutors was the respected historian, Ernest Lavisse, who was an Academician and director of the Ecole Normale, a school where the teachers were strongly influenced by the teachings of Jaurès, the French Socialist. Henri, with his preceptor, the Abbé Thomas, visited the poor quarters of Paris which tourists do not see, and was shocked at the misery of the French people.

Thus, to whatever tasks he bent he found influences guiding him in the same direction—Left. Henri was not, at this point, in direct line for a claim to the French throne. The claim descended to his uncle, the Duke of Orleans. In 1926, however, the Duke died. Henri's father became the Pretender and Henri the heir. In coming into his inheritance he also lost his birthright. Automatically, by a law of June 23, 1886, the family was barred from France. Exile is one of the most cruel of all punishments to suffer. As far as Henri knew, the odds were overwhelmingly in favour of his being banished for the rest of his life, from Paris, the green garden of France, and the French environment that seems in many ways more precious and alive to a Frenchman than a native land means to the citizen of any other country. The family obeyed the law, moved, and took up residence in Brussels, in the Manoir d'Anjou.

Henri also began his rigorous and macabre training, the careful grooming required of a Dauphin who aspires to a throne that does not exist. This was a depressing career to undertake, especially for someone of Henri's nature. By instinct a man of action, whose response to any challenge was to charge, he prepared to devote the rest of his life to an inactive cause, and one apparently bound to end in sterility and disappointment. Nevertheless he took up the task with enthusiasm. He joined the *Faculté des Sciences* at Louvain, learning civil rights, and absorbing more and more of the philosophies of the liberal and socialist writers. On July 25, 1929, for his twenty-first birthday, his father gave him the title of the Count of Paris. Life, even in exile, however, was good. The Orleans family was rich, richer than many of the families with thrones, the family wealth issuing mainly from real estate in France and in North Africa. Henri drove a red Bugatti at characteristically royal speed, flew his own airplane and went on military manoeuvres with the Belgian Army.

In the middle of his studies, while only 22, he fell in love. The "most beautiful woman in Europe," like "the richest man in the world" is an easy title to throw around, and an impossible one to establish. It has been claimed many times for Isabelle of Orleans-Braganza, and in truth, she was a girl—and is today a woman—of the most astonishing beauty. From the top of the brow to the tip of her nose there is almost no indentation; it is the classic profile of a Greek goddess. Matching her beauty is a vivid intelligence and a gay versatility. When Henri met her she was nineteen years old, but even then she was capable of enchanting a sculptor, testing an Academician with her conversation, or, as a matter of interest, milking a cow. Her personality may have stemmed from an unusual royal background, her blood being Brazilian-Portuguese, French and Bohemian. Had Henri been a prince in line for a real throne instead of a dormant one, the match would have been an exciting one in the affairs of the world. As it was, it is remembered as the most important royal wedding of the decade. Isabelle was the daughter of Dom Pedro of Alcantara and the Duchess Dobržensky von Dobrzenicz, and a descendant of Dom Pedro II, the last Emperor of Brazil. She and Henri met in Brussels, and when she was about to leave he begged her to return. In the summer of 1930 they met in Morocco. In the autumn they met in Sicily. In the winter they met in the mountains of Bohemia where Isabelle's parents had estates. In December their engagement was announced.

The world of unemployed royalty can be an enervating one, lacking direction, reason, or even much dignity. All at once this society had thrown together two people who would have electrified any society and, who, lacking a destiny, would, by their natural momentum and drive, create one for themselves. That they became engaged so young is among other things an indication of the solemnity with which they faced their royal duties.

The engagement reception was impressive and slightly crazy. For one thing it lasted forty-eight hours, and, as it was held in Paris, the exiled fiancé could not be present. For hour after hour in the Hotel Lambert, the Paris residence of the Orleans-Braganzas, the monarchists filed past to pay homage to the future Dauphine. One peasant old enough to remember the Emperor Louis Napoleon, who had lost his throne sixty years earlier, walked forty miles to see her.

The reception had been held on March 14 and 15. The wedding took place a month later, in Palermo, Sicily. For political reasons no invitations had been issued, except to relatives, but the world's monarchists were not to be left out. Eight hundred, led by Charles Maurras, turned up from France in a chartered steamer. Scores of princes attended. Thirty Brazilians came from Rio do Janeiro to show that monarchist sentiment in Brazil still flourished. The witnesses were the bride's father and the Duke of Apulia, Don Carlos de Bourbon and Prince Czartorysky. Near the bishop's throne sat Queen Amélie, widow of the murdered Dom Carlos of Portugal. Britain, the United States and Belgium were represented by ambassadors. Isabelle wore a gown of white silk with a train twelve yards long, and a mantilla and cape of old lace.

Writing in the temper of the times, the London *Daily Express*, on April 29, 1931, reported, "A crown prince who will never be a King and a royal princess who will never be a Queen were married in Palermo Cathedral this morning. It was pathetically appropriate that this wedding of puppet royalties should have been celebrated in Sicily, the traditional home of puppets."

Two people less pathetic and more unlike puppets than Henri and Isabelle could scarcely be imagined. From the beginning they were determined that they were not going to allow themselves to be mirrored by Maurras, and, exiled or no, they would make their own impact on French thinking. They bought a castle in the Ardenne on the Belgian border, without gas or electricity but from which battlements they could "see France." Henri guessed that, sooner or later, Charles Maurras, brilliant as he was, would follow the fate of all rabble-rousers. To undercut the power of Maurras he opened an office in Brussels and started, in all the departments of France, monarchist groups independent of *Action Francaise*. In December 1934, he began a monthly bulletin for his supporters which he has maintained ever since. In this he sums up his views on world affairs and the monarchy. The clarity of his style and the sense of his observations made an immediate impact. He wrote a book called "Essay on the Government of Tomorrow," which sold 40,000 copies in France in the first three weeks after publication. His theme was, "Monarchy is not a Party." His father, the Duke of Guise, a tall, vague gentleman in a gray goatee beard and shabby suit, sometimes issued statements to the press, and these began soon to assume the style and punch of Henri's writing. A manifesto published in November, 1937, signed by the Duke of Guise, but more likely the work of Henri, declared:

"I have to dissipate a misunderstanding. There is a confusion in public opinion and among royalists which leads one to believe that *Action Francaise* is our interpreter. . . Only the House of France, of which I am the chief, is the repository of the royal doctrine. Only this House is qualified to forecast what tomorrow's monarchy will be."

The Anglo-French humiliation at Munich, in 1938, so exasperated Henri that he slipped secretly and illegally into France in an ambulance, called a press conference at Magny - en - Vexin to denounce the appeasement of Hiter, and departed as secretly as he came. Daladier, the Prime Minister, was furious, troubled, it could be, by his conscience as well as by a monarchical crisis to add to his other problems. Henri was taking serious risks by holding up such authority as existed then in France to such contempt. A prince who meddles in politics runs the one risk he cannot afford, of being wrong. But Henri's instinctive bravura drove him ruthlessly forward. He was incapable of passivity. He was making enemies, particularly among his cousins, but the fall that always seemed imminent did not happen. He was showing a flair for appearing to stay ahead of politics, while actually he was living by them. He whizzed so fast that his skates left not a crack in the thin ice. He was assisted by one skill, unusual in princes, that appealed to Frenchmen. He wrote well, and his bulletins were earnestly studied. In the meantime Isabelle produced six children in the first eight years of her marriage. She was not included in the 1886 statute of exile, and visited Paris regularly with her family.

July, 1939, found Henri on holiday in Brazil. Smelling war in the air he rushed back to France and received a rebuff which he did not expect but which was scarcely surprising in view of his political machinations. President Lebrun refused to let him enlist in the French Army. Lebrun was a weak man but not without humour and he knew the temperament of the dashing, scheming prince. Solemnly he made Henri a secret agent and sent him off to use his personal friendships to get information out of Victor Emmanuel of Italy, the Regent Paul of Yugoslavia, the Tsar Boris in Sofia, and King George II in Athens. Henri went off happily enough, but the German invasion of France in May, 1940, brought him back to Paris like the wind. This time, Paul Reynaud, who had other things to worry about, with France on the point of collapse, consented to let him join the Army under another name. So Henri joined the classic regiment of secret souls, the Foreign Legion, enlisting under the same name that his father had used in World War I—Orliac. *"Citoyen Suisse. Né a Geneve."*

Occasionally he was recognised but generally he was accepted and packed with the rest in third class carriages, with the murderous, scabrous, fabulous *lie du monde* of the Legion. Machiavelli said that the business of the Prince was war, but this certainly was not what he had in mind. Henri was enjoying himself, but he was also learning the home truths and some of the illusions of his comrades. "That Leopold," said a Belgian Legionnaire. "He has never been any good. But, Orliac, do you know who was his go-between when he was dealing with Hitler?"

"Who?" asked Henri innocently.

"The Count of Paris."

"Really."

Henri had not even finished his basic training when France fell and Pétain signed the armistice. That was not all. Irony is something that accompanies a prince like his own shadow, something that over the years he grows to live with. The "Royal Highness" of Riviera head waiters, the "Emperor" of a Cannes villa, the "Commander-in-Chief" of a retired, sparetime aide-de-campe-in-exile, are as much a part of the Mediterranean scene as the Casinos. But Henri was now to experience a real and shattering irony. Within a few weeks of the incredible calamity of France's defeat he received news that sent his future, once so clearly defined, whirling out of his control like a spinning-top. A cable from Larache stated that his father was dead and Henri was now the head of the

House. He took a special plane and arrived in Morocco to attend the funeral and contemplate his own strange position. There he stood, over the open grave, Pretender to the throne of France. . . Not only was there no throne. There was no France either.

# V

# The Count of Paris

## "The Flying Heart"

The philosophers must become Kings in our cities, or those who are now called Kings and potentates must learn to seek wisdom like true and genuine philosophers, and so political power and intellectual wisdom will be joined in one.

—*Plato.*

*H*enri, Isabelle and their children moved, during the war, to a little village near Rabat in Morocco. Their house, *Oued Akreuch* was pleasant but small and uncomfortable. It was wartime and there was no electricity in the evening, only oil lamps; and often there was little enough fuel for those.

The Countess, one morning, found herself alone. The children and servants were sleeping, and her husband was in Rabat. As usual, she was expecting a baby, and all at once she felt her first pain. She telephoned Henri but could not locate him. She telephoned the clinic and was told to come over immediately. "I cannot," she said. "My husband has the car." The clinic told her that there was no gasoline in Rabat for transport. This was an unpleasant situation. Accompanied by the children's governess, she hurried through the silent house to the garage where one of the earlier inventions of M. Renault had been standing for the last few months.

She did not know if the car contained water, fuel, or was even roadworthy. With her pains coming more regularly she could not afford to care. She pressed the ignition and nothing

happened. She pressed it again and it groaned. After five minutes the engine coughed itself into some arthritic kind of action. It rattled uncertainly out of the garage and on to the
deserted, dusty road to Rabat. There was no sign of wheeled
transport, no trucks, no military vehicles. A breakdown now
did not bear thinking of. Still she kept her foot on the accel-
erator, trying to think of nothing beyond the next kilometre
gained. The Countess clenched her teeth and kept her head.
Not so the poor, loyal governess who with each succeeding
minute came closer to hysterics, and the Countess found herself having to laugh and joke, despite the pains, to keep
up the woman's courage.

Eventually she chugged triumphantly up to the clinic
where Henri, the doctors and nurses, were waiting in a sweat
of anxiety. As gracefully as though she were stepping down
from a Coronation carriage Isabelle alighted, went to her
room and delivered herself of twins. They were christened
Jacques and Michel and brought her score up to nine—so
far.

Tribulation had knit the family close. In the evenings,
when the oil lamps were working, they would gather in the
drawing room, and sitting on the floor, they would hear their
father read from a book aloud, according to Merry Brom-
berger, a French biographer of the royal House. Sometimes
they would dream and talk about a possible return to France.
This time their exile was not such a lonely one. It was a
dream they shared with all the Frenchmen who adhered to
the colours of General de Gaulle, with the prisoners in Germany, and with the French Normandy Squadron which was
fighting on the Russian front in Russian planes decorated
with the tricolour.

Sometimes, after the bath, the family would play Brazilian
records, dressing up in the skirts and scarves they had bought

in Brazil before the war, and dance mad sambas. At bedtime the French Royal Family would kneel on the floor and make their devotions together. Isabelle was at all times a loving mother with only one occasional failing. She tended to get her children mixed up.

Morocco was nominally under French control and the Germans were rarely seen, but no one was fooled by that. Only the blindest of Pétainists believed that France was capable of freedom of action while the Germans controlled more than half the country directly and the rest indirectly. Henri continued to write his monthly bulletin, but now it had to be smuggled through both the Germans and the Pétainist police. One of his directives said, "On every occasion act as a Frenchman and by every possible means create opposition to invaders."

Meanwhile, in the Allied camp his own fortunes were prospering, although he probably did not know it. As early as November, 1940, General de Gaulle's headquarters in London was receiving the following secret intelligence from Free French agents in Tangier:

"The Count of Paris is merely waiting for the occasion to act and throw off the Vichy mask which he keeps for the form's sake. Maurras, who suspects this and is playing on the German side, is from now on in opposition to him. The Count of Paris has studied the possibility of an action in North Africa based on British support. Desirous, if possible, of acting. . . in liaison with Weygand he has made him offers of cooperation. Weygand's reply arrived on November 13. It is favourable in principle. Subject to certain reservations Weygand . . . consents to rally eventually to the Count of Paris. We might, when certain details of Anglo-American support have been settled, see the Count of Paris, with Weygand's backing, proclaim the resumption of war, using North Africa as a base. . . . "

Two years later, Britain, with the United States now in the war by her side, began building up forces for an assault in Morocco. Henri knew what was coming and could see with a terrifying vividness the schizophrenia which blinded the French authorities to the truth. He knew that General Nogues, an old-fashioned general infatuated with Pétain, would fire against the American and British troops, and the prospect filled Henri with shame. He flew to Vichy to see Pétain, pleaded with him to leave France for North Africa, or at least to give orders to Nogues not to oppose the landings. Pétain just smiled. "The man is neither deaf nor innocent," Henri exclaimed.

He tracked down Laval and dined with him. Laval laughed at the very idea of an Allied landing. "You are still very young," he said to Henri. "Too young." Henri admitted defeat, at least in metropolitan France. He wrote to his representative in the so-called Free Zone of France, "The painful and even revolting details of this visit I don't want to talk about. These people don't know what they are saying and do not judge anything at its true value. . . I did not fail to tell them the truth. . . Their cowardice disgusted me."

In October, one month before the landings, he went to Rome and called on the Pope. This did nothing to lift his morale. Pius XII was obsessed with fear over what would happen if Russia won the war, and could think of nothing else. Henri's gloom only lightened when he observed the German and Italian soldiers, both of whom seemed equally convinced that Germany would lose the war. With new hope he returned to Morocco and watched the Americans arrive. As he guessed, Nogues ordered his soldiers to open fire but French resistance soon collapsed from lack of enthusiasm.

The events of the next few weeks were busy, confused and, as far as the Count was concerned, they ended in humiliation and failure. After the liberation of North Africa his followers made the first moves to have him mediate between General de Gaulle and General Giraud, both competing for the moral leadership of the Free French; but others felt that the Count's sympathy lay too far on the side of de Gaulle. The white French population of Algiers was strongly pro-monarchist at this time and tried to elect him as head of "Council of the French Empire" in opposition to the Pétain regime now virtually imprisoned by the Germans in Vichy.

De Gaulle's emissary who arrived in Algiers on December 19, was General François d' Astier de la Vigerie. His brother Henri was the leader of the movement which aimed at bringing the Count of Paris back into power. But effective power was in the hands of Admiral Darlan, who had been a notorious Vichyite before the liberation of North Africa and had now turned his coat with an alacrity which had startled public opinion in all Allied countries. The two brothers d'Astier were planning independently to bring Darlan down, François serving de Gaulle and Henri serving the monarchist cause.

On December 24, 1942, Darlan drove to his offices in the Palais d'Eté in Algiers. As he arrived he was shot down by a youthful fanatic and died an hour later. The assassin, Bonnier de la Chapelle, to his own great surprise, instead of receiving a Legion d'Honneur was executed by a firing squad two days afterwards. De la Chapelle had been closely implicated with Henri d'Astier, but there was no evidence to suggest that the murder was occasioned by anything other than a rush of blood to the boy's head.

Nevertheless it had done the Count of Paris no good, and it led directly to another cruel stroke of luck. It could only have been bad luck that forced him to have his showdown with his worst enemy, General Giraud, in the very brief period when the General was in a position of authority in the Allied team. The Giraud affair is only momentarily relevant to this story but, briefly, he had been taken prisoner in 1940 and had escaped from the Germans. Some Allied leaders, particularly in the United States, distrusted the Free French movement of de Gaulle and welcomed Giraud as a more conventional figure to put up as the symbol of French resistance. De Gaulle was obliged reluctantly to deal with Giraud, and in this period, the period of the assassination of Darlan, Giraud was Civil and Military High Commissioner in Algeria, and complacently considered himself the effective head of the French war effort.

He was sitting in his office in Algiers when he heard that the Count was asking to see him. In front of him he had a list of hypotheses for the assassination of Darlan, and it was an ugly one.

"Did the Germans do it? The Vichy French? The Royalists? The Gaullists?" As to the first he had written, "Unlikely, no reason. Vichy, ditto." The royalist hypothesis gave him pause. He wrote, "Disturbing thought," and against the Gaullist hypothesis he wrote the same. There was no doubt which interests he intended to crush. He wanted no other figure to share the centre of the stage which he believed—erroneously—he was occupying. He looked forward with pleasure to the visit of the Count of Paris, whom he had never met.

The Count arrived and went into an eloquent plea for a reprieve of Bonnier de la Chapelle. Giraud realized with delight that the Count did not know that the assassin had already been executed. He let the Count have his say without interruption. Henri pleaded that though the boy had committed a crime he had been moved only by a twisted but passionate patriotism, and that he was a "good Frenchman."

Only when the Count had finished did Giraud look up from contemplating his desk. "Too late," he said, and revealed that the boy was already dead. Henri went white and was silent. After a while he recovered himself and began to cover the situation as it concerned him and the possibility of acting as the central figure in the French war effort. Giraud launched into a stream of abuse, ending with the assertion that the Count of Paris was in Algiers illegally. Henri bore the attack with dignity. Only one exchange lifted the quarrel to any level worth recording. Giraud said with a sneer, "Why don't you join the Army again? We might make you an *aspirant?*" (roughly, an officer-cadet).

This taunt produced an instinctive response in Henri's sense of royalism. "The head of a royal House," he said, "is permitted to hold one of two ranks, either Commander-in-Chief or Private Second-Class," and he took his leave. It was a good exit, but he had to admit he had taken a beating. Giraud ordered him not to set foot in Algeria again. Tired and depressed, Henri left for Larache and fell so seriously ill that Isabelle felt, and still feels, that he had been deliberately poisoned. Had things worked out better the Count might have ridden side by side with de Gaulle into liberated Paris. As it was, barred from Algeria as well as continental France, his war effort ended. Giraud soon afterwards lost his struggle for power with de Gaulle, and went into eclipse, but the damage was done. Sick and defeated, Henri was left to contemplate this, the low-water mark of his career.

With his family he moved first to Spain and then to Portugal, Isabelle, her fertility unaffected, producing children at each stopover. The total had now reached eleven. One more child, and the President of France would automatically, by French custom, become its godfather. Henri, oppressed by the low state of his fortunes, was not in any mood to enjoy the paradox and Isabelle's child-bearing stopped one short of the Republican dozen.

The worst enemies of royalty cannot accuse the royal families of sterility, but the amazing number of children born by the Countess of Paris is one of the most endearing aspects of the French House.* Their constant traveling added to their novelty. Five of the children, for example, were born in Belgium: Isabelle, Henri, Hélène, François and Anne. Diane was "the Brazilian," born at the beginning of the war. Jacques and Michel were born at Rabat, and Claude at Larache. Chantal, "the Spaniard," was born at Pamplona, and Thibault, the youngest, "the Portuguese," at Sintra, near Lisbon. This enormous family sometimes left itself open to misrepresentation. Once, in Switzerland on a family holiday, the Count of Paris was offered reduced prices by shopkeepers who were under the impression he was the headmaster of a seminary.

In Portugal they lived as farmers. The Countess and her daughters milked their forty cows, while the Count and Henri, his eldest son, tended 150 sheep. The family affection remained profound. The Countess was known in the family as the Minister of Fine Arts, for her interest in the theatre and art exhibitions. Some time ago, Isabelle, the eldest daughter was asked, "Would you like to have as many children as your mother?"

"Why not?" said Isabelle. "Look at my mother and tell

* The Countess's brother, Dom Pedro, Pretender to the throne of Brazil has eight. Some sort of modern record, however, must belong to Robert, Duke of Bourbon-Parma (1848-1907) who, by two wives, produced twenty children, amongst them the Empress Zita of Austria-Hungary, and Prince Sixtus who became famous in World War I while serving in the Belgian Army as the intermediary between the Allies and Austria. Another, Felix, is the consort of Charlotte, Grand Duchess of Luxembourg. Most of them are still alive and three are nuns in the Benedictine convent of St. Cecile at Sarthe.

me if she is not younger, slimmer and more beautiful than a lot of women of her age who have no children at all."

In 1948, France's opposition to the Count started to soften. Permission was given by President Auriol for Prince Henri to come to France and study at the Lycée in Bordeaux.

In 1950, the long exile came to an end. The 64-year law barring both the Bourbon and the Bonaparte Pretenders from France was repealed. Prince Louis Napoleon had been living unofficially in Paris in the Boulevard Suchet for years, but he had never been a person of consequence in French royalist circles. The Count's ancestral home was made ready for him, the magnificent Chateau d'Amboise on the Loire near Tours which had been rebuilt in the 16th century by the Bourbons on Roman foundations.

The Count, however, needed a home near Paris. Leaving the Countess behind in Portugal, he took a suite at the Crillon and went house-hunting. He found the house he was looking for at Louveciennes, a tumbledown, almost derelict mansion. A past obviously more gracious than its present inspired its name, *le Manoir du Coeur Volant*, the Manor of the Flying Heart.

As if they had never left it, the Count and Countess of Paris and their family were immediately integrated into French life. The Count's sons prepared for military service; only his elder son, Henri, was taken aside to prepare to carry on the family fight into the future, should the Count be unable to win it in his lifetime. The Count was allowed the rights of every citizen except two. He could not be elected President, either of the Republic or of the National Assembly.

Since he has returned to France the Count of Paris has made himself a permanent and important figure in political life. He has steadily expanded the circulation of his bulletin so that it is now read by 40,000 people, amongst them the leading journalists and politicians in the country. He has regular contacts with parliamentarians, economists and trade union leaders. Of all Pretenders in all the republics he is far and away the most influential.

Nothing brings out the monarchists more noisily than a royal wedding. The Count and Countess, in 1957, had two. The first was the wedding of their second daughter, Hélène, to the Belgian Count Evrard de Limbourg-Stirrum, after which, in the pioneer spirit that characterises the family, Hélène turned her back on Paris society and went off to a remote ranch which her husband runs in Rhodesia, near Salisbury.

The second was more important. It united Prince Henri, the eldest son and the Dauphin of France, to the Duchess Marie-Thérèse of Württemberg, daughter of Duke Philip of Württemberg and the Archduchess Rosa of Hapsburg. Henri was a humorous, pipe-smoking young man of twenty-four, with a fondness for practical jokes and a Canutist attitude to his rank. Once he was complimented on the number of girls he attracted round him. Henri claimed it was simply because he was a prince, and elected to prove it. Dining before a dance he ordered a pungent meal *à la provençal*, and arrived on the dance floor in a blue mist of garlic. He was right. The girls still flocked round. Over their shoulders and to his friends, he winked.

Like young Henri, Marie-Thérèse was a descendant of Louis Philippe. She was twenty-two years old, and her father, grandfather and great-grandfather had all married Austrian arch-duchesses. Member of a pious Catholic House of Germany, Marie-Thérèse could one day be a German Queen of France and a link between two of the most mutually-suspicious nations of the world.

The wedding was an occasion which cost the Count an estimated $150,000, and brought the many-sided medal of monarchy glittering in all directions. General de Gaulle sent the Count a letter which belongs in the realm of curiosa. "The marriage is a reason for each Frenchman to rejoice," he wrote. "But also, my Lord, because the life of your family identifies itself with our history; because everything coming from you now is exemplary for the country; because your future, that of Prince Henri, that of [your family] are bound up with the hopes of France. I salute the union which God is going to bless, as a great national event."

More than three thousand guests turned up in 95 degrees of heat, the greatest round-up of royal Houses in years. They included King Paul and Queen Frederika of Greece, with their daughter, Sophie. Ex-King Umberto of Italy came in company with Dom Duarte of Braganza, Pretender to the throne of Portugal; ex-Queen Victoria of Spain, widow of Alfonso XIII; her son, Don Juan, Count of Barcelona, the legal King of Spain; Grand Duke Jean of Luxembourg and his wife, the former Princess Josephine Charlotte of Belgium; the Princesses Beatrix and Irene of Holland, and princes and princesses from Bavaria, Saxony, Yugoslavia, Denmark, Hanover and Liechtenstein. One House was notably absent, the House of Windsor.

Not all was gaiety. There was an ominous undertone to the festivities. Charles Maurras, the rabble-rousing royalist, was dead, but his spirit was not. The Count had reluctantly agreed to permit the *camelots du roi* to direct the crowds. They had not changed over the years. As a type they resembled American Legionnaires in convention fever. Forty-seven years earlier they had made nuisances of themselves at the funeral of the Duke of Chartres, the Count's grandfather, and had been ordered to leave the ceremony by the Duchess who shouted after them during the oration, "Tell those fellows to clear out. They are not wanted here!"

This was the best opportunity the *camelots* had had in years to throw their weight around, and there were soon scuffles. From the press box came yells from the French journalists of, *"A bas les Camelots du Roi! Vendus! Collabos! Fascistes! Salopards!"* Which made an unusual background chorus for a royal wedding.

The observer, wandering through the crowds of royalists would also notice a badge that had not been seen in France for a long time, a tiny hatchet set on a marshal's baton in blue and white with gold stars, the *francisque* of Marshal Pétain, usually worn by some elderly woman or couple from provincial towns. There is nothing much the Count of Paris can do about that either. *Aspect de la France* has now replaced *Action Francaise* as the non-official mouthpiece of the royalists, and it reflects the same old sentiments, anti-Semitism, Anglophobia (*L'ennemi héréditaire*), militarism and the rest of it, just as unpleasant as *Action Francaise*, but without the genius of Maurras to give it stimulus. A new semi-Fascist organisation, *Jeune Nation*, scrawls *"Vive le roi"* on the walls of Paris. Sometimes it is accompanied by remarks about *"Juifs."* This is the old man of the sea around the Count's neck, strangling his aspirations because he is historically associated with the Right, and he wishes to be just the opposite. "I think," he declared in some desperation, "that I am the most capable man for saving republican ideals," and many agree with him, but the French nation as a whole still cannot conceive of having a King and a Parliament at the same time.

To consider the future of the Count of Paris is to deal in incalculables. One thing, however, seems clear. He is closer to a return to some sort of constitutional power than he was a year ago, and France is closer to a monarchy than at any

Archduke Otto of Hapsburg, Pretender to the throne of the defunct Austro-Hungarian Empire, with his wife, the former Princess Regina of Saxe-Meiningen.

Albrecht of Bavaria. Although his country formally became a republic after World War II, the House of Wittelsbach, which he heads, continues to rule.

Prince Louis Ferdinand, head of the House of Hohenzollern, with his wife and children. The gayest and most human of the German Pretenders, the supremacy of his House is due mainly to his personality.

Ex-King Michael of Rumania and his wife, Princess Ann of Bourbon-Parma, after their wedding in Athens, 1947.

Don Juan, Pretender to the Spanish throne, with the former Queen Eugenie of Spain (left) and his wife, the Duchess of Barcelona, as they leave for a Buckingham Palace dance.

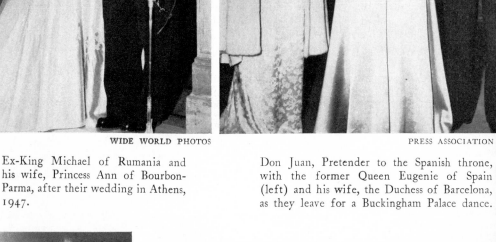

Above, Italy's ex-King Umberto (left) poses with his daughter Maria Pia, and her fiancé, Prince Alexander of Yugoslavia (right)

Left, the last picture of ex-King Umberto of Italy as Crown Prince.

time since 1870. General de Gaulle is undoubtedly a monarchist in sentiment. "De Gaulle thinks Maurras was so much in the right that it drove him [Maurras] mad," said Jacques Dumaine, former Head of Protocol at the Quai d'Orsay. It is hard to visualise a day—any day—when the General will be happy to bequeath his proud new constitution to the politicians, to Debré, or Mollet, or Pflimlin.

De Gaulle's constitution is his bequest to his country. It is always hard for a man in his position to see at what moment he ceases to be indispensable, unless he finds himself able to yield graciously to a figure as symbolic and as non-political as his own. And who better than the Count of Paris?

The Count is esteemed throughout the country. He is respected by Frenchmen who do not respect the monarchy. He can afford to wait. He is in his early fifties. No one is more aware than he of the inevitability of change. The change may occur in the nation as it did in Greece, or in the man as it did with King Leopold. The Count of Paris sees no need to change himself. He is what he is and he has kept faith with himself. And France is changing before his eyes.

# VI

# *Paul and Frederika of Greece*

## The Dangerous Way

"*I*f a nation does not want a monarchy, change the nation's mind. If a nation does not need a monarchy, change the nation's needs." This advice was given by General Smuts during the second world war to a pretty German princess, with the round *gamine* face of a child and the ambition of a Prussian. Later and unexpectedly, but not unprepared, she came to the throne of Greece with her husband, and sits there today.

Queen Frederika has followed Smut's advice so well that Greece, the most republican-minded of all the Balkan nations, is the last Balkan monarchy left. Established monarchies to the north and east have died while Greece was making up its mind what kind of country it wanted to be. A republic in a period of monarchies, it is now a monarchy in an age of republics, an aggressive, right-wing monarchy in the heart of Communist East Europe.

To rule Greece one needs courage as well as astuteness. Not a single King has seen his reign out in peace. Otto of Bavaria, who was called to the Greek throne in 1829 after Greece had been liberated from four hundred years of Turkish domination, might have had a better place in history had he been luckier. He had a Bavarian genius for government and a sense of the ridiculous which, when events go right for a man, can sometimes get him acclaimed a genius. Once, at a Cabinet meeting, one of his ministers crawled under the table and began to bite his colleagues' legs. "Leave him alone," called Otto. "He will do good work at the Ministry of Finance." As it was, his throne rocked on the crest of two revolutions before he decided he had had enough and abdicated. George I, brother of Queen Alexandra of England, who came to the throne from the Danish House of Glucksburg, almost made it. He reigned skillfully for fifty years as a constitutional monarch. In 1913, however, he was assassinated by a mad Bulgar.

King Constantine who followed him was married to Sophia, tragic daughter of the tragic Empress Frederick of Prussia. The union of a Constantine to a Sophia was popular at first. It provoked dreams of a new Byzantine empire with Greek troops marching through the streets of Constantinople. Constantine sought to be an authoritative King after the manner of Otto, and quarreled persistently with the Greek statesman, Venizelos. Nothing went right either for Constantine or Sophia. They opposed joining the Allies in the first World War and were forced off the throne by French and British pressure. They were later restored and then thrown off again; and both died in exile, penniless and embittered by the violent attacks made on them from what was their favourite land, Britain. This is something no monarch can shrug off. Nothing stings a King more painfully than criticism from England who, through Victoria, mothered them all.

King Alexander, Constantine's brother, reigned three years and died after being bitten by a monkey, a disaster received with a heartless lack of sympathy by the Greeks, who said that with Greece surrounded on all sides by enemies and threatened with obliteration, a King had no right to be wasting his time playing in a garden with dangerous animals. Constantine's elder son, George II, was called to the throne, deposed, recalled twelve years later, in 1935, after a rigged plebiscite, thrown out again by the Germans in 1941, recalled for a third time after a referendum in 1946, six months after which, exhausted, he died. This chronicle of misfortune suggests that, to put it mildly, the principle of monarchy has not penetrated too deeply into Greek philosophy.

It is difficult today, seeing Frederika among her people, to realise that the girl who fled before the Nazi onslaught of 1941 had to recompose herself and make herself over as a completely different being. She and Bernhard of the Netherlands alone were Germans among the exiled monarchs in the Allied Camp. Frederika, like Bernhard, had been pro-Nazi for a period before the war. In 1941 she could have said with accuracy that every lesson she had been taught, every loyalty she had grown up with, and every ambition she had treasured, had been reduced to rubble.

Frederika Louise Thyra Victoria Marguerite Sophie Olga Cecille Isabella Christa, Princess of Hanover, Princess of Great Britain and Ireland, Duchess of Brunswick and Luneburg, was born on April 18, 1917 in the fortress of Blankenburg, Hanover. The weight of history she carried in her names was well-matched by the curious vendetta which had marked her family history for nearly half a century.

The union of her father and mother was a union between two royal Houses, Hanover and Hohenzollern, previously sworn to eternal enmity. In the brief Austro-Prussian War of 1866, blind old King George V of Hanover had sided with the Austrians and was defeated at the Battle of Langensalza. His country was over-run and his Kingdom absorbed into Bismarck's empire. On his deathbed George made his son Ernst

August swear that he would never renounce his claims to the Kingdom of Hanover. Ernst August was only too happy to comply. He had no love for Prussia. Nor had his wife, Thyra, a Danish princess still bitter at the loss of Schleswig-Holstein. They lived in retirement at Schloss Dmunden, using their traditional English title, the Duke and Duchess of Cumberland.

Their son, Ernst August, Frederika's father, bore the family cross of vengeance. But love is a notorious enemy of vendettas. He fell in love with—of all people—Princess Victoria-Louise, only daughter of the Kaiser Wilhelm. By the time they married, Germany was at war with England and Ernst August's title to the Duchy of Cumberland soon went the way of the Kingdom of Hanover.

Despite defeat and the exile of the Kaiser the German royal tradition continued. If Germany was the beaten-down, lovable father, England was the affectionate but rich and haughty aunt. Frederika, with her brothers, Ernst and Georg Wilhelm, were brought up in the standard royal German way to consider themselves almost as English as they were German. The rise of Hitler caused agonized heart-searchings among the German princes. Most of them, conscious of their political impotence, remained aloof. Frederika, unable to remain aloof from anything, and at seventeen too young to know better, defended Hitler and took the German side in every crisis, but by the time she was twenty-one she had mellowed a little and was having doubts.

By then, she was in love with a man considerably older than herself, vastly taller, but intellectually, compared with her, a lightweight. Prince Paul of Greece had spent most of his young manhood on the Riviera, when his brother King George II was overthrown in 1923. Exile had demanded its usual price of him, the sacrifice of responsibility or any call to discipline, and Paul had been a sports-cars-and-girls prince in the Umberto manner. In 1935, when the monarchy was restored, Paul followed his brother back to Greece and it was in Athens, shortly afterwards, that he met Frederika. The love of the thirty-six-year-old Paul and the small German princess dated almost from the start and has continued without slackening ever since.

Paul was agreeable and well-meaning, with the aimless tranquillity of a prince deprived of a future. George, after all, was only eleven years older than he, so Paul was unlikely to become King until he was very old, if at all. The first couple of years of their marriage were concerned with little more momentous than keeping house on the small budget allowed them by George. Princess Frederika, however, was from the start the First Lady of the land, as George II had divorced his wife, Elizabeth, the sister of King Carol of Rumania, in 1935.* It was a difficult and delicate task for a prim Hanoverian to find herself burdened with, among a volatile, superstitious, tigerish people like the Greeks.

George II, who was born in 1890, was an interesting man and an interesting King. He was thoughtful and devoted to his duties to an extent that excluded all other considerations, whether they were hobbies, sport, social life or women. He liked, respected, trusted no one; never smiled or revealed any human emotion at all. His cynicism made him malicious, and while his ministers feared him, they respected him too. George spoke Greek well but with a strong Danish accent. This he neither apologised for nor tried to improve. It was enough for him that he was a Glucksburg, a member of the oldest ruling family in Europe, and therefore divinely qualified to fill any throne which happened to become vacant.

Once, Frederika, standing by his side at a long public cere-

* Queen Elizabeth died in November, 1956.

mony, and three months pregnant, whispered in his ear, "I think I am going to be sick." George replied coldly, "No Greek princess has ever been sick," and Frederika remained on her feet for four hours.

The war split Frederika's emotions apart. Pulled by ties both to England and to Germany, every new battle diced her loyalties more finely. She had a loyalty of sorts to Denmark which had been occupied by the Nazis. Greece, under the dictatorship of Metaxas, was fundamentally Fascist and sympathetic to Hitler.

Mussolini's invasion of Greece, from Albania, solved Frederika's problem for her. Greece was thrown, willy-nilly, on the side of Britain, then fighting alone. Frederika helped to mobilise Greek women and opened a campaign to provide clothing for the ill-equipped but fine little Greek Army. The Italians were thrown swiftly out of Greece and back into Albania. But the Germans invading from Bulgaria were a different matter. They swept over the country, wiped out the Greeks and forced the British Expeditionary Force into the sea, a habit by that time so familiar it moved the British to re-christen the B.E.F. the Back Every Fortnight. This exasperating sense of humour no doubt helped to win the war for England, but not all her allies were in a position to smile, however grimly, with her.

The Greek Royal Family were rushed out of Athens in the bomb bays of an aircraft; and took refuge in Crete, where they were promptly bombed. Paratroopers followed the bombs. In a few weeks resistance there, too, had ceased and Frederika, Paul and her two children escaped just in time to Egypt. Weary and tense, Frederika and Paul arrived in Cairo where King Farouk, handsome and not yet fat, but already possessed of habits that have since become familiar, tried perfunctorily to seduce her. He did not know who she was, but found her talking to his wife, Queen Farida. He ordered his wife out of the room and switched off the light. "I was quite terrified," Frederika said years later. "If I slapped his face, I knew it would cause all sorts of international complications." Her wits worked quickly. She told the Egyptian King sternly. "That *very big* man outside in the naval uniform is my husband and I love him very much." Farouk switched on the light, sneered and walked out. When Frederika indiscreetly told of this incident to a reporter after the war, representatives of the Egyptian Government called quietly at the Greek Foreign Office, and when the story was confirmed, retired aghast. We do not know in what order the straws were laid on the Egyptian camel's back, but Farouk was thrown out eighteen months later.

The Greek Family kept moving south, and arrived in South Africa, a country almost symbolically remote for an exile. Frederika was still in her twenties and unusually lovely. The hours at first passed bitterly for her. It must have seemed that her life was as good as over. Where, after all, was the slightest room for hope? The Germans were apparently unbeatable. Confidence in ultimate victory was a luxury that only the British could afford. The Nazis had overrun her adopted country and reduced it to starvation and despair. The stories of starvation and brutal oppression which came out of occupied Greece were horrifying. The resistance flowering in the Greek mountains was largely Communist. The royalist resistance movement which had also sprung up, found itself engaged in fighting not only the Nazis but the Communists as well. We have the word of the Greek political leader, Spiro Markezinis, himself a leader of the royalist resistance, that his men were outnumbered by the Communists four to one. In every way the outlook for the Greek Royal Family was a bleak one, and it seemed that even should the Germans lose the war, the prospects for a restoration of George's unsmiling, Fascist-tinted monarchy were faint.

It was at this moment, the lowest in Frederika's career, that she met a man who was to change her entire way of thinking. He was Jan Christian Smuts, Prime Minister of South Africa. By the immensity of his stature alone Smuts had put his schizophrenic and resentful country into the war with the rest of the Commonwealth, and more even perhaps than Churchill, he symbolised what was most inspiring in the British Empire.

Frederika, in her lifetime, had become accustomed to greatness in one form or another and she had learned to appreciate it. She had listened to the words of Kings and Communists, some of the best statesmen and some of the worst dictators in Europe. She now sat at Smut's feet and listened to some of the wisest words she would ever hear. The rest of the Royal Family moved to England to be closer to the war; Frederika stayed in South Africa.

To Smuts everything was quite clear. Nazi Germany would be defeated, and a period of great uncertainty would settle in Europe. No institution was in more danger than the institution of monarchy, and nowhere more so than in the Balkans. Accepting a desperate situation, what could a clever princess do about it? When you return to Greece, he said, you must prove to the Greeks that they are lucky to have you. You must show that monarchy is both advantageous and economical. Prove to them that you are cheaper than a President would be. Show that a Royal Family brings outside money in. Keep the robes and coaches for state occasions and the greeting of foreign dignitaries. For the rest of the time be simple, and make yourself one of the people.

The war ended and the Germans lost, but in the six-year war no nation had suffered more grievously than Greece. Her bravery had cost her everything she had. The cities were in ruins, the educated class almost wiped out. The population was starving, the mountains overrun with Communist guerillas, the economy flat on its back, and the whole country bankrupt. Greece was liberated by British troops, with guerilla aid, in October 1944, but the guerillas refused to disband and by the end of the war the country was in a state of full civil war, with British troops defending the established government in Athens, and rebels holding the mountain villages.

The rebellion was more or less suppressed and elections were held on March 31, 1946. With the Communists silenced and waiting for their second wind, Rightist bands took their turn at tyranny. They roamed the countryside, intimidating the peasants as they went to polling booths. One band threatened to burn down an entire village if it did not yield a majority for the monarchist candidate. The Left boycotted the election and the monarchists won 231 out of 354 seats. An Allied team of observers said the election was fair, but British and American correspondents on the spot thought differently.

Nevertheless, fair or foul, it meant that the Royal Family was on the way back. Seven months later, Greeks, in a referendum, voted 70% for a restoration of the monarchy. Ignoring the ominous signs from within the country, George II, in London where he now lived, set off for Greece, jeered on his way by the London *Economist* which said, "The only thing his return will help to solve will be the housing problem in Mayfair."

No sooner was the Royal Family back on Greek soil than the civil war erupted all over again. In Macedonia and Thessaly Communists repulsed the Greek Army units. Terror fought terror. In the middle of this ghastly crisis for the Greek nation, George II died. Paul became King and Frederika Queen.

This was the moment for which Queen Frederika had been trained by Smuts. She and Paul put Athens behind them and went out to make themselves living realities for every citizen in Greece. They travelled to every town and village in loyal hands, and sometimes beyond. They were often too fearless for their own good and for their officers' comfort. Fighting was still going on in the streets of Konitsa when Frederika and Paul turned up, bumping in their jeep the first civilians seen there in months. Another time, Paul, at the wheel of a jeep, swung Frederika through an uncleared minefield.

They were tireless and bold. Frederika, climbing up into the mountain villages and circulating among her soldiers, did a remarkable and until then unthinkable thing for a Queen. She allowed people to touch her. Soldiers slung her on their shoulders and peasants crowded round to put their hands on her to see if she were real.

The war could have dragged on forever, and might have continued to this day but for the good fortune of Tito's break with the Kremlin in 1948. Until then the rebels were taking refuge freely in Yugoslavia, recrossing the border refreshed and re-equipped. With Yugoslavia suddenly closed, the Greek Army saw its chance. It raked Greece from the bottom to the top, squeezed the rebels against a Yugoslav border that was suddenly closed to them, and then wiped them out as a military force. By 1949, Paul and Frederika were undisputed monarchs the length and breadth of their exhausted land.

The shooting had stopped but disaster has a way of perpetuating itself. Greece went on to suffer horribly from earthquakes and floods. Somehow, Paul and Frederika were always there, helping the homeless and afflicted. Often they were on the spot before the rescue parties. All the time homeless children in the thousands, a pathetic directionless flood, came pouring into the cities from the mountains. Frederika organ-

ised fifty-two Children's Towns, where eighteen thousand or-
phans were cared for and educated. Older youths were taught
mechanics, industry and agriculture.

Inevitably their power grew, which effectively meant Frederika's power, for Paul, though conscientious and able, was
without the spark which made Frederika the centre of any
activity she undertook. She was, above all things, determined
she should never be tagged as an alien monarch, as some of
her predecessors had been. She knew she would never be able
to master Greek to such an extent as to sound like a native,
but she was resolved if she could not speak like one she would
behave like one. "I was born a barbarian and came to Greece
to get civilised," she said once, to the delight of her Greek
hearers. She made it a point that her son, Prince Constantine,
should not learn German at school. "I can teach Tino German
myself," she said, and at home the Royal Family speak English.

Superficially the monarchy in Greece looked and still looks
good. Both Paul and Frederika are popular, and the political
equilibrium of the country gives them the support of all parties. Even the Communists, who are outlawed, are ostentatiously pro-royalist in the hopes of gaining respectability there-
by. In "Red" Salonika, the pictures of Lenin may be in the
drawer, but the picture of Frederika is on the wall. The monarchists back the Royal Family as the best shield against
Communism, and the republicans back it because they fear
what dangers might overwhelm them if the door of republicanism is opened.

The two monarchs glow with charm, Frederika with
her perenially child-like beauty, Paul with his good looks and
gentlemanly manners. The one possesses wit, the other humour. One foreign dignitary presented to Frederika had the
misfortune to be wearing a watch with a built-in alarm bell

which went off just as he was shaking hands with her. The Queen recovered quickly and said politely, "I hope that does not mean you have to leave already." An American diplomat complimented the King on the quality of his Scotch. "It ought to be good," said the King and showed him the bottle, " 'King's Ransom.' "

Among their own people they live and dress simply. Frederika shops for bargains in the Athens stores. She prefers to cook her own meals, and leads a domestic life in their summer home at Tatoi. This has been partly dictated by necessity. The Greek Royal Family is the poorest of all the reigning Houses and has been besieged more than once by angry creditors.

For ceremonial occasions and foreign visitors only, Frederika and Paul bring out the decorations and tiaras; and one suspects that it is at moments like these that Frederika is most in her element. She was born of royal blood and has lived her life in the milieu of royalty. Visitors have mistaken Frederika's informality, by overdoing informality themselves. One, rising to say farewell, was asked by the Queen, "Don't you think you should wait to be excused first?"

Smuts said something else. "Bring foreign money in." Ordinarily she would have had little time or patience for the expatriate Greek millionaires. Their money was abroad, and their passports conveniently Latin-American and they were altogether valueless so far as the Greek economy was concerned. Frederika decided that something had to be done. There was nothing she could do directly, except receive them socially. So she received them socially and encouraged Niarchos and Onassis to compete for the franchise of the Olympic Airlines. Onassis won and it is now one of the best airlines in Europe.

The children, Constantine, Sophia and Irene, have been

brought up carefully in the hard, German royal tradition. There is none of the democratic diminutives which made Beatrix of Holland "Trix", or Elizabeth of England "Lillibet." The Greek children have been addressed as "Prince" and "Princess" since they entered their teens. All have been educated in the severe Salem training system, described in detail later in this book. Sophia and Irene attend a country-house school with ten girls in each class, girls drawn from different classes of Greek life. They return home for lunch with the family unless there are important guests to entertain; and behave like continental children, the boy kissing one's hand, while the girls bob.

Constantine, born in 1938, is delicate, but he has been built into a self-confident boy, German-blond and immensely tall like his father, interested in everyone and full of questions. Sophia is shyer, in the royal English manner, more like Queen Elizabeth of England at the same age. At one time she wore braces on her teeth.

But a coalition-popularity as the Greek Royal Family's is, carries with it the seeds of its own danger. The Greek is a political animal who likes to take risks, and if a Royal Family plays politics with him it risks getting hurt. The temptations are conflicting. On the one hand, Paul and Frederika have the admirable influence of George I and George II to guide them along the difficult road of constitutional monarchy, and on the other the almost irresistible urge to become monarchs in the Byzantine tradition expected of them by the peasants. The Byzantine Empire, coupled with centuries of foreign occupation, has conditioned the Greeks in their relationship to the monarchy. The peasant expects the king to rule in the grand manner. The glory of Byzantium is with him every day of his life. The whole *mise-en-scene* of the Greek Church is Byzantine, and the image of the King merges, for the peasant, into the image of the Church. Consequently, the King is being constantly pushed into politics and getting into trouble as a result of it. The Greek has a primitive sense of loyalty. He is devoted to his family, his island or village, his Church, and in an abstract way, to his nation, but not to the state itself which means oppression and alien forms. It is a problem the King faces that if he exerts power as one section of the people expect him to, another section will identify him with the hostile state. General Smuts had nothing to say about that.

The attitude of Paul and Frederika to this tightrope problem is revealed in a statement the Queen once made. "We are national symbols, but that does not mean we must be figure heads. What an awful bore that would be." Both have thrown themselves into politics, in particular against Field Marshal Alexander Papagos, Greece's most eminent modern soldier, who is credited with the defeat of Mussolini's Italian army in Albania, in 1940-41, and of the Communists, in 1948. Some Greek observers feel that Papagos was one of the fortunate children of military history, given credit for gigantic victories which they symbolised rather than engineered. Similar sentiments have been expressed at various times against Eisenhower, MacArthur and Montgomery, and to such critics those men and Papagos received a wealth of idolatry out of all proportion to their accomplishments.

True or not, Greeks idolised Papagos to an extent that seriously worried Paul and Frederika who saw themselves sinking in stature to the level of a King Victor Emmanuel of Italy, lower than which it is difficult for a monarch to go. When Papagos entered politics their fears increased and they interfered in every way they knew how to obstruct him. The intricacies of the situation are too complicated to be worth detailing here, but the Royal Family lost the battle. Papagos was elected, but died in 1955, leaving Paul and Frederika to breathe again.

The dispute with Britain over Cyprus has opened up another menace to the position of the Royal Family. Frederika has never been very pro-British, but Paul is an Anglomaniac to an extent that has disconcerted important American officials in Athens, Anglophilia being rare these days, and not a force often taken into account in the formulating of American foreign policy. The passions aroused in Greek hearts over Cyprus cannot help having radical and possibly revolutionary aftermaths which would be dangerous to the monarchy. All Greek ministers from Konstantinos Karamanlis, the Prime Minister, down, have played the crisis slowly, aware that a break between Britain and Greece would split apart two countries which have always had a profound affection for each other. Love between countries is a rare but potent force in the relations of the world and it is not something to be lightly sacrificed. It is possessed, for example, by the United States for Finland and the Philippines, by all the South American nations for France (France, of course, loves only France), by Britain and Holland for each other, but more intensely than most, between Britain and Greece. King, Queen and ministers realise that a falling-out between such friends would be a calamity for the world. But this matters little when tensions are high. If Greeks don't like their ministers' attitude they can replace them. If they begin also to resent their monarchs' attitude (and an attitude is devilishly difficult to hide at any time, no matter how enigmatically one smiles) it is the throne itself that is menaced. Frederika has done her best in a difficult situation, to the extent that John Gordon, the London columnist has called her "Britain's implacable enemy," and attacked Prince Philip for taking her arm at a German royal wedding.

Frederika disarms by admitting her faults before one can present her with them. "I can't resist sticking my nose into everything," she says, a remark which indicates a little more trace of British good humour in her than she would publicly admit. Certainly from the leafy little royal palace in Athens, guarded by fiercely moustached Evzonnes in their skirts and pom-poms, there spread political tentacles far more widely than would be considered decorous in other monarchies. All political parties woo the Queen, who influences the King, who helps or obstructs operations in proportion to the intensity of his feelings. As long as the political equilibrium remains as it is, at the moment of writing, in Greece, this can be tolerated and even valued, but it creates a treacherous precedent for the future.

One other aspect of the Greek Royal Family remains—to be set forth briefly—to give some anxiety to monarchists. Since ascending to the throne, and particularly since 1956, the King has become more and more deeply absorbed in religion, and has developed some superstitions that are almost peasant-like. He goes to church every day and devotes much of his attention to the Greek Orthodox organisation Zoi (meaning "Live") which is influential in the running of schools. Every morning on rising, the King seeks benediction from his private priest, Father Kotsonis. This is mentioned only because an excessive devotion to religion has never been considered "a good thing" for a monarch, and has often brought destruction and defeat in its path. The effect of eastern mysticism on the cold northern mind has one historical precedent, that of Alexandra Feodorovna, the last Tsarina of Russia, far too tragic for anyone to wish to see repeated.

Royalty is a lonely state at best, and nowhere more so than in Greece. Here there is no native aristocracy to form a natural circle of friends for the Royal Family, only a rich and cynical bourgeoisie. Nothing but loneliness and the desire to find a husband for her daughters can explain why Frederika organised her two cruises for members of European royalty a few years ago. If she were taxed about it she would probably say that she did it to increase the tourist business in the Greek islands (which it did) but it was in bad taste, in direct contradiction to Smut's warning against display, and caused much indignation among the bone-poor Greeks.

The compensation for loneliness is, and has always been, power, and this Paul and Frederika do possess. Occasionally it is given to Greek citizens to see a demonstration of both the loneliness and the power of their Royal Family, although it is likely that they recognise only the latter. A town suddenly finds itself alive with policemen. The traffic is cleared. The lights go green. Motor cyclists roar through at high speeds, yelling instructions and warnings, Police cars whine. And then, the tiny gem in the Pinkerton van, a red M.G., with Paul at the wheel and Frederika at his side, races by at a terrific clip. More cyclists follow. Then the traffic begins to roll again and the flow of the community returns to normal. The King and Queen have passed.

# VII

# *Otto of Hapsburg*

"L'Empereur? . . . Jamais!"

> Question: How ought subjects to conduct
> themselves toward their sover-
> eigns?
> Answer:   Subjects ought to behave toward
> their sovereigns like faithful
> slaves toward their masters.
> —Catechism for school-children in
> the Austro-Hungarian Empire.

*I*f loneliness is the price of sovereignty it is a price most monarchs consider well worth paying for their thrones. It is true that in 1935 King George II of Greece was not too eager to leave the comfort of Brown's Hotel, London, to return to a land that had kicked him out twelve years earlier. But that was not because he shrank from the servitude and grandeur of Kingship. He simply did not want to be kicked out a second time (and as it happened, he was). Loneliness for the sake of power is one thing. Loneliness for the sake of principle, exile for a dream of royal power, demand altogether more impressive and perhaps more sinister virtues in a man.

From the windows of a small stucco mansion in a Bavarian village, the scion of a family which once claimed nearly all Europe as its own estate regarded the world around him and took comfort.

Down in the village of Pöcking, workmen whistle at their job as the hammers banged and the planks clanked. Thirty kilometres away, Munich had grown from the rubble of 1945 into as tremendous a city as ever it was, and a more prosperous city than it had ever been. Otto of Hapsburg, a man who sees books in brooks, sermons in stones and good in everything, has watched the *Deutsche wunder* from the start. He has seen the miracle of a people who have pulled themselves up from an obliterating defeat and made themselves the most powerful nation in Europe in scarcely a decade, and he has applied the principle to his own cause. "With victory comes relaxation," he says, "and with defeat comes the necessity for even greater effort. Defeat is good for a man who does not allow himself to be defeated by it. Look at Churchill, Roosevelt, Adenauer."

Otto's defeats have been many. Some have been humiliating and some heartbreaking, but he has borne them with dignity. He is a swarthy, handsome man, now in his forties and slender with good health, young-looking despite his receding hair. His brown eyes are alight with a sense of mission, which to him is everything. He does not smoke. He is indifferent to drink, dress or food. Unlike most princes, he is not interested in sport. He lives only for the cause that sustains him. Should he ever allow it to die, he gives the impression he would soon afterwards fade away into a ghost. Naturally a shy man, he has used his exceptional intelligence to realise that shyness will get him nowhere in the direction he wants to go. He has accordingly cultivated a political campaign heartiness, bursting in through doors and making his supporters wince with bone-crushing handshakes. His many visits to the United States have impressed the American type not a little on his personality. When he speaks English it is with a slight American accent. At the table he eats in the American and not the European fashion, with his fork in his right hand. He has also developed one of America's more deplorable habits, a taste for coining synthetic words. He speaks not of "restoration" which belongs, he believes, to the past, but of "instoration," which suggests something new (and painful). He talks with brilliance and understanding of foreign affairs, which is at once the gift and the weakness of princes. Since James I became the wisest fool in Christendom, princes have impressed listeners with the breadth of their knowledge, only to fold up when practical issues confront them.

This Otto is not likely to do. Already he has achieved something that no other Pretender, not even the Count of Paris, can match. He has gathered to his cause a group of monarchists in Austria, which may number between one and two million, who are fanatically loyal to him personally, men interested not in the Hapsburg family but in Otto of Hapsburg. At the end of 1958 Otto made a sudden but carefully thought-out decision. He went through the formality of renouncing his claim to the Austrian throne in order to be allowed to return to his native land. Few people who knew Otto were under any illusions that he had abandoned his lifelong ambitions. On the contrary, his cause had prospered so dramatically at home that Otto could no longer endure the frustration of being separated from it. Otto today does not insist on becoming King. President will do. Many serious political observers believe that Otto would be very close to the Presidency were it not for Austria's neutrality pact with Russia and the fear that a Hapsburg as President would antagonize a currently amicable Moscow. To understand the extent of Otto's achievement one must remember in what tatters his father left the reputation of his family, and what a weight of history Otto has had to climb over. For the Otto story and how he has done what he has done, one need go no further back than to his childhood.

He was four when the Emperor Franz Joseph died. On his deathbed the Old Emperor said, "Nothing has been spared me," and indeed, little had. His wife, the Empress Elizabeth, had been assassinated by a fanatic. His brother Maximilian, who had been made Emperor of Mexico, was shot. His son,

Rudolf, committed suicide at Mayerling, and his nephew, Franz Ferdinand, was assassinated with his wife at Sarajevo.

Franz Joseph was 86 years old and had reigned for 68 years. He had lived through the sweet but poisonous autumn of an Empire in the last stages of maturity, and even as he died he could see it collapsing. His funeral, on November 21, 1916, marked the first public appearance of the exceptionally pretty, dark-haired little boy of four years old, the Archduke Otto, who walked solemnly between his father, the new Emperor Charles I of Austria and IV of Hungary, and his mother, the Empress Zita, a princess of Bourbon Parma. After his physical beauty the most noticeable thing about Otto was his almost unearthly solemnity. It was more than mere gravity. He gave the impression that in his short life so far, no smile had ever lightened his lips.

Zita's personality completely overwhelmed that of her husband. Charles was a good man, but mediocre, always ready to act on impulse and then blame others. Zita was ambitious and so had the deciding voice at court. The Dual Monarchy was on the point of collapse, the flower of its young aristocracy killed on the Russian front, bled white by a war it was fighting at the skirts of its mighty ally, Germany. No one could blame the present regime for that. Zita loathed the Kaiser Wilhelm, and with the hunger for secret intrigue that had historically characterised her family, was soon putting out feelers to the Allies for peace.

Meanwhile, little Otto was taken to Budapest for the Coronation. It made a deep impression on him and from that time forward Hungary remained the country he loved best.

The collapse of the Central Powers found Charles and Zita at Vienna, with chunks falling out of their Empire like parts out of a Mack Sennett automobile. The atmosphere at Schönbrunn reflected the degradation. In a Court where proto-

col had been greater even than that of Spain, the white-uni-
formed Life Guards, all six-feet giants, now lounged at their
posts or dozed fitfully in the corridors with their huge feet
outspread, while children played around the desk of the list-
less Emperor. Charles was advised to get out of Austria and
follow the example of the Kaiser Wilhelm who had scampered out of Germany into Holland. But he was not without
courage. He went with his family to the Castle of Eckartsau
near the Danube, and declared that there he would stay in
spite of the formation of a Socialist government and the desti-
tution of his rights as Emperor. In Britain alarm was felt for
his safety and a British officer, Colonel Strutt, was dispatched
to Austria to protect him and make him see reason. The officer
was blunt. "Look here, Your Majesty," he said, "There has
been a lot of blood shed in this country, and if Your Majesty
does not go, there will be more."

Charles, it is said, was "a man born to shiver in the draught
of an open mind." He agreed and elected to depart at once.
By this time the kings of Europe were gone or going. To
the mass of Europeans who had had their fill of dying for
the ambitions of kings, names like Hohenzollern, Hapsburg
and Romanoff were still the names of fiends. It remained for
Charles, whether for better or worse, to reduce them from
fiends to fools.

Charles, Zita and their children, now numbering five with
a sixth on the way, moved to Switzerland and decided at first
to live at Warteg, on Lake Constance, where they could be
near to Austria. But that was just what the Swiss Government
objected to. From their neutral frontiers they had watched
Charles and Zita operate. They had seen Charles's manoeuvres
for peace behind Kaiser Wilhelm's back, and they knew from
experience Zita's passion for intrigue. Politely, but firmly, they
moved the family to the Castle of Hertenstein, on Lake

Lucerne, and kept a careful watch on all roads leading into and out of Austria. They had forgotten about Hungary. Hardly a month passed before couriers, whispering in Magyar, were sneaking to and fro across the Swiss border. Irritated, the Swiss authorities moved the family once more, to the Castle of Pragins, near Geneva, where they had a splendidly therapeutic view of republican France.

There the family remained for two years while Zita had her sixth and seventh children, and the plots and conspiracies went on because Charles and Zita, with a thousand years of middle-European intrigue behind them, were incapable of anything else. Austria, they had given up for lost, but Hungary was a different matter. Admiral Horthy, in November, 1919, had ridden into Budapest at the head of his Nationalist Army and announced he was acting as lieutenant of his sovereign minister, Charles, to whom he would cede power as soon as circumstances permitted. He was forthwith elected Regent.

This had filled the conspirators in Switzerland with joy. They Magyarised their names and insisted the children speak Hungarian. Liaison was set up with legitimists in Hungary, but, although he tried, Charles was not able to get in touch with Horthy, who remained brusquely non-committal. Finally, with a gesture so ludicrous it would be surpassed only once in his lifetime (by another gesture from the same person), Charles decided to enter Hungary on his own, and claim his throne. Alas, poor ex-King. He had fallen to the most insidious of royal temptations. Fed by reports of his sympathisers, he imagined he needed only to set his foot on his native soil to fire his subjects with devotion.

On March 26, 1921, he disguised himself in goggles and a false moustache, crossed the border secretly into Austria and through to Hungary. From within the Hungarian border he despatched at night two trusted couriers to the Regent

Horthy. He borrowed an officer's uniform, travelled to Budapest and admitted himself to the Prime Minister's residence, where he settled down to wait for his Regent.

Horthy was horrified. He had sent his ambassadors for guidance to various foreign capitals, to inquire as to whether they would permit Charles to return as King of Hungary. In Rome, Count Sforza, the Italian Foreign Minister, had clapped his hand to his brow and exclaimed, *"L'Empereur Charles? Jamais!"* That was pretty uncompromising, but mild compared to the reaction in Prague of Edward Benes, who said flatly that a restoration of the Hapsburgs would be considered by Czechoslovakia and the other members of the Little Entente a *casus belli.*

All this Horthy, a good patriot and an instinctive monarchist, turned over in his mind as he set out for what would inevitably be a delicate and embarrassing interview. The trouble was he also *liked* the King. Charles was waiting for him in the courtyard of the Prime Minister's residence, sitting on the side of a fountain in his Hungarian officer's uniform, watching the water play and munching salami which he was cutting from a large sausage with a knife, not a regal picture. At the sight of Horthy he threw the salami away and with a cry of delight flung his arms around him. Calming down after his first emotion, he inquired why no Guard of Honour had been turned out for him. He reminded Horthy that this was their first meeting since two and a half years before, when the Admiral had given him the news of the surrender of the Hungarian fleet. He said how happy he was to be back, and how horribly he was treated in exile by the beastly Swiss.

Horthy listened in a dismayed silence. When his turn came to speak he chose his words carefully. He assured the Emperor that if he (Horthy) could recall him it would mark the happiest possible termination of his office. "Your Majesty should consider, however," Horthy went on, "that the very moment I hand the reins of office over to the King, the armies of neighbouring states will cross our frontiers. We have nothing with which to oppose them in the field. Your Majesty will then be forced to return to Switzerland. Hungary will be occupied by foreign troops, and the evil resulting from renewed occupation will be incalculable."

Charles had been warned in advance by Zita to bluff it out. He played his trump card, and announced that he had come with the approval of the Allied powers. Horthy blinked in astonishment. As Horthy himself put it, "I could not doubt for one moment that His Majesty was speaking in good faith." In other words, he knew that Charles was lying.

Courteously, Horthy asked for details and Charles, his bluff called, muttered sulkily the word "Briand"—Aristide Briand, Prime Minister and Foreign Minister of France, and a man whose word few of the nations of Europe would then care to dispute.

Horthy persisted. "Has Your Majesty had a personal conversation with Briand?"

"No. Only through intermediaries."

Remorselessly pressing for details, Horthy elicited blurred assurances which seemed to suggest something to the effect that Prince Sixtus, Zita's brother, had talked to somebody who had talked to Briand about something or other.

Horthy relaxed. "Should Briand accept the responsibility," he said, "I shall gladly restore your hereditary rights to Your Majesty. Should the answer be unfavourable I shall have to beg Your Majesty to leave the country immediately before your presence here becomes more generally known."

The discussion had lasted two hours. Charles, thick with emotion, now presented Horthy with the Grand Cross of the Military Order of Maria Theresa and conferred upon him the title of Duke of Otranto and Szeged. Otranto was a naval base which Horthy had commanded with distinction. Charles was doubtless in too confused a state to recall that the title of Duke of Otranto had also been conferred by Napoleon on Joseph Fouché, the French turncoat who had spun round to accommodate himself to so many different regimes that in the end he ran out of regimes and ended his life in discredited exile. When Charles had gone, Horthy contemptuously threw the decoration aside and ignored the title.

Charles was sent to the border under military escort and slunk back to Switzerland. When the news leaked out, everybody was furious. The English, the French, the Yugoslavs, the Italians deafened the unfortunate Hungarian Foreign Office with protests. The Czech Minister in Budapest called threatening blood-curdling reprisals, and he looked in again every day thereafter as new and more devastating variations on the theme occurred to him. In Switzerland the authorities vented their own anger on the Royal Family and warned them on pain of expulsion to get up to no more tricks. How could they understand that intrigue to Charles was not a conscious thought process but an instinct?

In October, Charles was back in Hungary again with Zita and four thousand *soi-disant* soldiers. He had taken advantage of some local elections at Sopron to fly in with the collusion of a couple of officers, Colonel Lehar and Major Ostenburg. These men shared Charles's conviction that he had merely to present himself to his people in Budapest for all the hideous past to melt into a gorgeous present. The two officers had under their command a band of conscripts who were more gendarmes than soldiers, simple Magyar peasants who took an oath of loyalty without question, being trained by instinct to passive acceptance of whatever their superiors told them to do. All boarded a train and chugged towards Budapest. Every-

body but the little train-load of laughing, simple people realised that this was civil war. In Belgrade, the Yugoslav government immediately called up three classes of reservists. Rumania prepared partial mobilisation. Meanwhile, the Hungarian army under General Gombos blew up the tracks, and
as the little band of bewildered mercenaries fanned out under
the orders of their officers, there was a rattle of bullets, and
a few of them fell dead.

With this sound Charles and Zita came to their senses. They
realised that they were responsible for the shedding of the
blood of their own subjects. All around them their soldiers
were packing up and heading for the woods. Charles and Zita
were left alone to face undignified arrest at Tihany.

Horthy's first words to his King were of cold anger. "Your
Majesties," he said, "must go." Charles, his nerve already
gone, yielded. He would go anywhere. But where? Both the
Czech and Austrian frontiers were closed to him, and his private plane had disappeared somewhere in the scuffle.

The Admiralty in London, always solicitous of Kings, sent
a naval vessel to take them down the Danube. But first Charles
was forced to sign a deposition renouncing his claims to the
throne. The question now was where they could possibly live.
Switzerland would have nothing more to do with them. Other
countries petitioned for asylum were either adamant from the
start, or else inquired first about the Royal Family's bank
balances, and became adamant when they learned the answer.
Eventually the Portuguese Government was persuaded to
give them a home in Funchal, Madeira, and the family was
glad to accept. Not so many years had passed since the Empress Elizabeth of Austria, falling ill, had been advised by
her doctors to go to Madeira for her health, and Queen Victoria had been gracious enough to place her own ship at the

Empress's disposal for the voyage. For Charles this may well have been the bitterest irony of all.

Now he, too, was on his way to Madeira, and most certainly it was for the good of his health, and one of His Majesty's ships was taking him, the destroyer *Cardiff* having put into the Adriatic to pick them up. The last Emperor of Austria, the last Apostolic King of Hungary, was packed off to exile in a remote and primitive island where, six months later, his spirit broken, he died. He was only thirty-four. Only six apocalyptic years had passed since the funeral, in the full pomp and majesty of the Austro-Hungarian Empire, of Franz Joseph and the accession of Charles to his thrones. Now Charles was taken to his rest and buried in the local cemetery, bequeathing the whole undignified *schweinerei* to little Otto, not quite ten years of age.

Otto was the eldest of a family of seven brothers and sisters, with an eighth on the way. The solemnity of the boy which had moved observers at the funeral of Franz Joseph, was more noticeable now and it was hardly to be wondered at. He had lived through a childhood which could be described as pathological. He had never been to the cinema or read a newspaper. His only playmates were his brothers and sisters, who addressed him as "Your Imperial Highness," and bowed or curtseyed to him in the nursery. Friends of the family had come to call him "*Weltfremd*," or "stranger to the world." But he could speak six different languages with dazzling fluency and understood others.

Alfonso XIII of Spain, seeing the penniless state of this once proud and still complex family, took pity on their misery. He gave them the hospitality of the Castle of El Prado in Madrid, where Zita had her eighth and last baby, the Archduchess Elizabeth. By now the tragedy of her life and the pigmentation of the Bourbon Parmas had taken their toll of

Zita, who was no longer pretty, and a relative who met her mistook her momentarily, by her appearance, for a servant.

From there they moved to the Castle of Steenockerzeel in Belgium, where the education of the Archduke continued as rigorously as ever. No story books, no sports, no sweet Viennese music. His was an education which was to make him one of the gravest young men of our times. But at Louvain University he passed two doctorates in Political Science and Economy.

After that he settled down, like the Count of Paris, to the serious business of being a King. So far as Hungary was concerned he was dead. True, under Horthy, it continued to call itself a Regency, but the smell of Charles's little coup d'état still hung in the air. Austria was a different matter. The legitimist movement was strong, and both Dolfuss and Schuschnigg, the Chancellors, were sympathetic, in principle, to the idea of monarchy. But the fierce opposition of the Socialists and the menace of Hitler unnerved them into immobility. As always, Otto's political sense was sound, but like so many princes he did not know what to do with it. He could see that Hitler was about to take over the country and in January, 1938, wrote Schuschnigg a long, hysterical letter, warning him of the danger. His idea for a solution, however, was an odd one. He urged that Schuschnigg resign and make him (Otto) Chancellor.

What an inexperienced prince of twenty-five could do that an experienced politician could not, he did not say. But in fact it was Schuschnigg and not Otto who was confounded by events. He dismissed both the warning and the suggestion with a respectfully contemptuous note, and less than two months later the Germans did what Otto had warned the experienced politician they would. In March, the Nazis occupied Austria and made it a part of the Reich. The dreams of many men

died on that day and with them the dream of Otto, at least
for a time, that he would ever be King.

The war scattered the Hapsburgs, most of whom prudently
took refuge in the New World, Zita moving to Canada and
Otto to New York. When America entered the war the Secretary for War, Henry Stimson, authorised the formation of a
Free Austrian battalion. Otto saw President Roosevelt several
times, and from one occasion he emerged elated and cried to
a friend, "I have never been so optimistic for my own prospects." But when he attempted to become the leader of the
Austrian Battalion the protests from anti-monarchists, both
Austrian and non-Austrian, were so loud that Otto felt compelled to resign. The time for princes was still not yet come.
The battalion which at first numbered five hundred volun-
teers, dwindled within weeks to twenty-nine and was then
disbanded for lack of interest. That was the beginning and end
of Otto's war effort.

Aimless, drifting, not knowing what to do, Otto followed
the armies and found himself on the borders of Austria but
denied a visa. Pining for some sight and sound of his country-
men he visited some camps of displaced persons in Germany.
In one of them, near Munich, a nurse was working, Princess
Regine of Saxe-Meiningen, daughter of a Catholic mother
who had married into a Protestant family. Regine's life, too,
had been in the tragic mould of twentieth century Middle
European nobility. She had been born in 1925 in the Castle of
Eldburg, in Thuringia, and was educated at the Catholic
Convent of the Ursulines. Her father, Duke George of Saxe-
Meiningen, was a jurist and magistrate. He kept his charge
during the war and was one of the few who survived his com-
plicity in the 1944 bomb plot against Hitler. He also managed
to keep Regine out of the Hitlerjugend. When the Russians
swept over their home, however, the Prince was deported and

"died in captivity," but Regine and her mother managed to cross over as refugees into the Western Zone.

The displaced prince and displaced princess met many times after that, and on May 10, 1951, they were married. From that moment Otto was a changed man. He became, in fact, a happy man. He began to laugh freely and to enjoy himself. He took his wife to the French fashion houses and helped choose her clothes. Four girls, including twins, have been born to this marriage so far. In the winter the children go tobogganing, and in the summer they are taken in the family car to the lake at Starnberg a few kilometres away. The little girls are happy in their modest existence. They are too young to know the intricacies of royal politics and that they were considered by the Austrian government too dangerous ever to be allowed into Austria for so long as their father insisted on his claim to the throne. Otto was not even permitted to travel as an Austrian citizen and used a Belgian diplomatic passport under the name of the Duke de Sarre.

By any standards Austria's Hapsburg Law was a brutal and preposterous thing, as is any law in a so-called free country that bars a man from his native land. It has not cured princes of ambition. On the contrary, it has steeled their characters. There seems no reason why Austria, Italy and Spain do not follow the civilised example of France in permitting the Pretenders to return. If a nation wishes a monarchy to be restored it is no part of a democratic government to prevent it. If a nation does not want it, enforced exile merely imposes a grievous extra burden of hardship on a prince and his innocent family. If Otto endured his position patiently, it must be said that his wife suffered deeply. Friends who have known Regine through the years say that the weight of her responsibilities have told on her. It was not easy to be called "Majestät" when one knows only too well that one is not, knowing that one is Queen of nothing. However, Regine, a lady of Christian piety, has borne her lot bravely and with devotion.

She knows that Otto lives only for a period beyond the present. It is interesting, at this point, to see how two supremely intelligent Pretenders, Otto and the Count of Paris, have faced similar situations and by a process of similar reasoning come to diametrically opposite conclusions, one characteristically Austrian and one characteristically French. Both have seen that basically a monarchy depends on a dual respect, respect for the institution and respect for the monarch himself. Ideally there should be respect for both, but the monarchy will get along as long as there is respect for one or the other, and will fall only when there is respect for neither. Belgium is an example of a country where the institution has survived unpopular kings and Greece is a country which has little feeling for the institution but enjoys its King and Queen.

The Count of Paris's first task was to persuade republican France to respect the institution which had become unfamiliar with disuse. In consequence he is jealous of his prerogatives and insists on being treated as a King at all times. In December, 1953, he was to have been chief witness when Otto's younger brother, Robert, married Princess Margherita of Aosta at Bourg-en-Bresse, but when he found that ex-Empress Zita was to be given precedence over him, he refused to attend at all. This was pretty stuffy, but it was done with careful calculation. The Count can never allow himself to be anything less than King of France. However, in emphasizing his unique position in France, his personality has been to some extent lost and he is still a vague and woolly figure to many Frenchmen.

Otto has no need to bother about the institution. In Austria the names of the streets, the parks, pillars, monuments, the paving stones themselves, are heavy with the Hapsburg tradition. Otto has had to concentrate on mending the personal mistakes of his father. He sees that of the remaining seven thrones of Europe, two, the British and Belgian, are in the hands of one family, the Saxe-Coburg-Gothas, and three, the Norwegian, Danish and Greek, in the hands of the Schleswig-Holstein-Sonderburg-Glucksburgs, and asks himself why these Houses flourish when mightier Houses like the Hapsburgs and Hohenzollerns are sunk without trace. He realises that the answer lies in personality. Both Families have been blessed with a series of brilliant princes.

Like the Count of Paris, Otto is a political prince because he believes Austrians should know where he stands; and like the Count of Paris, he is liberal. He is heartily in favour of such new ideas as the political integration of Europe and the common market. The Count, incidentally, who speaks for an eternally chauvinist France, is against such ideas.

Otto says that regimes fall because of their own shortcomings, adds that there is no point in restoration itself, which, even should it happen, would be a restoration of sentimentality and a return to the past. He and the *Monarchistische Bewegung Osterreichs*—the Austrian Monarchist Movement—which claims to number one Austrian in every five, have sought to evolve a Technological Age monarchy. Otto feels that some branch of the government should be strengthened in order to meet the new technological pressures which the traditional democratic orders were never created to expect. But to strengthen the executive means a dictatorship, which is unacceptable. The legislative cannot be strengthened because when it is prominent it leads to sterility, as in the case of France. There remains the judiciary. Otto and his supporters seem to think that an answer may lie in a closer relationship between the judiciary and the executive, with a monarch serving as combined head of the state and as a sort of Chief Justice of the Supreme Court. Whatever emerges, Otto, at least, has new ideas for an old institution that are quite revolutionary.

"Mine is not a one-man operation," he says, "I am one of a team." And he has now gone home to captain it.

"So, you have seen Otto?" Louis Ferdinand's large, almost hypnotic eyes are curious, and though he smiles he asks the question with his full attention. "And tell me," he adds, "Is he still planning to revive the Holy Roman Empire?"

There is laughter all round. The face of the legitimate Kaiser of Germany, splits into a laugh, but his eyes remain inquiring. Prince Louis Ferdinand is only half-joking.

How sane is the world of unemployed royalty? Do the princes really think that these things matter, that they will be given back their crowns and palaces and all the panoply of corrupt and artificial deference of which they have been deprived? We in the Western democracies know better. Kings have no real place in our lives. If we are to be blown to pieces we demand the right to elect the man who pushes the button, and in the struggle of Christian against atheistic Communist the Russians will at least die at the hands of a democratically elected enemy. In the face of such grave problems Prince Louis Ferdinand worries about Otto of Hapsburg and the Holy Roman Empire. He must be mad. We, the victims of our democratic logic, laugh hysterically.

Yet we can see that monarchy is only dead in Europe if we choose to think it so. If monarchy stopped at the activities of busy Pretenders it could be left to the mercy of death and decay. But in fact it is not so. Monarchical feeling spreads in a great complex through European existence, deriving life from religion, patriotism, the land, the army, national literature and political philosophy. Many of the leaders of Western Europe are monarchists at heart. The fact that their principal concern is with other matters, with foreign policy, diplomacy, law and financial administration, does not alter the fact that the enormous potential is there should some change exist in the structure of Europe that would throw monarchy up as a logical alternative issue.

Wherever monarchists meet in Europe the subject quickly comes down to the Archduke Otto of Hapsburg. What is he up to? What does he want? Is he still planning to revive the Holy Roman Empire? During World War II, when the State Department was full of schemes for the dismemberment of Germany, one plan which was given serious countenance envisaged the separation of the Catholic German states from the more militaristic Protestant states. Austria, Bavaria, Württemberg and the others would form a perhaps loose union. The question of monarchy did not arise, but the author of the scheme was reported to be Otto.

In fairness, Otto has denied this specifically and, in fact, advised against it when it was put to him in Washington. Nevertheless, forces are at work in Europe to keep some such idea very much alive.

There is a castle in South Württemberg, near Liechtenstein, the Schloss Zeil, the ancestral home of the princely family of Waldburg-Zeil, which is the headquarters of a group calling itself *Neues Abendland*, and the honorary President is the Archduke Otto of Hapsburg. The word *Abendland* generally signifies Christian Europe as against *Morgenland* of the pagan East, and was used as early as the Crusades. In its present particular context it means a land which preserves European monarchist traditions and virtues, especially the Catholic virtues, against the Russian and conceivably even the American menace. The organisation is backed by rich middle-European Catholic industrialists and businessmen as well as by the large fortune of the Waldburg-Zeil family. A few Protestants are represented but by and large it is held in deep suspicion by the Protestant monarchists of northern Germany. A certain loss of momentum occurred in the movement in 1953 when the head of the House, Prince Erich August von Waldburg zu Zeil, was killed in a motor accident at the age of fifty-four, but the work continues under his son, the new head, Prince Georg.

*Neues Abendland* which brings out an occasional magazine of a high intellectual quality of the same name, reflects the unmistakable fact which lies at the root of the whole political problem in Germany today: namely the rise of the Catholic Church to power in the Federal Republic of Germany today, in contrast to the Germany of yesterday which has always been a bulwark of Lutheranism. Ideologically, Germany today is in a state of suspended animation. Once the flood gates are opened, Germany could well change shape in all sorts of ways including a re-forming of the South into a Catholic Carolingian union. Such a union would be dominated by conservative and ultimately monarchist elements and it may well be that an enterprising scion of one of the contending princely houses will seize his chance once he sees it.

# VIII

## The Germans

### The Republic of Kings.

The greater part of Europe . . . would
regard the Hohenzollern restoration . . .
as a comparatively hopeful event . . . This
is not because [the Kaiser Wilhelm's] light
shines brighter . . . but because of the increasing darkness around. The victorious
democracies in driving out hereditary sovereigns supposed they were moving in the
path of progress. They have in fact gone
further and fared worse.
—Winston Churchill, 1937.

*W*hile the head of the House of Hapsburg
works like a bee in a modest villa at Pöcking, the head of the
House of Wittelsbach, thirty kilometres away, in the sprawling
yellow Castle of Nymphenburg, shrugs his heritage away and
goes shooting.

Otto is a King in name only. His fellow-Catholic, Crown
Prince Albrecht is a King in all but. Through two wars, a republican revolution and a Nazi revolution, Bavaria has never
ceased to be—at least *de facto*—a monarchy. It is true that
Ludwig III was obliged to abdicate after World War II, but
the Wittelsbachs went on reigning as if nothing had happened.
They had, after all, ruled Bavaria for more than seven hundred years and an occasional abdication did not mean much in
such a long context. Today they even maintain official relations, or indeed, reign in collateral glory with the Bavarian
administration which freely acknowledges their pre-eminence
in the state.

The Wittelsbachs are most certainly not unused to anomaly.
From 1913 to 1916 they acknowledged two kings at the same
time, Ludwig III who was crowned King in the lifetime of

King Otto who was mad. This act aroused doubts among Legitimists and forebodings among the superstitious and, as it happened, the long Wittelsbach reign ended officially only a few years later. But the Wittelsbachs have always understood their people and this is the principle source of their strength. They have a flair for mixing, an ability to enjoy with equal sincerity the company of poet or peasant, and a way of making themselves comfortable in a castle, a rooming house, or a hovel. In this way they are royal in the very best sense.

For a generation the word Wittelsbach was associated with insanity, but as both royal brothers, Ludwig and Otto, never married, the mad strains in the family were cut off without infecting the present members. The most appealing of all the Wittelsbachs was Ludwig II, with his long flowing hair and Byronic beauty. Trying always to escape from a world of reality into fairy tales, he built wild eyries and castles like the castles of Neuschwanstein and Herrenchiemsee, which still survive, monuments to a spirit that longed for freedom. At the end of his life Ludwig hated eyes and forbade anyone to look at him, ruled by leaving little bits of paper where people could find them, or pushing messages under closed doors. Servants who entered his rooms scratched at the door and bent double when they entered. His mania drove him to build and build until the exchequer could stand no more; penniless and desperate, Ludwig actually planned to exchange all Bavaria for an unspecified French island. He died in 1886, aged forty-one. On being declared insane he lured his doctor, von Gudden, whom he hated, to a lonely spot on Lake Starnberg where they were both subsequently found dead in a few feet of water. No one knows exactly the circumstances of their death, but there are not many alternatives. Poor Ludwig, he lived only for beauty and imagination, but his legacy proved more enduring than that of many sane monarchs. His dreams survive in his crazy castles and he will always be acknowledged as one of the most important patrons of Richard Wagner.

On his death the crown should have passed to his younger brother, Otto, but he too was mad, incarcerated in the Castle of Fürstenreid where he lived like a ghost, his white face pressed to a window for hour after hour and year after year, comprehending nothing. Otto went mad young and then lived on to 1916 to the age of sixty-eight. As he was incapable of ruling, his uncle Prince Luitpold became Regent. Luitpold was as sane and normal as can be. So was his sister, Princess Alexandra, who felt the weight of the family curse on her spirit, entered the Church and became Abbess of St. Anne's Convent in Munich.

Nothing has had any effect on the family's traditional popularity. Few monarchs have been so favoured by their subjects. The Bavarians love their Kings no matter how they behave. They loved Ludwig I when he was making himself ridiculous over the Irish adventuress Lola Montez. They loved Ludwig II. They loved Otto. They loved Prince Luitpold who faithfully followed the Wittelsbach tradition of longevity and died in 1912 at the age of ninety-two. They loved Ludwig III even though they were constrained to chase him from the throne in the confusion of October and November, 1918.

But the best-loved King of them all was never crowned. He was Crown Prince Rupprecht who succeeded Ludwig III and died in 1955, aged eighty-six. Rupprecht was truly a King, one of those old-fashioned knights who inspired awe by the catholicism of their gifts and talents. He was a splendid soldier and by 1955 he was the last of the Kaiser's field marshals still surviving. Like all the Wittelsbachs he was intensely artistic, and was particularly an expert on Chinese and Indian art. He climbed mountains and swam until he was eighty. He could

turn a nice phrase and wrote good books. He was a first class
shot. In 1921, when he was impoverished and fifty-two, he won
the heart of a princess, Antonia of Luxembourg, thirty years
his junior; and had six children by her to add to his only son
by his first marriage. His last child, Princess Sophie, was born
when he was sixty-six years old. As a symbol of the superman
he was to intelligent Bavarians much more real and tangible
than any Hitlerian myth. During the hard days after World
War II, his appearances in the devastated streets of Munich
were greeted as raptuorously as those of King George VI in
London. He accepted the title "Majesty" as easily as if he
were entitled to it, and in 1933 he almost became so.

At that time the Bavarian legislature worried about Hitler's
increasing influence in Munich, and thought that one way to
counter it would be to proclaim Bavaria a monarchy. The
Minister-President called on Rupprecht at Nymphenburg and
told him about it but Rupprecht was dubious, and the idea was
soon afterwards declared unconstitutional. Next, the idea was
proposed to make Rupprecht a *Staatskommissar* of Bavaria, a
rank not dissimilar to that of Governor of an American state.
This Rupprecht thought was possible, and a popularity con-
test between Rupprecht and Hitler promised, at least, to be
a good fight. Then nerves began to go. No one except Rupprecht really relished the thought of baiting Hitler. General
von Blomberg warned the Minister-President that any kind of
separatist move on the part of Bavaria might result in troops
being summoned. Rupprecht did not believe it, and the Cabinet urged him to press the claim. When, however, he realised
they were pushing him without backing him, he withdrew and
the idea failed.

In World War II, Rupprecht's wife, Crown Princess
Antonia, was arrested and sent to Buchenwald where she was
cruelly tortured. Rupprecht himself was harried out of Bavaria

and driven into hiding at the home of a friend in Italy. At the end of the war Antonia was moved to Switzerland to recuperate, but died there from the treatment she had received.

Rupprecht had lived a long life in the shadow of family tragedies and political instability. He had been born in 1869, the year before the Franco-Prussian War. He went on to survive the Kaiser, Hitler, and two world wars, and he lived to see the rebirth of his beloved Munich from the ruins of World War II. In May, 1954, on the occasion of his eighty-fifth birthday, the Müncheners let him see what they thought of him. Brass bands and a thousand torches led the enormous crowd up the Nymphenburgerstrasse to the Castle. The crowds roared out Bavarian songs, shouted "Long Live our Lawful King!" and sang the Bavarian national anthem. Bavarian students enjoy demonstrations at any time, all the same this was a moving show of affection for a prince who Theodor Huess, President of the German Republic said in a telegram of tribute, "has been active and sharing in our sorrows." Inside the Castle, secretaries sorted out thousands of letters and telegrams of congratulation, many from England, more from Scotland. Nominally Rupprecht was the Stuart Pretender to the throne of England* and was from time to time even proclaimed King by Oxford students on a spree.

Rupprecht did not take this last claim very seriously and he might be said to have implicitly renounced it when he attended the Coronation of King George V in 1911. He permitted his

---

* The direct line of the Stuarts ended in 1807 with the death of Cardinal York, brother of Bonnie Prince Charlie, who might have been England's Henry IX. His death made the head of the family Charles of Savoy, King of Sardinia, and a descendant of Maria, daughter of Charles I. Victor Emmanuel came next, and was succeeded by his daughter who married the Duke of Modena. With the Modenas the claim rested and descended to Rupprecht's mother Princess Marie Therese of Modena, the last of that family.

daughters to wear the Stuart tartan when they put on the kilt, and when he died in the following year the Royal Stuart Society in London went into mourning.

Between Rupprecht and his son and successor Crown Prince Albrecht there is a vast difference of personality. Albrecht is popular because it is the pattern of his family to be popular. But the instinctive regality of Rupprecht has gone. Albrecht is a complicated man. The family love of hunting is a passion with him. He hates royal protocol and royal appearances, and he is happy in the forests and the mountains. He likes talking to peasants, to dress as a peasant, and speaks German with a broad Bavarian accent. When he became the head of the family he recalled for the benefit of the Court that it was a former convention of the Wittelsbachs that no one be styled "Royal Highness" until they were eighteen, and even after that "Highness" is preferred. He used this half-forgotten tradition as an excuse to escape from the title of "Majesty." He spends many months a year out of Bavaria in Brazil, where he is interested in forestation and wild life schemes.

One speaks of the Wittelsbachs first because they are the most powerful and the most royal of the German Houses. At the same time the Hanovers remain well entrenched in Hanover, and the House of Baden commands great respect in the country. Two other Houses have recovered from bitter family losses. The Hesse family lost five of its members in an air crash in November, 1937,* but are still influential in royal affairs. The Wettins of Saxony were crippled by Russian occupation and compromised by family scandal, the last Queen

* Archduke Georg: his wife, the Archduchess Cecilia (third sister of Prince Philip), the Dowager Archduchess Eleonore, Prince Ludwig and Prince Alexander. The aircraft crashed at Ostend while carrying the family to the wedding of Prince Ludwig and Miss Margaret Geddes, sister of the present Lord Geddes, now the Archduke and Archduchess of Hesse. A baby born at the instant of Cecilia's death was buried with her.

of Saxony having run off, firstly with a Belgian gentleman and subsequently an Italian. However, the present head of the family, Margrave Meissen, married the wealthy Prince Thurn und Taxis, scion of a family which once held the postal franchise in Germany and is still rich from it. *"Macht Euern Dreck alleene,"* said King Friedrich August in course Saxon when he signed his abdication declaration in 1918, meaning, "Make your mess by yourselves," but in fact all the German Royal Families have done well, save one, the most important of them all, the Hohenzollerns. And the fact that the Hohenzollerns are still supreme is not only due to the legitimate tradition but also to the personality of the present head of the House, Prince Louis Ferdinand, not perhaps the most brilliant of all the Pretenders, and certainly not one of the most influential, but easily the gayest and the most human of them all.

Louis Ferdinand—"Lulu" to his friends—has had to fight hard for his position. Tough and uncompromising, long-nosed and with piercing brown eyes that give him the look of a fierce sparrow, he flourishes the cursed name of Hohenzollern as challengingly as Cyrano de Bergerac his white plume. Confronting a world that he senses to be fundamentally though incomprehensibly hostile, he squares his shoulders, throws back his head and assumes a glare that does not lose its defiance even when he laughs, which is often and raucously.

The word Hohenzollern which still inspires distrust and hatred in many breasts he utters lovingly. Try to suggest that the Hohenzollerns are latecomers, *arrivistes* on the German royal scene and he demands angrily whether you would question the legitimacy of his ancestor who fought for Barbarossa or of the ancient Dukes of Brandenburg who rode out of the darkness of the twelfth century and made the Hohenzollern name feared and famous. Accuse the Hohenzollerns of militarism and Louis Ferdinand stands flabbergasted at the preposterousness of the charge. The word "Prussia" which is a bad word in almost any language, falls gently from his lips and his eyes glisten when he talks of a Prussia under the Communists. Louis Ferdinand, in short, has no apologies to make to history.

He has another quality which sets him apart from all but a handful of his fellow-men. This is a conscious contempt for the arts of discretion or diplomacy. He says what he thinks and cares not a damn to whom he says it. Before the war he was warned by William E. Dodd, the American ambassador in Berlin, "The Nazis will hang you one of these days; I shall come to your funeral but that won't do you much good." Calculated indiscretion is a risky art, and it needs a genius, a Churchill or a Bismarck to play it ("Don't imagine" said Bismarck to Disraeli, "that my illness is the result of the French war; its cause is the horrible conduct of my King." Even Disraeli lacked the flair. He replied, "I have not seen any of this two-facedness in the monarch I serve. She is frank and upright.") In a man like Louis Ferdinand, who would not make any claim to greatness for himself, his indiscretion reveals a remarkable sophistication and self-assurance. When he talks about himself he speaks of such earlier phases of his career as an addiction to alcohol, a foolish love affair, a brief sympathy for Hitler, and a considerable Anglophobia, frankly and without excuse, leaving his hearers to draw whatever conclusions they feel like, and to hell with them.

Louis Ferdinand was born in 1907, in the Royal Palace at Potsdam, and had thus reached the impressionable age of eleven when he watched the German Empire collapse. Before that he had shown signs of incipient royalism, his favourite game being to go into and out of doors so that the guards could salute him. His first recorded words to his English nannie at the age of five were, "If you don't get out at once I shall have you shot."

Nothing about his childhood suggested that he would one day have to lead all the royal Houses of Germany through a republican wilderness. He was only the second son of Crown Prince Wilhelm, "Little Willie," of the World War I cartoons, eldest son of the Kaiser. Louis Ferdinand's elder brother, Prince Wilhelm Friedrich, was heir to the throne.

The 1918 defeat instead of depressing him, elated him. He had outgrown the militariness of his childhood, and was simply relieved that he would not have to attend Plön, the German cadet school. Without cares or responsibilities, the whole world opened for him and he set on two decades of travelling and wild-oat sowing which made its own modest contribution to the international scene of the late twenties and early thirties. In 1929 he went to the United States and there met two men who were to influence his life. The first was Franklin D. Roosevelt whom he described as "an aristocrat in the best sense of the word, but also," he added thoughtfully, "a great enemy to my country." The second was Henry Ford. One of the most formative experiences of his early years was to watch the great motor pioneer sit with his friends or crawl under his cars to make sure everything was being done properly.

Ford liked the Prince and put him on his payroll, and there Louis Ferdinand remained, on and off, for twenty years. When he proceeded to fall wildly in love with Lili Damita, the French film actress, a complicated chequer game began, with his various patrons moving him here and there out of the girl's way. After he saw Lili Damita in Berlin, his grandfather, the Kaiser Wilhelm in exile at Doorn in Holland, shipped him off to America. When Lili went to Hollywood Louis Ferdinand followed and declared his love not only to

Lili but to most of the assembled newspaper reporters of Los Angeles. Hurriedly Henry Ford had him transferred to South America. Louis departed tearfully, but the girl he left behind was not alone for long. The Royal Navy put in to port in Southern California, and among the British officers was another Prince, George, Duke of Kent. Soon Lili Damita and Prince George were being seen together in Hollywood gatherings regularly, to the great indignation of Louis when he opened his newspapers. This was the first of some elemental lessons which Louis absorbed in the field of man-woman relationships.

Returning to the United States he took up with Lili again, but he found that no matter how carefully and secretly they arranged to meet, the newspapers always reported it next morning, while all the time Henry Ford and the Kaiser Wilhelm were growing more and more angry. Slowly it dawned on the boy that one of the two of them must be tipping the reporters off. Understanding followed. For an experienced actress the attentions of a young and lovesick prince were worth a fortune in publicity. Louis also found out that when a prince falls in love with a showgirl it may be he who provides the car but it is also he who gets taken for the ride. And so the affair dragged to a close, without ill-feelings on either side. Damita went on to marry Errol Flynn.

By 1933 Louis was in his mid-twenties and he had covered much ground. He had met Mussolini and found him "like the maitre d'hotel of a *trattoria*," and Hitler "a man who looks like Charlie Chaplin and talks like an Austrian railway porter." Lloyd George gave him a piece of information which depressed and perplexed him. "You know, Prince Louis," said the Welshman who had been Germany's bitterest enemy in 1918, "we over here never expected nor intended the fall of your dynasty. In the face of public opinion at the time, it would have been impossible for me as Prime Minister to conclude a peace with either your grandfather or your father. But we all thought that a Regency for your brother Wilhelm would be set up under your mother or one of your uncles. If your family had remained in power I am certain that Mr. Hitler would not be giving us headaches right now."

Field Marshal Hindenburg died and in his will declared his wish that the Hohenzollerns be restored, but by that time Hitler was at the German helm and remained there for the next eleven years. But the day was approaching when Prince Louis would have to grow up. His elder brother, to the stunning distress of his grandfather, decided to marry a commoner, Dorothée de Salviati, and renounced his rights to the throne. Louis was now the heir. In fact Louis would have become heir anyway, in due course, because Wilhelm Friedrich died after wounds received in the French campaign in 1940. In spite of his youth and wildness Louis had an unquestioned faith in the destiny of his family, and in spite of the Damita incident he believed implicitly in *Ebenbürgligkeit,* or the "eligibility of equality of station" in affairs of the heart. He resigned from Ford and prepared to train himself for his new duties.

In 1938 he met the Grand Duchess Kira Kirillovna, a great grand-daughter of the Tsar Alexander II. After the heat of the Damita affair this was circumspect in the extreme. The formality bore arduously on Louis's high spirits, and he soon gave up, in a scene which Kira describes in her own words:

"In the evening," she said, "we played poker. I later found out that this was the only game anybody has ever induced Louis to play, and the poker we played that night was a riot. Louis was more interested in the golden Rhine wine liberally poured by my hostess. In the intervals of sampling it he staked wildly, and when he won, gave half his chips away. He rejoiced finally when he was broke. He stopped playing and devoted his undivided attention to the delights of the grape."

Fortunately the dark and lovely Kira possessed a sense of humour as keen as Louis's. She decided she liked him, and Louis, with characteristic ebullience, having proposed, went on to marry her three times. The first was at a civil ceremony in Potsdam, the second at a Russian service in Cecilienhof, his home, and the last at Doorn in Holland, so that the exiled old Kaiser could witness it.

When the war began, Louis joined the Wehrmacht but was soon released. Hitler had ruled that members of the princely families should be gradually dismissed from the services. Those that remained were to be kept away from the front line. Hitler did not fear their death, but was determined that they should be given no chance to show heroism. Consequently, Louis, his family increasing with royal regularity, retired to his favourite estate at Cadinen, in East Prussia, and remained there until the advancing Russians were less than twenty-four hours away. To flee galled his Hohenzollern pride and he almost decided to stay put, but as he explained it, "We had not the slightest ill feeling against the Russians and tried to be objective about the Soviet system, but we had no assurance that the Soviets would feel the same way about us."

Back in Cecilienhof he intrigued casually with the anti-Hitler conspirators, sufficiently that after the failure of the bomb plot in 1944 he went underground, like Crown Prince Rupprecht, until the war ended. Afterwards the ever-loyal Ford Motor Company made him their German representative, which made him, incidentally, the highest paid unemployed King in Europe.

Today the Crown Prince lives near Bemen, at Borgfeld, in the Villa Wümmehof, a house even less pretentious than Otto's home at Pöcking, and one which would be considered definitely undistinguished in Westchester County, New York, or Oxshott, Surrey.

He devotes himself to his wife, four sons and three daughters, all of whom enjoy the carefree, jolly existence that only a large and deeply affectionate family can understand. Louis is a gifted composer and spends much time with his music and going to concerts. From the remains of his once great fortune he looks after his old retainers, paying pensions to courtiers and servants, although in the end there is not a great deal left over for himself.

His royal attitude is exactly the opposite of that of Otto or the Count of Paris. "I am not a political prince," he says. In April, 1957, he gave an interview to the German news magazine, *Der Spiegel* and said that if he came to power he would strengthen and protect democratic institutions in Germany. "Under no circumstances must there be another dictatorship. I will fight it as I fought the Third Reich."

Like the other Pretenders, he is unsure how to translate a widespread desire for monarchy into a practical movement. He has said he would accept his name being put forward for the Presidency of Germany providing that there was evidence of 'overwhelming support.' He adds that in such circumstances he would insist on a seat of government being transferred to Berlin, but then, realising that he has put a very small cart before a very large horse, he amplifies his stand in typically humorous manner. "Do I find evidence of a groundswell?" he asks rhetorically, "Perhaps. I received one vote at the last Presidential election. Unfortunately I could not draw too much comfort from it because my cousin, Ernst August of Hanover, got one vote too."

Unfortunately for Louis and his prospects his most loyal hereditary lands and oldest Hohenzollern preserves, the

Marches of Prussia, are now in Eastern Germany and no one knows what traces of royalist feeling still remain there.

Louis Ferdinand, though the senior Pretender among the German princes, has less active support, fewer local roots than his Hanoverian Protestant cousins, his centuries-old Wittelsbach rivals, or even the Austro-Hungarian exiles at the Starnberger Lake. In 1954, a secret meeting was planned by representatives of the various dynasties to make a formal acknowledgment of Prince Louis as Chief of the German Houses, but old Prince Rupprecht took umbrage over a technicality and refused to attend, so the meeting was abandoned. The reaction of most of these families towards restoration is to pay lip service to the idea but in practice to let well alone. They are doing well enough in the mock-monarchies in which they live. Why stir things up? Consequently Louis Ferdinand stands isolated and frustrated, willing but not powerful, while the Wittelsbach and Hanovers, though powerful are unwilling.

The main hope, remote though it is, remains in the basic royalism of the German people, and even here Louis's thunder could be stolen by Otto with his irrepressible dynamism, and his intense ambition. A readable but tiny magazine called *Tradition und Leben* published in Cologne by an overworked and dedicated couple, the Baron and Baroness Heinrich von Massenbach, devotes itself to spreading the monarchist faith with particular emphasis on the Hohenzollerns, but this is toy artillery compared with the big guns of Otto with his powerful Austrian organisation and the well-financed activities of *Neues Abendland*. It is not surprising that Otto causes anxiety to Louis who sees his beloved country, or much of it, lost to a rival whose wiles he cannot hope to match and dominated by a religion which is alien to his northern Lutheran mind.

So far as Nazism is concerned the hands of the German royal Houses are fairly clean. Wilhelm of Hesse was briefly

Nazi and so was one of the Kaiser's younger sons, but Hitler distrusted the princes and despised those who joined him.

Louis Ferdinand must regard with ambiguous humour the fact that the branch of the Hohenzollern family to cling longest to its throne was a branch that was disavowed by the family during the First World War because their country made common cause with Germany's enemies, the Hohenzollern-Sigmaringens of Rumania. And of all Europe's Hohenzollerns it was the last of these, King Michael, who bequeathed the greatest credit to the family name. Otto of Hapsburg says, "Regimes fall as a result of their shortcomings." One of the few exceptions is Michael. He became King of Rumania twice, which is unusual. He also became King twice in the lifetime of his father, which must be unprecedented. Almost alone he can say to the world that he lost his throne through no fault of his own and his curious history will be considered now.

*IX*

# Michael of Rumania

## King Among the Communists

"Where are we going now?" I asked
Mummie sadly. "We shall not know until
the King gets here. You will have to learn
a lesson I learned many years ago, Sandra
. . . You must learn to live one day at a
time. Tomorrow is always soon enough to
think of tomorrow."
—Queen Alexandra of Yugoslavia.

*T*he monarchs of Rumania whirl out of the
shadows of the past as out of a dream. Surely they never
existed; Carmen Sylva, the poetess-Queen, running barefoot,
all twelve stones of her, through the dew, her hair flying.
Immoral English Marie and her sniggering husband, King
Ferdinand. Debased, debauched Carol II, jowled like a spaniel,
and his mistress Magda Lupescu. Only Michael seems to
have been thoroughly normal, and it was Michael who lost
his throne. Eccentricity clearly suited the Rumanian temperament better.

The line does not go back very far. Rumania had been a
constant battleground for three mighty neighbours, Turkey,
Russia and Austro-Hungary. By 1861 she had been granted
an uneasy independence and looked around for a King.

The country's leader, John Bratianu, summoned a Hohenzollern prince, Karl, to run the Turkish blockade and accept
the throne. Karl was smuggled into Rumania as Bratianu's
valet and on his arrival declared, "Now I am a Rumanian."
He called himself Carol and founded the Rumanian Hohenzollern dynasty, although he was not crowned King until 1881,
after the defeat of the Turks.

King Carol I built an important state out of what had once been a Turkish vassal province. But he and his poet-wife, Queen Elizabeth, who wrote under the name of Carmen Sylva, had only one child, a daughter, who died young. Carol named a nephew, Ferdinand of Hohenzollern, as heir-apparent in 1889. Like his uncle, Ferdinand turned himself into a Rumanian, but against the fearless and regal King Ferdinand was an uninspiring sight. He was scrawny and dirty and his face was yellow as though he suffered from a perpetual *crise de foie*. When nervous he giggled. Ferdinand showed early some of the traits which his son, Carol II was to inherit so liberally. A sleazy affair with one of Carmen Sylva's ladies-in-waiting earned him the thorough disapproval of his aunts, uncles and cousins in various royal families. When seventeen-year-old Princess Marie, the daughter of the Duke of Edinburgh and granddaughter of Queen Victoria, accepted his offer of marriage, the entire royal community of Europe was aghast.

The most cursory look at the young couple together, however, would have shown which of the two would be the dominating figure. Photographs of Marie at the time, indicate a quite startling similarity to Queen Elizabeth II of England. There are the same cool, straight eyes, the same defiant mouth. The material she had to work with, the tongue-tied Ferdinand, was not promising, but she had made her choice and she was not a person for regrets.

Marie and Ferdinand were married at Sigmaringen in 1893. A year later they called on the Empress Frederick of Prussia who commented that "Missy (Marie) looked sweetly pretty and quite a baby, and very transparent and delicate, and he, poor dear, more unprepossessing than ever. She seems quite happy, but she is young and inexperienced . . . At eighteen she rejoices in life and change and beauty. She has all the buoyancy of youth, and luckily for her no very deep feelings. She says her little boy (Carol) is well."

The early years for Marie in Rumania must have been a nightmare. Between Carol I and the nitwit Ferdinand there was no family love or affection. The King bullied and abused the poor prince so publicly that the servants laughed in his face. To hide her humiliation Marie joined the tormentors of her husband and cuckolded him outrageously. "I fear she gets into scrapes," wrote her aunt, the Empress Frederick, in a breathless orgy of Victorian euphemism. "Like a butterfly, instead of hovering over the flowers (she) burns her pretty wings by going rather near the fire."

By 1914, when Carol died, the stuffing had so been knocked out of King Ferdinand that no opinion prevailed at Court save that of Queen Marie's. Beautiful, domineering, devious, she schemed with politicians from her home in the Sinaia Palace and filled out the horizons of her five children so completely that nearly forty years later an American psychiatrist was telling her daughter, Princess Ileana, "You must get rid of your mother-complex and stand on your own feet." The death of Carol I meant the end of German influence in Rumania. Marie was a loyal niece of Edward VII and detested the Kaiser, a sentiment that may be explained by the fact that once, when she was travelling through Germany, the Kaiser Wilhelm said that he had no wish to see "that English harlot" at his Court.

In 1916 Marie swung her husband into declaring war against the Central Powers. The German Hohenzollerns, furious, wrote Ferdinand out of the family, and the German Army speedily obliterated Rumania. Ferdinand's nerves shattered like glass and he actually wrote to the Emperor Charles of Austria for asylum in Vienna. This extraordinary request appealed to Charles's sense of humour and he agreed. But by that time Queen Marie had heard about it and dragged her husband off to Jassy where the remnants of the Rumanian Army, nation and Court were holding out. By this one action Marie saved the throne of Rumania and enabled Ferdinand to survive the war as the only reigning Hohenzollern. A letter Marie wrote to King George V at the time of the Armistice indicates her stature, and shows what a formidable precedent of grandeur she set those who come after her.

"My dear George," she wrote. "You will never know what it meant for us, the first communication with you all again. We were like buried alive, smothered, cut off from the living, and suddenly light broke in upon us with such a rush that we were nearly blinded . . . I can only tell you, dear George, that I held firm as only a born Englishwoman can. Nothing shook me, neither threats, nor misery, nor humiliation, nor isolation . . . I knew you would win, and I kept my people from giving way even at a moment when many had become doubters, luck having been from the beginning so dead set against us. And even if you had not been victorious, I would have stuck to you; for me there are no two forms of fidelity. . . ."

Young Prince Carol, Marie's son, had served without distinction in the war. He was a pretty youth and his mother loved him. She was, after all, young enough to be his sister. The problem of finding him a wife was an important one. He had considered the Grand Duchess Olga, eldest daughter of the Tsar and Tsarina of Russia, but Marie had hastily scooped him away, suspecting that the girl might, like her mother, be a carrier of haemophilia. Carol, left momentarily on his own initiative, promptly married a Rumanian *mondaine* called Zizi Lambrino, and had a son by her whom he sentimentally called Mircea, after a brother who died in infancy. The shock throughout Rumanian ruling circles was great and a divorce was hastily rushed through the Rumanian Supreme Court, separating the lovers, leaving Zizi in Paris, heartbroken, a condition which did not inhibit her from suing Carol for ten million francs.

Marie's scheming mind was at work on a suitable match, and she married Carol off to Princess Helen of Greece. She also married her daughter Elizabeth to Helen's brother, King George II of Greece, and another daughter, Marie, to King Alexander of Yugoslavia. This, on the face of it, was adroit matchmaking, but all were to end in bitterness, the first two matches ending in royal divorces, and the last in assassination, all in Queen Marie's lifetime.

Carol made Helen pregnant and forgot about her. He took up with an astonishing, plump, snow-faced, red-headed Jewess called Elena Lupescu, with whom he was to spend the rest of his life. Lupescu had been miscalled Magda in a European newspaper and the name stuck because it savoured so much of sin. She had been born Wolf but Latinized her name to Lupescu. During the war she had been popular with the troops and one, an officer called Tampeanu, went as far as marrying her, but she shed him when she met Carol. After a violent quarrel in the Sinaia Palace with his parents, Carol stormed out, renounced his claim to the throne in a rage, accepted a royal hush-hush cheque for $400,000, and went to live in Paris with Magda. Meanwhile the loveless union between Helen and Carol yielded a boy, Michael.

It was into a family stunned with shame that the golden-haired child arrived. The name of Michael's father was not mentioned in his home. And when, on July 20, 1927, Ferdinand died, aged sixty-two, it was Michael and not Carol who was proclaimed King.

Michael issued his first inaugural proclamation to his troops in 1927 at the age of six, and the tone of the document gave a good idea of the years of fantasy that were to lie ahead.

"Soldiers!" the document began. "After a reign, brilliant and glorious for the race, the fatherland and the army—a reign conducted with great sacrifice and stern decision—our great and beloved King has closed forever his eyes, which never ceased to contain unlimited affection. Under his leadership you have conquered, you have forged a national unity of all Rumanians, and with laurels gathered in the battlefields you have crowned his brow and your own.

"Soldiers! We are confident that all, from the chiefs of the Army to the humblest soldiers, will give proof of that spirit and discipline which is the pride of the Army, and that you will remain worthy of the confidence which your country has placed in you, devoting all your strength and souls to the fatherland and the throne. Signed MICHAEL."

In Paris, Carol and Magda Lupescu were furious. His mother and sisters begged him not to return to Rumania and prejudice his son's chances. Carol ignored them. He was living as "Mr. Tampeanu," and with the most casual of malice aforethought he tossed two words into the Rumanian camp which rocked it like a bomb. When reporters knocked on the door he sent a message via his secretary that he—Carol II—had nothing to say.

Forces in Rumania were moving to his advantage. Expressions were heard more and more loudly that a King playing in his nursery and his Greek mother were not enough to keep Rumanian politics from sliding deeper into the swamps of corruption. In 1930, Julius Maniu, the Prime Minister, agreed with all parties to recall Carol, and Carol graciously accepted. He also accepted the all-important proviso, that Lupescu be left behind. The abandoned Magda rose to the occasion before the assembled newspaper reporters of Paris. "My enemies say I am a woman scorned," she cried. "The choice is entirely mine. I renounced my perfect love and gave my heart over to the executioners to be crucified and tortured as they saw fit, and the least my enemies can do now," she added rather querulously, "is to give me credit for the sacrifice I made."

Nobody gave a thought to the child King who turned to his distraught mother and asked, "How can Papa be King when I am King?" So ended the first reign of King Michael and the beginning of the reign of his father, who at the age of thirty-seven, could, if he wished to be introspective, say honestly that he had ruined everything he had ever undertaken. He had broken his father's heart, alienated his mother, humiliated his wife and deserted his son. George V of England had called him "that bounder," and refused to receive him when he came to London. The London *Daily Express* headlined him "Carol the Cad," and he was officially declared *persona non grata* in England in 1928, after he had brought his Balkan intrigues on to British soil. The King who landed at Baneasa airport in Bucharest to salute a guard of honour, may have been royal but he was far from regal. With his pale eyes sagging from whisky, his heavy Hohenzollern snout and small Hohenzollern chin, the weakness emphasized incomprehensibly by a drooping moustache, he was the picture of inbred, dissipated, royal decadence.

The moment he arrived, his loved ones scattered. His ex-wife, Queen Helen, quit the country and his mother, Marie, headed for the seashore. The bewildered Michael was packed off to camp for the building of bone and muscle. Three weeks later, King Carol summoned Maniu and greeted him with tears in his eyes. He told the Rumanian statesman that he was unable to live without Elena Lupescu. "She is the other half of my being, the other half of my mind." He revealed between sobs that Lupescu was back in Rumania. Maniu realised that, for a clever man, he had been most easily duped.

A turbulent period began. A Lupescu cabal ruled at court. A green-shirted organisation called the Iron Guard grew powerful in the country, hunting down the Jews and aping the Nazis, a curious creation which tried to wed orthodox Fascist terrorism with the romantic Rumanian mind. It was recruited almost exclusively from the students and intellectuals and clad its political doctrines in a queer quasi-religious mysticism. But there were no doubts about its intentions. When the Dean of the University of Jassy suggested that more time should be given to study and less to pogroms, his students murdered him.

Queen Marie died in 1938, lonely, isolated, bitter. Elections held in the same year disappointed Carol, and declaring them null and void he whipped up a hasty oral plebiscite which gave him a free hand and made him the only royal dictator in Europe. Trying to play off the Great Powers of Europe against each other he signed worthless treaties and pacts, winning great victories of diplomacy that got him nowhere.

In his spare time he ate like a glutton and designed ever more magnificent uniforms. His passion for uniforms which became an international joke began at a boy scout jamboree. Carol turned up in a simple scout uniform, and the boys, not recognising him, hailed his military aide instead. Carol was enraged and never made such a mistake again. Over tumblers of Scotch he invented new decorations and orders and lived with a regal splendour unrivalled in the Balkans, or, for that matter, anywhere else.

There was also a credit side to Carol's reign. He encouraged the rival powers to interest themselves in Rumania's riches, oil and wheat, and was responsible for a considerable economic boom. He reformed the army and brought it up to first-class fighting trim. He supervised Michael's education strictly and made sure that he was not mollycoddled by his friends. In this toughening-up normalising process, the one prince whom Carol wanted Michael to associate with most of all was a boy of Michael's age called Prince Philip of Greece. There was not much money in Philip's family and Rumanian officials approached Philip's mother, Princess Alice, and asked if she would allow Philip to go to Rumania. As it happened, Philip was on his way to school in England but he and Michael managed to see a good deal of each other and became firm boyhood friends.

The fall of France ended the phony war with a vengeance and there was no place in Europe for a royal clown in an oil-rich country like Rumania. Germany leaned ever so lightly on the Rumanian house of cards and Carol collapsed. The Iron Guard converged on the palace shouting, "Give us the King! Give us Lupescu, the she-wolf!" Like his father before him in a previous war, Carol lost his nerve completely. He appealed to Hitler for asylum in Germany. "All right," said the Fuehrer without enthusiasm, "but I won't take the woman." Marshal Ion Antonescu, the swaggering chief of the military junta, appeared at the Palace to demand Carol's abdication. While the King haggled for terms with a whine, Michael, next door, aged nineteen and absolutely baffled by it all, burst into tears.

Switzerland offered to give Carol transit facilities, and the King signed. Antonescu provided an escort to Bucharest railway station where the royal train had had steam up for two days. The entourage consisted of Carol, Lupescu, and their faithful aide, Ernesto Urdareanu, three military aides, the director of the royal train, the Commander of the Royal Guard and several servants, two Pekingese dogs and three poodles, a saloon car and eight other cars packed with trunks and even motor cars. On the way, word came that a crowd of Iron

Guards were waiting in Temisora to take out Lupescu and shoot her dead. Lupescu collapsed in hysterics. The train which had planned to take on water in Temisora went roaring through the station, taking the Guards by surprise. Lupescu had taken refuge in the bath-tub and Carol gallantly hurled himself on top of her for protection. In the bath-tub with his mistress, King Carol II of Rumania left his native land for the last time.

Michael was once more King and under the most humiliating circumstances. He loved his father, yet was forced to read the Bucharest newspapers which were full of abuse of the former King. Antonescu was determined to keep the boy in his place, and Michael himself, full of hestitation and self-doubts, wilted quickly under Antonescu's unconcealed contempt. "You are a child and know nothing," he said, if ever the King made any kind of protest. The dictator also kept Michael in a state of insecurity by threatening to transfer the crown to the family of Michael's aunt, Princess Ileana. Ileana, a woman of great beauty was married to Archduke Anton of Austria and had two sons and four daughters. She was Antonescu's protege and the dictator succeeded in driving a wedge between her and Michael which persists to this day. Ileana, living in the United States as "Mrs. Issarescu" and Michael living in Switzerland, have no communication with each other.

Antonescu announced publicly that he had invited Michael's mother to return to Rumania to "complete her son's education." When Queen Helen arrived, she found Antonescu's stupid and ambitious wife taking precedence over her and signing her letters "Maria" in the royal manner. A friend of Michael's from Germany called in to see him and found the King tense and nervous. "What do you hear from your father?" the friend asked.

"I can't write," said Michael, looking round uneasily. "Not allowed."

It was a quiet, melancholy court now, after all the alarums and scandals of Carol's reign and after the brilliance of Queen Marie's circle. Michael was not a boy to examine things too deeply but was struck by the fact that in his lifetime he had never had a father and a mother at the same time. "When I needed a mother I had a father, and when I had a father I needed a mother," he reportedly said.

Michael was a good boy and a quiet King. He could not have been a greater contrast to his father. He preferred comfortable English sports clothes to uniform. Wherever he went he was followed by a large dog, firstly a Great Dane, and then when it died, a German police dog. They seemed to be his only companions. Carol had done a good job on Michael's education. Michael was now six feet three inches tall and broad-shouldered. His passion was for mechanics and motor cars and he had worked in a Ford motor factory for a while. He smiled seldom and had little sense of humour, but he had a fine sense of resolution and intellectual integrity, and when he did smile he dimpled deeply.

He had been back on the throne a year when Antonescu took Rumania into the war on the German side and joined in Hitler's attack on Russia. Rumania, thanks to Carol's reforms, fought a brave war. She supplied more troops, conquered more territory and fought infinitely more bravely than the Italians who were ostensibly Germany's principal allies. The Rumanians outfought the Russians, captured an annexed Odessa, plundered huge areas and carried out mass executions. But the tide turned. Russia began to push the Axis troops back, slowly at first and then in a great massive sweep from Leningrad to the Black Sea. Ultimately they washed up in their great grey hordes against Rumania's frontiers and the situation in the country was desperate. For the non-Fascist European conservative in those days, nothing was more agonizing than the anomaly of the alliance between the United States, Britain and Russia. More and more Michael and his secret advisers believed that the only hope for Rumania was to get out of the war and throw themselves on the mercy of America and Britain, who, they hoped, would temper the barbarity of Russian occupation.

Between them and their plans stood one man, the ruthless Fascist dandy, Ion Antonescu. Antonescu knew what the King was thinking, but he dismissed the boy's fear contemptuously. "It shall never be my hand that signs a document agreeing to the entry of Russian troops on Rumanian soil," he told Ileana. "We learned in the last war what it was like to have them as friends. What would it be like to have them enter as victorious enemies?"

In his Bucharest palace, Michael sat alone wrestling with a terrifying decision. It was life or death, now or never, and the twenty-three-year-old King had resolved on a showdown with the dictator, a man who intellectually and mentally was his superior, who could throw at the young King an assurance of authority and wealth of experience that the King could never match. Michael steeled himself to his task like a schoolboy preparing to face his headmaster. He summoned the dictator to a memorable interview.

Antonescu's rough heavy face was impatient when he came in and his salute was perfunctory. "Long live your Majesty," he said.

Michael put his hand below his desk and silently switched on a dictaphone, so that nothing might be lost. "There is no time to lose," he said. "In spite of the representations I have made to you, you have brought the country to a situation from which only the immediate cessation of hostilities and expulsion of the Germans can save it."

Antonescu sneered and turned to go. "You are mistaken," he said rudely.

Michael snapped back, "Please accustom yourself to addressing me correctly. What is this 'you'?"

Antonescu was taken by surprise and started to stammer. "You—Your Majesty . . . is nervous today."

"Yes, because when I called you this morning you treated me as a mere nothing." Michael thumped the table and shouted. "I do not permit you to take liberties with my person. Do you think I can permit you to usurp my prerogatives and simply look on like a fool while my country crumbles away?"

"And who is destroying it?" demanded Antonescu, as angry as Michael.

"All of you," said the King wildly, and becoming incoherent. ". . . You have no time for the King of this country."

"I wish to tell you that you are mistaken if you think you can save the country by an armistice."

"I have not called on you to ask your advice or for your opinion. The purpose for which I have called you is for you to transmit this telegram concerning the cessation of hostilities to the United Nations."

He handed a slip of paper to Antonescu, who read it coldly. "Who composed it?" he asked.

"What does it matter to you?" said the King. "If you do not accept it I shall send it myself."

"How can you imagine the Marshal can betray his German allies and throw them into the arms of the Russians?"

Michael began shouting again. "Who is doing the betraying, you or the Germans? Did you guarantee Germany's frontiers, or Germany Rumania's?"

"I am not deaf. Why are you shouting?"

"Yes, you are," said the King. "Otherwise you would have heard the murmuring of the country. In short, Marshal, will you send the telegram, or no?"

"No, in that form, no."

"How then?"

"I must contact Germany."

"What?" cried the King. "Are we bargaining here, Mister Antonescu?"

"*Marshal* Antonescu."

"*Mister* Antonescu. For the four years you have been usurping my rights, you have had neither my confidence nor my sympathy. For months I have been working with the opposition to save my country. You, I know, consider me a stupid, stammering child. My Rumanians will judge that. But if you consider me to be a traitor, you will be completely disillusioned. I am the King of my country and your King. I wish to save the country," and here Michael thumped the table and shouted at the top of his voice, "and nobody can prevent me."

"Your Majesty is young and inexperienced," said Antonescu.

"You are wrong," said Michael bitterly. "Suffering is an experience."

"You cannot dispose of the country if. . . ."

"I am the commander of the Army and the order has been given."

Antonescu was thunder-struck. "Given? What order? Does your Majesty know that your Majesty might lose the throne?"

"Are you threatening me?" said Michael furiously. "Do you think you have the power to order anyone any more? Here and from now on, I will make the decisions. You are under arrest."

The King pressed a push-button. The doors of the King's study were thrown open, and a handful of the King's guards pushed through with their guns. Antonescu wheeled round and yelled, "What! I, the Marshal of the country? No!"

The King was calm now. "Nonsense," he said. "Take him away."

The King's men then closed in on Antonescu's bodyguards and disarmed them. Antonescu's ministers were arrested. The German High Command was told that Rumania had taken herself out of the war. The Rumanian soldiers who had been Germany's most faithful brothers-in-arms were suddenly told to fight no longer, and waited nonplussed to see what would happen next. All the time the Russians were advancing, overrunning German and Rumanian posts alike, with everyone shooting at everyone else. The country was in chaos.

Michael telephoned his mother at the Sinaia Palace. He told her to leave at once. "I will join you," he said. "Go to sister Elizabeth's house." Helen slipped a gun into her handbag and set off. Michael, speeding from Bucharest, ran into a German motorized column and veered away as the column opened fire. Michael's Rumanian escort fired back, eluded the Germans and arrived safely at the villa.

It had been a fantastic adventure, but as the war left Rumania behind and swept into Germany, a new sequence of events began for Michael, even more incredible than what had gone before. Michael's coup had attracted the admiration of America and Britain. Until that moment Michael had shown to the world only the picture presented of him by grace of Antonescu, that of a vacillating and ineffectual youth. The abrupt emergence, instead, of a rocklike monarch and friend took the Western allies by surprise, and they lost him before they could take advantage of him. Out of Moscow now came a band of Rumanian expatriates, many of whom Michael had never heard of, and were efficiently taking over the country. Michael, dazed, tried to form a government in the traditional way. He called in old Prince Stirbey, a former lover of Queen Marie's, who had once had his face slapped in public by King Carol. Instead, he found himself face to face with Andrei Vishinsky, specially flown in from Russia, who "suggested" that he appoint a Moscow stooge, Petru Groza, a wealthy, land-owning Rumanian Communist.

The war ended and the cold war began. A Red façade, called the National Democratic Front, took over, and Michael found himself dealing with politicians completely alien to anything in his experience. Not the least extraordinary figure was his new foreign Secretary, a woman called Ana Pauker, who had not even bothered to change her citizenship back from Russian to Rumanian. She was a big woman, quite attractive and even girlish in her personal manner, with intense blue eyes and a baby's smile. She was believed to have denounced her husband to the Communists and had him shot.

Michael became more and more of a royal curiosity. He was the only King reigning behind the Iron Curtain. Every moment it seemed he would be deposed, yet he hung on from day to day and month to month, until it began to stretch into a year and then two years. The Communists seemed perfectly happy to put up with a King, and the scene would have done justice to a London musical comedy. After all, if Communists accept the King as titular head they must accept the forms of monarchy too, and this the Rumanians did. The craziest paradoxes prevailed. Patriotic rallies would be decorated with huge pictures of Lenin, Stalin, Groza, Ana Pauker —and King Michael. The Russians decorated the King with the Soviet Order of Victory. Communist policy was declared in speeches from the throne. On social occasions the Red leaders appeared before the King in white tie and tails. But the Royal Family was desperately lonely. It is an illustration of the family's isolation that they were obliged to turn for friendship to Ana Pauker a notorious murderess. Ana enjoyed the royal patronage. Princess Ileana, Michael's sister, tells how Ana after taking tea with her, asked politely, "Should you dismiss me, or should I leave? I have enjoyed this charming conversation so much that I have forgotten just what the protocol is."

Only here and there did the Communist tyranny penetrate through to the Royal Family, as when a broken, white-haired ghost of a woman confronted Princess Ileana in Bucharest and asked her for a phial of poison which she could hide and use in case she was tortured further. The Princess recognized with horror that this was Maria Antonescu, wife of the former dictator who had been crudely and brutally executed.

The royal farce could not last. The Communists could not afford, even with the nicest sense of humour, to keep the King as a rallying-point for anti-Communist sentiment in the country. The Government well knew that there were not more than a thousand Communists in all Rumania before the war. The moment Communist discipline was relaxed everybody who hated the regime, which meant nearly everybody in the country, would flock around Michael.

In August, 1947, the country celebrated the second anniversary of the overthrow of Antonescu. The whole Cabinet was present in the theatre where the celebration was being held. Groza was cheered vociferously. Michael, entering the royal box, was greeted with a freezing silence that would have unnerved the bravest. The King sat impassively as Groza covered in detail the events of the glorious day when Rumania left the war on the German side and became the comrade of the Russians. There was one interesting omission. He spoke not a word about the part played by the King in getting rid of Antonescu. It appeared that the entire credit belonged to Groza. In his speech he said, "We are moving forward to the elimination of the last traces of Fascism." There was a pause, and the Cabinet, as one, turned to focus their eyes on the King. The next day the King was seen walking thoughtfully in the grounds of Sinaia, alone, save for the German police dog at his heels.


Meanwhile, in the non-Communist half of the world, the summer of 1947 found two marriages being arranged, both of considerable interest to Michael. Princess Elizabeth, heir to the throne of England, had become engaged to his childhood friend, Prince Philip of Greece, now a handsome, embarrassed young man in the Royal Navy. And in faraway Brazil, Magda Lupescu, on her deathbed with an incurable ailment, was finally united in marriage to King Carol, her joy being so great that she recovered almost immediately.

In London, King George VI announced that the wedding would be a quiet affair in harmony with the austerity existence which Britain had willed herself since the war. The military escort would wear battledress and the pomp and ceremony would be kept to a royal minimum. For once the King had failed to assess his subject's feelings correctly. The nation wanted no austerity for their future Queen. They wanted colour and the opportunity to go wild. The pre-war regalia was brought out for the first time since 1939, the bearskins and the redcoats taken out of storage, and the nation prepared to resume its pre-war tradition of sumptuous royal weddings.

Invitations went out to all of Elizabeth's and Philip's royal cousins, and in they poured, the Hohenzollerns and the Hapsburgs, the Orange-Nassaus and the Bernadottes, the Saxe-Coburg-Gothas and the Schleswig-Holstein-Sonderburg-Glucksburgs. Also the Bourbon-Parmas, among them a pretty princess, Anne of Bourbon-Parma, who lived in Switzerland.

From Bucharest, in his private plane, came the Iron Curtain King, Michael I of Rumania, attracting, in some ways, the most curious glances of all.

What, the others wondered, does two and a half years of Communism do to a King? Michael, they noticed, looked pale and strained. He was simply uniformed, unsmiling and reserved. His manners were poor and he was boorish and bad-tempered to servants. One could see he had been through a severe strain and few people present were inclined to criticise him. King Peter with his usual jolly ebullience and lack of tact buttonholed him. "Look here, Michael," he said. "You will either be killed or moved out very soon by the Russians. Why don't you take your chance and stay here?"

Michael said something non-committal about having to clear up a mess, and changed the subject. As his holiday progressed his gloom lightened. Princess Anne was a girl of spirit. She had arrived penniless in New York during the war when her parents, Prince Rene of Bourbon-Parma* and Princess Margrethe of Denmark, escaped from occupied Copenhagen, and she had earned her living as a salesgirl. Returning to Europe, she enlisted as an ambulance driver in the French Army, seeing action in Casablanca, Algiers and Italy, and following the advance of General de Lattre's advancing troops as far as Stuttgart. For her services she had been awarded a *Croix de Guerre*. She was the very image of the graciousness for which Michael had been starved.

The Western press which speculated on whether Michael would return to Rumania at all, underestimated the strength of Michael's character. But from Rumania there seemed to be a brooding silence difficult to define but which boded no good for the King. Those who felt it most strongly were his re-

* One of the score of children of Prince Robert.

latives who went to meet him at the station in Bucharest on his return. They noticed that the streets giving access to the station were closed and there was an unnatural air of desertion in the station itself. Soldiers were at every entrance, obviously to bar demonstrations of welcome. The ministers who had come to the station to greet the King looked glum, only Groza and Ana Pauker bothering to greet the royal relatives. Michael, everyone noticed, looked better than he had looked for years. He was so exuberant he did not notice the coldness of his reception or the deserted avenues. At the palace he gave out the news and gossip about his English relatives, showed photographs of Princess Anne. He and his mother were full of plans for converting Michael's bachelor apartments at Sinaia to make them suitable for a wife.

Michael asked Groza formally for permission to marry, but was met with an ominous hedging. Christmas passed and there was no word from the Government. The word was on the way, however. The date for the fall of the final curtain was December 30, 1947, but the stage was set the evening before. The snow was falling outside the King's residence, Sinaia Palace, and Michael had been planning a New Year party for a few family friends, and working on his New Year message to the nation. At 8.30 p.m. while the King and his mother, Queen Helen, were at dinner, Petru Groza, summoned him to the capital the following morning "on important business."

Michael did not like Groza's tone, and said curtly, "Make it tomorrow afternoon. I shall drive down to Bucharest then." And with that he returned to his dinner table.

Ten minutes later the telephone rang again, and Michael, really annoyed, picked it up and heard Groza insisting that he must keep to a morning appointment. With bad grace, Michael agreed. He parted the curtains and looked out into the night. Below him the river had torn a torrential, purple gash out of the snow, and the white-hooded Carpathian forests rolled down from the mountains to the river's edge.

Next morning, the royal car with King Michael at the wheel, Queen Helen by his side and the King's equerry and duty A.D.C., behind, drove into Bucharest. Immediately Communist officers closed in on them, separating the King and his mother from their suites. Michael saw that the guards at the doors were strange and unfamiliar to him. Over the past two and a half years Michael had grown accustomed to Groza and almost liked him. What made him grow tense was the sight of another minister, Gheorghiu-Dej, Secretary-General of the Communist Party. Gheorghiu-Dej could have no interest one way or another in whether Michael married Anne of Bourbon-Parma. In spite of all the crises through which they had gone, Michael and his mother were utterly taken aback when Groza handed over to him a parchment containing a declaration of abdication.

The solemn blue eyes of the King looked up to the faces of the two men in front of him. "If I refuse to sign this," he said, "you cannot force me."

"No," Groza admitted. "But I warn you, Sire, that guns are trained on the city. Blood will flow. Thousands of your supporters will be arrested. Rumania will enter a period of horrible suffering and those who love you now will hate you for it."

"Can I have time to think it over?" Michael asked quietly. He was given twenty minutes. Michael and Helen argued but it was useless. Michael signed. A passport was handed to him. His citizenship, he was told, was not to be taken away from him. For what it was worth, he would still be permitted to travel on a Rumanian passport.

The long argument over abdication threw up one dramatic moment, and a testimony to the King as vivid as it was indirect. When it was all over and the document signed, Groza lifted the flap of his side pocket and showed Michael and Queen Helen that he was carrying a gun. The Communist leader giggled at the Queen's alarm. "I was taking no chances," he said. "I wasn't going to let you do to me what you did to Antonescu."

As the cold year of 1947 turned into the no less chilly year of 1948, Michael left his country by train, seen on his way by a slovenly so-called Guard of Honour who gawped at him stupidly, and by officers who sneered in his face. The train stopped at Brasov, still ruined from the bombardments of the war. Michael looked out for some demonstration of affection by the people, but all he saw were thick clusters of Red Guards lining the station to prevent just such an event. The muddy plains of Russia now buried under the snow, rushed past him. In his carriage with his small entourage and bound for the freedom and exile of Switzerland where Anne of Bourbon-Parma was waiting, he was sunk in gloom and consumed with a sense of failure which did him credit. He blamed only himself, not Groza, not Ana Pauker, not even his father who had brought such ruin upon him.

It was all over. He was only twenty-six, yet the period from the beginning to the end of his reign was not much shorter than that of George V of England. And in that period he could honestly say he had never known a single day of sane, normal, constitutional rule. Nothing but madness.

Customs formalities at the frontier were perfunctory. Rumania was left behind to its fate. Ana Pauker later sank into disfavour and on last reports was working obscurely in a Rumanian publishing house. Groza died of cancer in 1958, aged 75. By that time other Communists still more anonymous had taken their places.

There were constitutional difficulties against the Orthodox Michael marrying the Catholic Anne, but no one was inclined to test the patience of the ex-King who had endured so much, and they were married in Athens in 1948. They lived for a while in a small house in Lausanne where their two children were born, and in 1953 they moved to Eyot St. Lawrence, where Bernard Shaw had lived. Michael had established many records during his reign, records not likely to be equalled. As an English gentleman farmer he had a new, melancholy record to his name. Of all the Kings in exile he was the poorest, poorer even than Peter of Yugoslavia.

Whatever money existed in the family was possessed by Carol, and this infuriated Michael. When Carol visited London he sent messages to Michael, but Michael ignored him. Carol had set himself up in Portugal where he and the new Princess Elena Lupescu were shunned by all the other exiles except the good-natured Umberto of Italy. While Michael made a meagre living farming, Carol's other son, Mircea, and his former wife, Zizi Lambrino, were reduced to penury. Mircea, in 1945, had managed to pay his way to Brazil for an audience with his father and was told by Urdareanu that "His Majesty knows no one by the name of Lambrino."

In April, 1953, Carol died, and many princes came to pay their respects to one of the worst, but certainly not one of the least, of their ilk. Carol had had his day of power, which is more than can be said for all. Michael sent a chilly word from England that his wife had just had a baby and he could not come. Prince Nicholas, his brother, was the sole family representative. "I hated Carol more than I ever hated anybody in my life," he said, "but he was my brother and my King." After the funeral, Magda Lupescu, grievously mourning, holed herself up with her memories and King Carol's fortune.

The various free Rumanian national committees scattered throughout the free world are mostly monarchist and loyal to Michael. In spite of his lack of formality, Michael likes to be recognised as King, and he maintains an equerry, General Petre-Lazar, in London.

Michael has had a succession of jobs, including one as director of a Swiss branch of a California aeronautical instrument firm. He is in poor circumstances but he has turned down an offer of $100,000 from an American magazine to write his memoirs.

Money apart, he is happy where he is and how he is. He likes to shoot and to spend his time with his family. Mention Rumania or King or Royal Family to him and a curtain falls on his good humour. He rarely discusses the past. He has pulled up the stem of royalty by the roots and does not want to think about it. Among his royal cousins he is not popular, consequently many people were surprised when he accepted an invitation to go on one of Queen Fredericka's royal cruises. 'What on earth are you doing here?' he was asked by one cousin.

"I like some royalty," he replied, unsmiling. "But not many and not much."

# X

# *Umberto of Italy*

## Wise Too Late

"If we win I shall be King of Abyssinia. If I lose I shall be King of Italy."

—King Victor Emmanuel in 1936 during the Italo-Ethiopian War.

*T*ime and timing are essential to the fortunes of a King. Michael of Rumania came to the throne too early. So did King Peter of Yugoslavia, who was played out before he was twenty-one. So, perhaps, did Queen Elizabeth of England, judging by the criticisms she received in 1957 and 1958 and which will be explored later. King Umberto is a man who came to the throne too late. By the time he got there he had acquired the stature and the flair, combined with a pleasing lack of imagination, to be a good monarch. The decision being put to the Italian people at a moment of history when he had not a chance of winning, he reigned for only twenty-six days.

Today his home is the village of Cascais, near Estoril, in Portugal, in the Casa d'Italia, a pretty villa in cream and white with a roof of bright orange tiles reminding one somewhat of Mr. Howard Johnson's ice cream palladia in the United States. Here Umberto keeps an admirable public relations establishment dealing with thousands of letters and hundreds of requests for audiences every year. He is accessible to all. Often he can be seen sunning himself on his bal-

cony in a plum-coloured dressing gown. Wave to him and
he waves back. Usually during the day he climbs into his small
black Fiat, sometimes alone, sometimes with one of his staff,
and goes down to one of the beaches. He likes mingling with
the crowd, where he ceases to be "Majesty," and becomes
simply the Portuguese "*O Senhor.*"

Charabanc loads of Italians, from Italy itself and from
Italian communities all over the world, call in to pay their
respects. The author was caught in the middle of one of these
torrents, the visitors being Italian-Americans in Portugal on
a cut-rate cruise. Umberto, flanked by his valet, his secretary
and by General Graziani, his aide, appeared at the top of the
stairs, smiling a small deep smile which seemed to spread
vertically rather than horizontally. His face radiated that
particular brand of health which always seems to be possessed
by bald, sunburned men. He greeted his visitors with a chuckle
that was once famous through all Italy, high-pitched and
throaty and at the same time, deprecating and mildly apprehensive, but completely engaging. The crowd surged around
him to shake his hand. Only the chuckle rising above the noise
gave any indication of where he was. The conversation was
loud and excitable.

"King, you are just the nicest man . . . The nicest. . . ."

Chuckle "So kind . . . so kind."

With requests for photographs the crowd opens out. "King
Umberto, will you let me take a picture of you with my daugh-
er?" Umberto sees the daughter and agrees willingly. He
takes her hand politely. The girl looks at him in adoration.
She is not the first. The pictures are taken. Then come the
autographs. Sometimes the crowd breaks into a stream of
Italian, but soon they stop. Italian for Italian-Americans con-
tains too many old-world connotations. It involves too much
"*per piacere,*" "*Signore*" and even "*maesta.*" Their accents

embarrass them. They find they are much more confident of themselves when they talk American. The King's amiability never deserts him. Nor does the dignity with which he greets each of his admirers.

A week or so earlier the author had been present at a similar scene in Belgrade for a visiting Hollywood film star. There were the same exclamations, the same excitement, the same hunger for autographs. The difference had been in the object of their admiration. Where the King had been modest the showgirl had swept the mob with her hauteur. The King was aware of every person around him, and gave to each in turn his full attention. The showgirl's smile was for the mass, fundamentally directed inward at herself. Only she was in focus, the rest was a blur.

It is of course an unfair comparison. The showgirl had risen in a few unexpected years from Woolworth's to wealth and fame beyond her dreams. The King has fallen into a low estate from an adulation which the Italians, more than any other people in Europe, gave to their Royal Family. From the time when the Milanese under Austrian rule roamed the streets crying *"Viva Verdi,"* which meant secretly, *"Viva Vittorio Emmanuele, re d'Italia,"* the symbol of independence, and even from 1918 when Victor Emmanuel was hailed as the *"re vittorioso,"* the drop to the Casa d'Italia is a long one, and, for Umberto, holds out little hope of reversal.

He has grown accustomed to adversity. The nearest he can get to Italy is when the Pan-American plane he always uses in Europe touches down at Ciampino Airport in Rome in transit. Then he stands at the top of the steps and looks out over the tarmac to draw what satisfaction he can from hangars and sheds. He was joined once in this mild contemplation by an American tourist.

"That Rome," said the tourist, "is a wonderful town."

"It is indeed," said the King.

"But, rubbishy, as the poet said, rubbishy."

"What poet?" asked the King, surprised.

"Are you Italian?" asked the American.

"Yes."

"Do you live in Rome?"

"No, I live in Portugal."

"Why don't you live here?"

"Because they won't let me," said the King philosophically.

"Oh", said the American, not quite knowing what to say. "Fascist, eh?"

The King laughed and returned to the plane. Although no match, intellectually, for men like the Count of Paris or Don Juan, Umberto has made himself, by his good nature, the best-loved of the exiled monarchs. Umberto was the only man who did not mind being seen in public with King Carol of Rumania, which shows, if nothing else, that he is a good fellow. The other exiles consult him about their problems or look to him to settle their innumerable internecine quarrels, particularly the various Braganzas, who are always squabbling.

To Italian immigrants he is often the last touch of Italian civilisation they see before setting out for North or South America. Towards them he is fatherly and wise, and the advice he gives them is usually sound.

He is alone in the world. After he ceased to become King he flowered as a statesman. He has every reason for bitterness, but possesses none. Instead he has achieved a sort of sincerity which he did not have before. His wife lives in Switzerland and his children are grown. Transformation of personality is not uncommon in a King, but few have changed as completely as Umberto.

It is hard, now, to conceive how propitious were the circumstances surrounding Umberto's birth. He came into the world at the Royal Palace of Racconigi on September 15, 1904, during the period of national prosperity that so often follows a military disaster. The humiliation of the Italian defeat in Abyssinia at the turn of the century had been shrugged off. The glorious days of Garibaldi and of the Risorgimento were still a living memory.

At the age of nine Umberto's education was entrusted to an army officer, Commander Attilio Bonaldi, and he took happily to military life. Umberto was a charming athletic boy, always laughing, a habit which, with the progressive deterioration of his fortunes, ceased to please, and caused him to be called in later years "the smiling fool of Europe."

When he was thirteen he met the girl he would one day marry. It was 1917 and Marie José, daughter of King Albert and Queen Elisabeth of the Belgians, was being educated, far from the war, in Switzerland. Marie-José was eleven years old, a violent, uncontrollable tomboy with a mop of hair so thick that British officers in Belgium gave her the nickname "Fuzzy Wuzzy" and "Gollywog." The Italians called her "*scugnizza*," a Neapolitan name meaning ragamuffin. Her mother had always surrounded herself with musicians and artists and this had been an important influence in the forming of her personality. Umberto and Marie-José liked each other well enough at first meeting. They did not meet again until shortly before they married.

Umberto grew up to be what the Italians call a *donnaiolo*, possessing an apparent irresistible charm for the opposite sex. In January, 1930, the Houses of Saxe-Coburg-Gotha and Savoy were united in a brilliant marriage when Umberto, the Crown Prince, married Marie-José, in Rome, after a week of festivities throughout Italy. Marie-José was beautiful now, and calm, vastly changed from the strange-looking little creature she had been as a child.

That same summer, Umberto was seen dancing alone with a well-known Roman beauty. There were other scandals. Though the royal couple respected each other well enough there was too little in common between them. Within two years the marriage, though yielding heirs, was dead, Umberto and Marie-José both returning to their old ways of life. Marie-José must have been one of the unhappiest princesses in the world at this time. Used to the milieu of culture in her mother's home in Brussels, the court of Naples was too crude for her to bear. The ordinary people of Italy looked up to her, but from Italian high society she had to put up with an unending battery of innuendoes and slanders of a nastiness of which only the cream of an ancient aristocracy is capable. No opportunity for a pinprick was lost. Once, visiting a palace with Umberto in Sicily where they were guests, they were greeted by cheering crowds who poured into the courtyard and stood beneath the balcony shouting for the royal couple. Marie-José was overjoyed. Afterwards the hostess said to the Princess, "See, Your Royal Highness, see how the people love the House of Savoy," with a slight but stinging emphasis on the word "Savoy."

Marie-José loved Italy itself, but she pined for the liberalism and democracy of Belgium. Rome and Naples under the thick, oppressive atmosphere of Fascism suffocated her. She would have returned home, but her brother, Leopold, whom she loved, reminded her of her duty to both the royal Houses.

This duty Marie-José continued lovelessly to honour. She produced, in all, four children, three girls and an heir to the throne, Victor Emmanuel.

Under Mussolini the status of the Royal Family steadily declined. Italians laughed at Victor Emmanuel who was so small that he needed a stool in order to mount a horse. The Duce received letters every day asking him to overthrow the institution, but he laughed and threw them away. Mussolini liked the King. "I don't want to throw out anybody," he said. In 1940, to the dismay of nearly all Italians, Fascist and non-Fascist, Mussolini took the country into the war on the side of the Germans, and ran into an almost non-stop series of humiliating defeats. The Fleet was sunk at Taranto. Two British divisions under General Wavell wiped out the entire Italian Army in North Africa. The British occupied Italy's East African Empire, and the Italians invading Greece from Albania were thrown out unceremoniously by a handful of brave Greeks. Milan and Turin were blasted by the R.A.F. who returned home almost without loss. Finally the Americans bombed Rome, and Victor Emmanuel, inspecting the damage at San Lorenzo, was booed by the crowds.

Since the start of the war Marie-José had been intriguing with the anti-Fascist underground. But she was one of those souls, beyond help, who had her every act misinterpreted. Like the tragic Empress Frederick, mother of the Kaiser Wilhelm, like her own brother Leopold, everything Marie-José attempted went wrong. In 1940 she visited Hitler to plead for leniency for Leopold and the Belgian people. With this act she alienated all the anti-Axis and anti-Fascist circles in Italy which she had been at such pains to cultivate.

She moved for safety to Switzerland. In July, 1943, Mussolini was overthrown and Italy switched abruptly from the German to the allied side. Hastily, Victor Emmanuel, Umberto and their staffs packed and fled helter-skelter from Rome through the German lines to the allies advancing in southern Italy. They joined General Badoglio who was forming a government to work with the British and Americans. They had, of course, little alternative. Had they remained in Rome they would have been immediately arrested by the Germans. But to Italian eyes this flight seemed to be the last

episode in a long dereliction of royal duty. Italians had set
their Royal Family on too high a pedestal. It had been created
for them by Garibaldi, and they expected more of it than
it was able to fulfil. Anti-Fascists had resented them with increasing bitterness for their placid subservience to Mussolini.
Fascists and anti-Fascists alike looked to them to restrain Mussolini from getting into a war which nobody in Italy wanted.
The Royal Family had done nothing—except run. The Italians were left under the Germans and without a King. For
twenty-two years the Duce had thrown a protective cloak over
them. Now suddenly there was no Duce and no Royal Family
either, and the sudden draft was too much for them. Romans
heard of the flight of the Royal Family with fury.

At Pescara a naval vessel was waiting. It took Victor Emmanuel, Umberto and Pietro Badoglio to Bari, where the
new Italian cabinet was working. Italian troops were re-forming to fight on the allied side and Umberto went to the front
with them. Like his late father-in-law, Albert of the Belgians,
he spent the rest of the war at headquarters, and made himself
a popular figure with the soldiers. Umberto, to do him justice,
had never been a Fascist, and he loathed the Germans, the
murderers of his sister, Princess Malfaldo, who had died in
Buchenwald. Winston Churchill in the House of Commons
and General Mark Clark, American commander in Italy, both
praised his conduct. But he was beyond saving.

In Switzerland Marie-José visited a prison camp where
Italian soldiers who had escaped from the Germans were
being held, and she tried to distribute gifts. To a man they
refused to touch anything from the Italian Royal Family. A
journalist watched this demonstration and asked the Queen
what she thought the odds were against her son ever becoming
the King of Italy.

Half dazed by her experience, the Belgian princess shook

her head. "It doesn't matter," she said absently. "He likes mechanics. He will become an engineer."

In April, 1944, Victor Emmanuel decided to save what he could of his House. He withdrew altogether from public life, remaining the *de jure* King but entrusting the reign to Umberto as lieutenant-general of the realm. At last serious responsibilities had settled on the Crown Prince. This was not the arrogant, aggressive Italy of before the war. He was at the head of a country which had been smashed with the full blast of battle and of post-war crisis. The fighting had raged up the length of the country. The paper lira bore the limp dirty look that comes to a currency exhausted by inflation. Starvation, poverty, the humiliation of defeat and occupation had reduced Italy to physical and spiritual beggary.

For two years Umberto handled his monstrously difficult task with dignity and quiet efficiency. But Italians were too absorbed in the problems of staying alive to notice. It was too late. The flight to Pescara from Rome could not be undone. The open breach between Umberto and his wife was too glaring. Public resentment against the Royal Family was carefully fostered by the Communists, who had swollen into Italy's largest political party. Marie-José, trying to help her husband in his work, found that the monarchists despised her. This did not worry her. What did distress her was that the anti-Fascist elements she had encouraged so much would now have nothing to do with her.

On May 9, 1946, Victor Emmanuel abdicated and a national referendum was called for Italians to decide whether they preferred to be represented by a monarchy or a republic. It was the worst of luck from Umberto's point of view that the royal referendum should take place at such a time, so thoroughly steeped in cowardice and disrepute had the House of Savoy become. The Communists had everything their own way. The Right was silenced by its Fascist past. The non-Fascist Conservatives were divided. Monarchist areas like Trieste were barred from the referendum because of their unsettled political status. The Communist bully boys roamed the streets, the self-declared heroes of the *partigiani*. They campaigned with the coarse theme:

> *Dimmi, conosci quel figlio di troia,*
> *Nome Umberto, cognome Savoia?*

Umberto himself took to the hustings and carried out a nation-wide campaign. During the elections, people walking late at night may have seen a strange and tragic sight, a woman alone tearing down the monarchist posters, a woman whom some recognized as the Queen of Italy, Marie José, sister of King Leopold of Belgium. When the nation went to the polls the Queen went too and voted Socialist—for the republic.

Umberto sat out the counting of the referendum in the apartment of a friend. He tried to shrug off the election and pretend he did not care one way or the other. All the forces of personality, of cheeriness and laughter which he could muster he brought out now. The result came in—twelve million for a republic, ten million for a monarchy. Umberto smiled a brave shadow of the Umberto smile and even raised the trace of the Umberto chuckle. He turned to the window and looked out into the street. "It is going to be a beautiful day," he said. Umberto and Marie-José had reigned for twenty-six bitter days. It had been a closer vote than people expected. Had the Communists been less rampant and the monarchists less timid the King would probably have remained King.

Before the Royal Family parted for exile there was a poignant incident, reported in the Italian press. Marie-José had voted against her husband, hoping she might be allowed to remain in Italy, but her claim had been disallowed. At midnight, on June 5, a lady-in-waiting in the Villa Maria Pia, Naples, called General Adolfo Infante, who was responsible for organising the Royal Family's departure.

"Her Majesty refuses to go," said the lady-in-waiting. "What am I to do?"

General Infante hurried to the Queen's presence and found her distraught. "They will say again that we run away," she cried. "I am not a Savoy. I do not want to run away. Can I stay even two days more?"

The General knew that this was the Queen's favourite home and one which she now occupied for the first time in three years. "I will telephone His Majesty at the Quirinale," he promised. He did so, but Umberto insisted that his wife must accompany him.

"When must I be ready?" Marie-José asked. He told her. "Four a.m. In four hours' time."

"I will be ready."

They left in the Italian cruiser, the *Duca degli Abbruzzi*.

In Portugal Marie-José took the title of the Countess de Sarre. At least she could claim Belgian citizenship. Umberto was not even allowed an Italian passport. The Portuguese police gave him a travel document and that is all he possesses to this day. The Casa d'Italia was purchased and the man who only a few months earlier had possessed forty palaces and half a hundred shooting lodges settled down to contemplate what to do next. Marie-José, however, had still to taste the dregs of unhappiness. She fell ill, not too seriously, but she had to be given a blood transfusion and by mistake she was given plasma from the wrong blood group. Shortly afterwards she became partially paralysed and completely blind. She moved to Switzerland for treatment and there she remained. Her sight was partly restored in so far as she was able to see downwards, but could not turn her eyes up. She bore this dark and hooded world with a noble dignity and devoted her time after that to a history—a friendly history—of the House of Savoy.

Financially the Royal Family was secure. Marie-José was wealthy from her own family with its vast interests in the Belgian Congo, a country which originally belonged outright to Leopold II. Umberto's main income was the interest from a £1,250,000 life insurance policy taken out by his grandfather and never cashed. His father, Victor Emmanuel, had died one of the richest men in Italy, leaving an estate worth $16,000,-000. When Italy became a republic the government seized this estate but Umberto sued in the Italian courts and won the right to four-fifths of it, the rest remaining with the Italian state. Apart from the estates, Victor Emmanuel also left the seven members of his family £1,500,000 in British banks.

Umberto's cause also receives money from the Mafia. This strange army of bandits, Sicilian in origin and inspiration, is unswervingly traditionalist in its ideals. It supports in Italy, Sicily and even the United States many honest Italian families of ancient lineage. Mafia agents are to be found high up in monarchist councils in both Palermo and Naples.

The 1946 vote showed that Umberto, in spite of everything, had left behind a large fund of goodwill in Italy. The south and Sicily were heavily for him and there were important royalist centres in the north, especially among the aggressive Piedmontese, "the Prussians of Italy." Much depended on how Umberto would behave himself in exile, whether he went politicking like the Count of Paris, or withdrew utterly from politics like Leopold, whether he behaved with dignity like his neighbor, Don Juan, or without like Peter of Yugoslavia.

Umberto refused to back the monarchist parties, or to lend himself to monarchist propaganda of any sort. "My political faith," he told Italians, "is that only monarchy which represents all classes can give my country the calm she needs for formulating wise counsels undistorted by partisanship. I shall return to the throne only if it is decided that it is clearly the people's will."

The odd result of this estimable policy has been that Umberto is more popular in Italy today than he was before his exile but he has less public support. He is treated seriously as a distinguished Italian in the press and in Italian councils. But the monarchist parties which back him earn no respect at all. They are mostly a mob of brawling hooligans, split among themselves, who ally themselves with the neo-Fascists in the Chamber of Deputies. The most famous monarchist in Italy, Achilles Lauro, as Mayor of Naples, became identified with boss-politicking in the old American school of Hague and Crump. Monarchists in elections usually poll about seven per cent of the total vote. Should another referendum be held on the monarchist question—which is not likely—Umberto would get a much larger vote than this, but a much smaller one than he received in 1946.

The Italians, in short, have lost the urge for monarchy. Conservatives and Liberals who clung to the monarchy in 1946 as a symbol of stability have grown used to doing without it.

So the Italian Royal Family today, held in higher esteem by Italians than it has been for years, is a family without hope. Umberto is reconciled in spirit and Queen Marie-José, who still lives in Switzerland, does her best to share from there the burden of her royal mission with her husband. The eldest daughter, Maria Pia, who bears a strong resemblance to her father, married Prince Alexander of Yugoslavia and settled in France. The second, Maria Gabriella ("Ella"), is the darling of the Italian illustrated magazines. A studious, attractive, unusually tall girl, five feet nine inches in height, she was born in 1940 and acts as her father's hostess. Inevitably she has been reported engaged to both of the most eligible Catholic princes, Baudoin of Belgium and Don Juan Carlos of Spain. A third daughter, Maria Beatrice, was born in Switzerland in 1943.

The heir to the throne, Victor Emmanuel, born in 1939 is an alert, quick-witted boy who has grown up with his mother. He is barred from Italy but has shown commendable initiative, and commendable contempt for a despicable law by smuggling himself across the Italian frontier in pursuit of girl friends. Victor Emmanuel has gone through the royal sporting and scholastic curriculum but has little time for royal routine. As his mother forecast many years before, he prefers to be an engineer and has little interest in the family destiny. So the burden of Italian monarchy is carried by Umberto alone. If the monarchy is to be restored in Italy it will be restored in his lifetime or not at all, and time is running out.

# XI

# Don Juan of Spain

This Year? Next Year?
Sometime? . . .

As for me I will, so far as I know and can,
God helping me, honour and safeguard each
one of you, according to his rank and dignity; and I will preserve him safeguarded
from all mischief, whether hurt or decep-
tion; and I will maintain for each the law
and justice which pertain to him.
—*Maximes du droit public francais,*
(Amsterdam. 1775).

As the example of King Michael has shown, the fundamental requirement of a King is to prove to his fellow-men that beneath the King exists a man, and within the man a heart. What only a few Kings have appreciated is that in some directions they can get away with murder, whereas one step in the wrong direction means exile.

Stupidity is not necessarily a handicap to a King. Nations have had their greatest days under Kings who were asses. Kings can be mad like George III of England or Ludwig II of Bavaria, or dissolute like Edward VII, or drunk like Henry of Holland, or deformed like Richard III. Frailty can unite the people around a King, as the British united around George VI, one of the most popular Kings England ever had. What cannot be forgiven is moral dishonesty. The ex-King who throws away his chances in petulance, in a parade of empty royalism, and aimless living, deserves what he gets, which is usually something less than contempt for contempt itself needs flesh to feed on rather oblivion which makes the man himself all the more pitiful.

Loyalty, then, to the country that exiles him and denies

him a passport, fortitude in adversity, patience in the face of injustice, and serenity in loneliness, all the things that go to make a man, can save a King. These qualities have been shown by Don Juan, the Count of Barcelona, the legal King of Spain, a man who has actually turned back the tide of history, and has, technically at any rate, won himself back a throne. One compromise and it could probably be his in fact. But it is a compromise he will not make, and the result may be that he will never seat himself upon it. But the moral victory will be his.

Where some kings have crumpled at the first sign of opposition, Don Juan has borne up under a series of blows tragic enough to crush many a worthy man. His father, King Alfonso XIII, was surely the unluckiest sovereign in Europe. Throughout his life it is said that many of his superstitious European cousins and relatives feared to pronounce his name, thinking it would bring them bad luck. When they met him, they crossed their fingers.

Alfonso's life began in the most ominous sort of grandeur. He was born a King, turning up in the world seven months after the death of his father. His wedding day in 1906 was celebrated by the loudest anarchist bang heard outside Tsarist Russia to that time. Alfonso was married to an English princess, Victoria Eugenie (Ena) of Battenburg. The wedding procession had arrived almost at the end of the Calle Mayor in Madrid when a bomb was thrown from an upper window by an anarchist. Many people were killed, including twenty-six equerries, some of them so close to the royal couple that Ena's wedding dress was bespattered with blood and ripped by flying glass. The British Ambassador, Sir Maurice de Bunsen, was the first to reach the dazed couple, followed by officers of the 16th Lancers, King Alfonso's British regiment. The Prince of Wales (later King George V) rushed up a few seconds later and assured his cousin that the explosion had been an accident, a cannon misfiring its salute.

The anarchists had better luck a couple of years later when they killed Dom Carlos of Portugal and his son, in Lisbon. In 1913 someone shot three times at Alfonso at point-blank range without hurting him. In 1925 an ambitious plot for his assassination was uncovered just in time. Six times in all Alfonso escaped assassination. He finished his reign in 1931, alive but in exile. Yet even all these shocks could be numbered among the lesser of his woes. Two of his children suffered from haemophilia, the royal disease which prevents the blood from clotting. Haemophilia is carried in the woman but strikes only her sons. Both haemophilic sons were killed in motor accidents, the eldest, Don Alfonso in 1938, and the youngest, Don Gonzalo, in 1934. Both accidents were comparatively minor, the deaths resulting from haemorrhages. Alfonso's second son, Don Jaime, was born deaf and dumb and renounced his rights to the throne.

Alfonso was forced into exile when Spain voted in a republican government. He died in Rome ten years later and was buried with his ancestors in Spain's Escorial Palace by special permission of General Franco.

One sound brother out of four is a macabre fact of life to have to accept, but the sound one was very sound indeed. Born in 1913, the year his father was shot at, Don Juan joined the British Royal Navy when his father was exiled and, completely absorbed in naval life, the idea of exile was a somewhat unreal one to him. Despite a Spanish accent which he has never lost, his outlook is almost entirely English. As a child he had had an English nurse, Miss Doherty, and an English teacher, Miss Dutton. With his mother and among his family he spoke English almost exclusively. The Queen was one of those women whose national habits are so ingrained that not even a life-time of living in foreign parts can change her. From her sensible shoes to her pearls and the aristocratic vagueness of her smile she was, and remains today, as English as a cup of tea. Don Juan grew up a big, well-muscled young man, a sports fanatic exceptional even among sports-mad royal cousins like Leopold of Belgium and Philip of Greece. He was happiest in a sail boat or on a golf course, or shooting big game in Africa. He also had a strong Spanish strain of thoughtfulness, and his combination of Latin ebullience and an English sense of humour made him a most delightful person to meet, but not necessarily the kind of material that a Fascist Spanish dictator, however royally inclined, would find himself at ease with.

He served in the cruiser H.M.S. *Enterprise* in Indian waters. In 1934 he was transferred to the training ship *Iron Duke*, and in 1935 to the destroyer *Winchester*, where he was promoted to lieutenant. In 1935 he married Princess Maria Mercedes of Bourbon, a girl of characteristically noble Bourbon beauty, and ten thousand royalists attended his wedding in Rome. The marriage produced two sons and two daughters.

When the Spanish Civil War broke out in 1936, Don Juan tried to enlist in General Franco's army, but the Caudillo, fearing perhaps a rival, would not permit him to enter the country, and stalled him off with vague promises about the prince being "kept for higher purposes," promises which, as it happened, Franco has done his best to keep. World War II found Don Juan, his family and mother in Switzerland. The blackest days in the life of an exiled prince are when history is being made and he plays no part in making it. He brooded away the war skiing, yachting and playing golf.

Don Juan's official court today is the Villa Giralda, a handsome modern house situated at the top of a hilly street appropriately called the Rua Inglaterra in Monte Estoril, Portugal, a few minutes' drive from King Umberto's Casa d'Italia. Don Juan lives in much greater style than Umberto, for the good reason that most of the bills are met by the Spanish Embassy in Lisbon. His chancery is elaborate with several aides and numerous servants. His wife, the Dõna Maria, has her own household. There is a gentleman-in-waiting and a lady-in-waiting in permanent attendance, each chosen from a list of members of the Spanish aristocracy prepared for him by his special assistant and secretary, Don Ramon Padilla. Everyone except the servants pays his own expenses. There are regular political conferences at the Villa Giralda. Grandees call in to discuss ways for easing the practical problems in the way of Don Juan's restoration. Following Umberto's example Don Juan makes himself available to Spanish admirers who come to Estoril to pay tribute to the man they call *el rey*. Money is no problem. King Alfonso, when he died, left a fortune of 25 million Swiss francs, some of which goes to Don Juan directly, and some to the cause of the monarchy. Don Juan's mother, Queen Ena, is the principal trustee of this estate. Don Juan also draws income of a kind from his extensive royal estates in Spain, but Franco, in this connection, is far from generous. He insists that the income is drawn at the pre-1936 (Civil War) rate of exchange when the peseta was worth two Portuguese escudos. Now the peseta is worth barely half an escudo.

The misfortunes that made his father the unhappiest monarch did not spare Don Juan or the Dõna Maria. Their second daughter, Margarita, was born blind. In 1956 their fifteen-year-old son, "Alfonsito," killed himself while looking down the barrel of a semi-toy rifle, the kind often used for indoor target practice. This was a truly shocking accident which prostrated the family with grief, especially Alfonso's elder brother, Don Juan Carlos, who was present and blamed himself for the tragedy. For a long time after that Don Juan Carlos seriously contemplated retiring into a monastery.

Negotiations for a restoration of the monarchy began after World War II. Don Juan, encouraged by Queen Ena, who is the driving force behind her sometimes indolent son, moved to Estoril. Dr. Salazar, the Portuguese dictator, was not too enthusiastic about having the Spanish Pretender as his own neighbour but he agreed at the request of Franco, who used for the purpose that indefatigable Portuguese lobbyist for monarchist causes, Dr. Ricardo Espirito Santo. Franco and Don Juan met for the first time in 1945 aboard the Caudillo's yacht, *Azor*, in the Bay of Biscay and Don Juan, in as many words, asked for his throne back. Franco hedged but he did agree to permit Don Juan's son, Juanito, to be educated in Spain. They met again in 1948, and disagreed about everything except the boy.

In the most curious way history was repeating itself, the problem of the Spanish succession raising its head all over again. It had last existed in 1869 with another military dictator in search of the right kind of king. In 1869 the search ended with the Franco-Prussian war of 1870. The issues are less vital today but they may well affect the entire future of monarchy in Europe. The question involves not only a throne, but what kind of a throne it must be, and on what foundations it will be based. A monarchy restored only to be overthrown would be a disaster to the institution everywhere. Franco's own attitude to monarchy is ambiguous. European monarchists who have met him many times are convinced that the dictator believes in a restoration of the Bourbons. But Franco's political background is republican. He founded the Military Academy at Saragossa in republican days, and after nineteen years of Franco dictatorship since the end of the Civil War the monarchy has not been restored in anything except name. Franco is

many things to many people, that is part of his devious genius.
He wanted to have Don Juan on call yet not so close as to
breathe down his own neck. So, knowing Don Juan's personality and the liberal English influences behind him, he laid
down conditions which he knew Don Juan would not accept.
Don Juan, said Franco, must be an absolute monarch as he
himself was an absolute monarch, and he must have ministers
below him who would do what he told them to do. Don
Juan's reaction was predictably forthright.

"That is impossible," he said. "We are not living in that
kind of an age any more. It is against the entire spirit of the
times." Franco shrugged and the matter was left there. In
1954 they met for a third time at the country estate of a
Spanish monarchist near the Portuguese border. They talked
for five hours without reaching agreement, after which they
gave up and went hunting. Franco now went through the
motions of becoming angry. To the Archduke Otto of Hapsburg, a mutual friend, he burst out that he wanted to give
Don Juan back his throne, but that the Prince was badly served
by his advisers. It was, in other words, all Don Juan's fault.

Don Juan was not a complicated man, but little by little he
was made aware that the cunning old Gallego in Madrid was
outflanking him. The Spaniards who came to visit him at the
Villa Giralda were hand-picked by Franco and expressed the
Franco point of view. There was not much Don Juan could
do about it. He was barred from Spain and could not investi-
gate for himself, and whether he liked it or not he was largely
in bondage behind the Franco chariot. Even his aide, Don
Ramon Padilla, although loyal, was a Spanish career diplomat
with the rank of Counsellor, and his salary was paid not by
Don Juan but by General Franco.

Don Juan discovered something about General Franco's
tactics which made him determined to fight him at every point

he could. While keeping Don Juan at a distance, the dictator had turned his attention to the young son, Don Juan Carlos. Don Juan noticed the change and telephoned his mother, who had read the signs too, and was as worried as Don Juan himself. Though no parties in the dispute would officially admit to such a thing, what is going on in the Iberian Peninsula as these words are written is nothing less than a struggle between a dictator and a father for the soul of a prince. The issue is undecided. Either side could win it, or, equally, both sides lose it. Few dictators in history have ever been able to dictate their successors, and the Spanish people may well elect to have no monarchy at all unless the monarchy becomes a *fait accompli* in Franco's lifetime.

As for Juanito, he was developing in every way that a father—or an *ancien régime* dictator—could wish. He had changed from the day shortly after the war when, at the age of ten, he had crossed the Spanish border and enrolled in a private school in Madrid. He was shy then and dressed in the short trousers and grey flannels of the typical English boy. The shyness did not last. He had had a lonely childhood in Switzerland, and the chance to be with other boys was all he needed. His comrades had been specially chosen, the sons of grandees, and they were warned to treat the prince carefully. So fast did Juanito progress, however, that when he graduated to a more senior school the situation had reversed itself, and Don Juan was obliged to send a message to the headmaster that, "should my son pick a fight the others must hit him back."

With the change in the royal climate General Franco began to take a greater and greater interest in the boy. When Juanito graduated the Caudillo took him personally round the Palacio de Oriente, one of the boy's ancestral homes. He showed him the gilded throne room with the ceiling frescoes by Tiepolo.

Afterwards Franco exchanged correspondence with Don Juan and they agreed that Juanito should attend the Saragossa Military Academy so that he should prepare to be of "the best service to the nation." Afterwards it was decided he would do naval and air force training and attend the University.

Don Juan agreed to all this but he was thoroughly alarmed. He himself was not prepared to be a monarch in the mould assigned to him by General Franco, and even less was he prepared to allow his son to become a puppet. "The boy must become a man before he can become a King," he exclaimed. Franco, sensing Don Juan's mood, played his next card. On July 18, 1957, the announcement was made that seemed, on the face of it, to put the throne at Don Juan's disposal, but which actually put it further away from him, than ever. On that day it was officially announced that when Franco dies or retires, Spain will have its "Very Catholic King" back. But neither the King nor even the dynasty was specified.* The Presidential Minister, Luis Carrero Blanco, outlined what kind of a King and what kind of a monarchy Spain would expect. "It will not be an absolute monarchy serving the privileges of a minority. Nor will it be a liberal monarchy which is no more than a crowned republic. It will be a traditional monarchy of Spain, adapted to the circumstances of modern times, the traditional monarchy in its epoch of grandeur, that of the (fifteenth century) Isabella and Ferdinand and the Yoke and the Arrows of the Falange."

* It is known that some members of the Falange, for strictly divisive purposes, are seeking to revive the 19th century issue of the Carlist succession. This began when King Ferdinand, after remaining childless through three wives, produced by his fourth a daughter Isabella, in 1830, frustrating the ambitions of his brother Don Carlos and his descendants. Isabella, a dissolute woman, was kicked off the throne in 1868. The Carlist Pretender today is Prince Xavier, born in 1889, yet another of the huge brood of Duke Robert of Bourbon Parma. Xavier was appointed "Regent" by his uncle Prince Alfonso Carlos when the latter died in 1936, aged 85.

The reference to a "crowned republic" in that extraordinary definition was a clear expression of contempt for the British style of monarchy, and indirectly an attack on Don Juan's Anglophilia. The next part dealt with the type of monarchy which Franco and Don Juan had argued and disagreed about. The final reference to the Falange, Franco's Fascist supporters, was certainly included in the knowledge of how much Don Juan and the Falange detested each other, and of the Falange's machinations.

At approximately the same time as this declaration, rumours began to circulate inside Spain and beyond, to the effect that Don Juan might be passed over in favour of his son. By the law of Spain Juanito, then nineteen, could not become King until he was thirty, but Franco could always change that. Don Juan knew what was going on and said brusquely to reporters: "Like everyone else, I have heard rumours that General Franco would prefer my son to take over the throne. I can only say I have no knowledge of General Franco saying this either publicly or privately. So far as I know the law of succession is unchanged." And Juanito loyally said, "To me my father is King."

But now there was another change in the type of Spanish visitor which Don Juan found himself receiving. These were representatives of the more important Spanish groups, the bankers, the industrialists, the politicians, the generals, all suggesting circumspectly that he should yield the title in favour of his son. Don Juan said flatly, "When the monarchy is restored the succession will naturally be mine."

In private Don Juan made arrangements that when Juanito finishes his Spanish education he should travel abroad and continue his studies away from the atmosphere of Fascist Spain.

The fight with Franco has changed Don Juan's philosophy

in a curious way. A throne that he had never considered worth fighting for so strongly for himself has become worth fighting for on behalf of his son. Had the critical issue not arisen he would probably have been content with his present existence. He may have been barred from Spain, but he was a welcome guest at Buckingham Palace, and a popular figure in his second country. Exile did not carry with it the pain that it carried for Otto or Umberto. Don Juan liked to play golf every afternoon, and busy himself with ambitious projects for Atlantic cruises in his yacht. But he was determined to fight to the extent of his admittedly limited power to get the throne and put it into shape for his son, a task which certainly requires the efforts of a man of his bull-strength and personality, if not that of Solomon.

For no matter how one looks at the Spanish scene the prospects for a sustained monarchy do not emerge brightly. Don Juan and Don Juan Carlos are caught between two bitter national pressures, and whichever side wins, they lose. The masses identify the Royal Family with Franco and the hated Falange. The Falange itself distrusts the Royal Family because it fears its own powers will be curtailed by a restoration of the monarchy. There is anxiety in the country about Don Juan's English orientation. Even monarchists did not enjoy having the hearty, blonde Mountbatten girl, Queen Victoria Eugenie, on the throne. They fear that under Don Juan the Court of Spain would take on the atmosphere of a Mayfair garden party.

All this hurts Don Juan, but it may help Don Juan Carlos. The son, brought up in the Spanish tradition, will be less aware of the menaces to the Spanish throne, which can be seen better from outside than from within. Spain is almost the last of the agrarian countries of Europe, and whether he likes it or not, the King would be held in power by a small landed aristocracy, supported by the Church, perhaps against the wishes of the peasants and the industrial workers. Don Juan has seen the danger and talks emphatically about the separation of Church and State. Don Juan is aware of the danger of the Roman Catholic Church to a Roman Catholic King in a Roman Catholic country. The support of the Catholic Church has proved the kiss of death to monarchy all over Europe. Only one Catholic monarchy, Belgium, remains outside the principalities, and even there the ruling family stems from Protestant ancestors. Today not a single Hapsburg, Bourbon, Braganza or Savoy is in power.* In all Catholic nations anti-clericalism is a political force in its own right, and grows with the power of the Church. There comes, inevitably, a moment when the anti-clericals command a majority in the nation. They cannot get rid of the Church, so they do the next best thing and get rid of the Royal Family. The fall of the thrones of Italy, Spain, Portugal and Brazil can all be attributed in one degree or another to the surge of anti-clericalism. The anti-clerical sentiment of the French-speaking Walloons was a considerable factor in the Belgian Leopoldine crisis of 1950. Anti-clericalism in France is the impulse that the Count of Paris has spent most of his energies trying to divert or accommodate. Don Juan understands the menace but here, as in other fields, his freedom

* Religions of the ruling Houses of Europe are as follows:

| | |
|---|---|
| Belgium: | Roman Catholic. |
| Denmark: | Lutheran. |
| Great Britain: | Church of England. |
| Greece: | Greek Orthodox. |
| Netherlands: | Dutch Reformed (Lutheran) |
| Norway: | Lutheran. |
| Sweden: | Lutheran. |
| Liechtenstein: | Roman Catholic. |
| Luxembourg: | Roman Catholic. |
| Monaco: | Roman Catholic. |

is limited. He cannot escape his own title, "His Catholic Majesty."

So far as Don Juan was concerned it was the most execrable luck that the Marquis de Portago was killed in the 1957 Mille Miglia auto race. Portago was only twenty-eight years old and he was both a liberal intellectual and an ardent royalist with strong political ambitions. Racing for him was a patriotic dedication, and he saw his own victories in terms of Spanish prestige. "Spain has had no national hero for many years," Portago said shortly before his death. "That is what the auto racing championship of the world means to me. I think I can reasonably hope to be foreign minister one day." As one of the world's great drivers he was idolised by the Spanish masses, and he, more than any other, might, had he been destined for a longer life, have helped to link the gap between the Spanish aristocracy and its peasantry. He always referred to Don Juan in his communications as "the future King of Spain."

Impotent as Don Juan is in Spanish affairs his meetings with Franco have been followed by certain stumbling moves towards the liberalisation of the Spanish regime, and some of the credit must go to the Pretender. To counter Franco and appeal to some of the more liberal elements in Spain, Don Juan took a leaf out of the Count of Paris's book and issued a political manifesto of his own, in which he declared: "Royalist Spain wants a world of justice and peace in the spirit of the United Nations . . . not only one party but the creation of independent parties . . . a free economy and the amelioration of the lot of the Spanish people who are so poor; these are the main points of the social policy of the Royal Family."

While battling with Franco, Don Juan had another problem on his hands, a family problem concerning his elder brother, Don Jaime, the Duke of Segovia. Born deaf and dumb, Don Jaime renounced his claim to the throne. In later years his condition improved to the extent that visitors often left him without being aware of his affliction at all. In 1935 he married a nineteen-year-old Franco-Italian society girl called Emmanuelle de Dampierre, and later claimed the marriage was illegal "because it did not have the consent of the Spanish Parliament." He subsequently angered his mother and family by marrying a Berlin singer called Charlotte Tiedemann.

To any member of a Royal Family the word "family" means something much more intense than it does to other people, which explains the Royal Family rows which periodically burst into flames across Europe. When the Family is involved the various members become blind to the outside world. At a "peace" meeting held in a Lausanne clinic where Queen Victoria Eugenie was undergoing an operation, Don Juan and Don Jaime met and clashed furiously, their faces white, ignoring the strangers around them. Don Juan said that Charlotte had no right to the title of the Duchess of Segovia (she hasn't). Don Jaime said, "I may have abdicated my rights to the throne, but I did not abdicate my right as head of the family." The new "Duchess" said, "What does my peevish brother-in-law want me to call myself, Mrs. Bourbon?"

The British Royal Family was caught innocently in the imbroglio, for in the middle of it King George VI died, and the protocol officers were presented with the problem of which brother should be invited. They picked Don Jaime, as head of the family, an astonishing decision which did not improve matters. Nevertheless it can be said that the Spanish Royal Family carried off their quarrel with more dignity than did the British Royal Family in 1936, the Dutch in 1956, or the Swedes in 1958.

The Don Jaime incident was an irritating distraction for Don Juan, who wished only to concentrate on his unending game of political chess with General Franco. It has been carried on, it must be said, with a singlemindedness of purpose which pays tribute to the intellect of both men. In all the manoeuvres and counter-manoeuvres neither Franco or Don Juan have lost sight of the central figure in the dispute, the young Don Juan Carlos. The young man who arrived in Madrid in 1955, on his way to the Saragossa Military Academy, was a different person from the shy boy in shorts of a few years before. He was tall, athletic, and romantically good-looking, much more Spanish in appearance than his father despite his fair, wavy hair. He had grown confident of himself as his education progressed. When cadets began to address him as "Your Highness," he replied sharply, "Drop that," and told them to call him "Juanito." His principal devotion is to his family, to his father, to the memory of his younger brother and to his sisters, Dõna Maria del Pilar and Dõna Margarita, a lovely appealing girl whose blindness has moved her to devote her life to the care of the sick and the study of languages. Juanito's Christian faith and sense of responsibility have kept him away from the easy temptations of princes. The only two girls whose names have been linked with his have been eligible princesses, Maria Gabriella, his neighbour, the daughter of King Umberto, and Princess Isabelle, eldest daughter of the Count of Paris, who is, however, several years older than he.

There was a grand demostration of royalist feelings in December 1955, when Juanito entered the Military Academy and, with other cadets, went through the ceremony of kissing the red and gold flag of Spain. A large monarchist crowd had gathered, and when it came to Juanito's turn they gave a tremendous shout of "Long Live the King." Tears fell from the eyes of some of the older officers witnessing the scene. It was an emotional, heady incident, charged with the passion of which only Spaniards are capable.

Don Juan was not there to see it. He was still exiled. However, he had guessed that something of the sort would happen, and he was worried. Juanito was only seventeen years old, and unprotected against sycophancy. A few days before the ceremony Don Juan went into his small study on the ground floor of the Villa Giralda. It was quiet there and from the windows the ground fell away to the sea. But the blinds were drawn against the sunlight and Don Juan was alone with the numerous photographs of his family. He sat down to write and what he wrote was a moving exposition of the royal conscience.*

"My dear Juanito:" wrote the father. "I want this letter to reach you on the eve of the oath-taking so that you may sleep carrying in your heart the thoughts I wish to impart to you as well as the assurance that I will be at your side in spirit during the ceremony. While I am sure the officers at the Academy have explained to you in recent days the significance of that act you will perform on the 15th of December I cannot let the occasion pass without impressing on you the eminently religious character of the oath, and that no oath may be taken blindly.

"Before all other things this oath signifies that one must, in all circumstances, maintain a spirit of discipline, of self-denial, of sacrifice—if need be, to the death—for the defence of the country and her flag.

"To those who have chosen a military career this undertaking may sound obvious. Nevertheless it implies with he who takes it the acceptance of an enormous responsibility. As long as one remains in the 'other ranks' it is a question only of obeying orders and doing only that which accomplishes them, but to the extent that one is led to assume command, responsibility increases, and it is important to understand where the true sen-

* As translated by the author, published with permission of H.R.H. the Count of Barcelona.

timent of patriotism lies and where God has established the limits of power and obedience.

"In so far as it concerns you personally your oath will make real for you the consecration of your life to the service of Spain. I now want to say these few words in order that you grasp in all its profundity the sense of the undertaking that you will accept when the oath is demanded. The fact that God has chosen that we be born in the heart of a family of royal blood has charged us with a series of responsibilities which are associated with a series of rights and duties. We cannot claim to exercise our rights except on condition that we scrupulously accomplish our duties. It is a condition then that all our acts are inspired by a high sense of duty, and imbued with such patriotism that no temptation to act otherwise would be conceivable. Quite apart from the splendid order for the march-past, this day of December 15th will be a great day insofar as it will mark the date when, fully conscious of your act, you will consecrate the rest of your life to the service of your country. I know the programme of your visit to Barcelona and I see you are going to have to do a great deal in a very short time. I rely on you to honour your standard, to be agreeable to all and to interest yourself in all you are taught. People form judgments from small details and it is important to pay careful attention to these, for the men to whom we address ourselves and who place their hope in us merit our esteem and all our respect.

"Once more, I will be with you on the 15th in my thoughts and with all my fondness.

"Your father who loves you and embraces you—

Juan."

# XII

# *Peter, Zog, Simeon*

## The Balkan Misfits

One of the few remaining prerogatives of Kings is to be called "ill-advised" when ordinary mortals are called fools.

—Ernest O. Hauser.

$\mathcal{J}$ohn Gunther's book, "Inside Europe," written in 1937 includes the following summary of King Peter of Yugoslavia, then aged fourteen:

"King Peter is one of the richest boys of his age in Europe, perhaps the richest . . . A throne and no playmates. Ten million dollars and nothing to spend it on. All the glamour of royalty . . . is hardly recompense for the formidable strain which will accompany the unlucky lad's adolescence. He should be playing football; instead he has a court chamberlain behind the curtains. He has moreover the most terrible prospect in the world; he can never change his job. He is King for life. He can never escape the steep walls of his own fortress."

Few single paragraphs could contain more ironies. What happened was that the steel walls themselves disintegrated. Not only did the King escape but so did his crown and his fortune. To-day King Peter II is the most spectacularly unemployed monarch on the Riviera. His financial problems are notorious. Like the fallen Pecksniff he "shows his elbows worn in holes, and puts his soleless shoes upon a bench and begs his auditors look there." Of all the Kings in exile none is held in lower esteem. He drove his wife to the edge of suicide, and he has commercialised to the maximum on his royal position.

In 1951 he put his rank publicly on the block. Through a Manhattan public relations firm he anonunced he "was available for consultant services and public appearances," adding that it was "for a limited number of prestige clients." This invitation, desirable as it may have sounded, yielded few offers. So hostile is the verdict of the British and the American press on Peter and his wife, Queen Alexandra, that they seem in a way to have accepted the verdict for themselves. Their two autobiographies do not spare themselves or each other. And yet it is hard not to feel that an injustice has been done. Few who condemn him could themselves have overcome the problems that Peter has had to face in his life. It must have seemed to him, sometimes, that he could scarcely get to his feet before some new disaster knocked him down again. He still pines for a country that, even in his short lifetime, has experienced regicide, revolution, enemy occupation, starvation, massacre and the lacerating zig-zag from Fascism to Communism.

The country that he came by chance to rule over looked to him to settle many of the problems they could not settle for themselves. An amalgam of different and hostile Slav tribes, the Croats and Slovenes were Catholic and until the end of World War I were part of the Austro-Hungarian Empire. The Serbs, who numbered almost half the country, had wrung freedom for themselves after four hundred years of Turkish rule, and established the dynasty by force of arms. In 1804, a Serbian revolt against the Turks was led by a peasant called *Kara Djordje,* or "Black George." He was subsequently assassinated by a rival, Milos Obrenovitch, and since then the

Prince Don Carlos, son of Don Juan, Pretender to the Spanish throne, said to be favored by General Franco over his father to be the next King of Spain.

Ex-King Peter II of Yugoslavia, ex-Queen Alexandra and their son, Prince Alexander. The most spectacularly unemployed King on the Riviera, he rushes hither and thither in search of money.

Former King Zog of Albania, 15 years after his abdication. Still one of the richest of the ex-kings, he lives in exile with his wife, his sisters (one of whom is shown above) and his dreams.

King Zog of Albania in 1937. A former tribal chieftain, he proclaimed himself King in 1928. When he fled the country in 1939, ahead of the invading Italians, the nation's gold reserves departed with him.

Exiled King Simeon II of Bulgaria (foreground) as a student at the Valley Forge Military Academy in Pennsylvania. Although his country is one of the most antimonarchist and firmly under Communist rule, Simeon considers himself King and believes that he will some day return to rule.

The line of Swedish succession in 1946. Left to right are: Prince Gustaf Adolph (killed in an accident in 1947), Gustaf Adolph (then Crown Prince, now King), King Gustaf (who died in 1950) and on his lap, Prince Carl Gustaf (the present Crown Prince).

Sweden's royal family poses after the opening ceremonies of the Swedish Parliament. Left to right are: Princess Margaretha, Prince Wilhelm, Princess Birgitta, Queen Louise, King Gustaf Adolph, Princess Sybylla with Crown Prince Carl Gustaf in front of her, Prince Bertil, and Princesses Christina and Desiree.

Yugoslav throne has been held either by a Karageorgevitch or an Obrenovitch.

In 1903 King Alexander Obrenovitch and his wife, Queen Draga, were brutally murdered by military conspirators. Alexander's place was taken by Black George's grandson, King Peter Karageorgevitch, a brilliant soldier, who restored dignity to the brawling court of Belgrade. Peter I was King when the Archduke Franz Joseph was murdered in Sarajevo, and when the first World War began he led the Serbian armies which were defeated after a gallant fight. In 1918 the Serbs, Croats and Slovenes combined, under Peter, to form a Triune kingdom, all still mutually distrustful but united by the aspiration to be part of a single, powerful South Slav state.

Peter I died in 1921. The heir should have been his elder son, George Karageorgevitch, a huge hooligan whose method of disagreeing with anyone began and ended with a blow of his fist. George, however, had been obliged to renounce his rights in 1909 after he had kicked a groom to death, and he had been prudently incarcerated as insane by the politicians, leaving his younger brother Alexander free and undisputed right to ascend the throne. Alexander was superstitious. Three members of his dynasty had been killed on Tuesday, so he flatly refused to undertake any public activity on that day. He was obliged to relax his rule when he paid a state visit to France in 1934, and in Marseilles on Tuesday, the ninth of October, he was duly shot dead.

When news came of the King's death, Peter, eleven-years-old, was taken, dazed with sleep, from his bed in an English private school, and presented to ambassadors, ministers and courtiers, all in tears. He was driven through England and France to Belgrade, where he found himself shaking hands with the Duke of Kent on behalf of King George V, (the Duke later died in an air crash), with his uncle King Carol of

Rumania (later removed from the throne), Prince Cyril of Bulgaria (executed by Communists in 1945), President Lebrun of France, the Duke of Spoleto of Italy on behalf of King Victor Emmanuel, Marshal Petain, Herman Goering and a multitude of lesser dignitaries. Afterwards his grandmother told him, "You know Peter, people will call you 'Majesty' now."

Peter broke down. "Grandmamma," he sobbed, "I am too young to be a King."

A lonely seven years began for the boy, seven years as King under a Regent, Prince Paul, whose wife was sister to the Duchess of Kent. His mother he scarcely saw at all in his early years. Queen Marie was a Rumanian, sister to King Carol, so lovely as a girl she was given the nickname "Mignon," and later became the Annie Oakley of European royalty, a pistol-packing, tent-wearing, chain-smoking, fireeater. Marie had three sons, Peter, Tomislav and Andrea, the two younger ones being lucky enough to come afterwards.

The second World War fixed Paul firmly into a cleft stick. Pro-British himself, he was forced by geography closer and closer to Italy and Germany until, in March, 1941, he signed Yugoslavia into the Axis. For this he was briskly overthrown, and Peter, at eighteen, became a King in fact as well as name. It was, for those lonely allies, Britian and Greece, a noble moment. Peter, almost alone among European monarchs, was untouched by any significant German blood. His second country was England and he willingly led his country towards those pitifully few days of resistance to the Germans. It took the Wilhelmstrasse a few hours to recover from the shock of Paul's overthrow, another few days for the Wehrmacht to prepare and in less than a fortnight it rolled. Within twenty-four hours the back of the ill-organised Yugoslav army was broken.

The Yugoslav politicians and generals were in a panic. They

hustled Peter into an airplane. A fifteen year old girl who was being prepared as Peter's future wife was pushed off the plane to make room for another politician. In the excitement nobody thought of the "mad" Prince George Karageorgevitch, still in prison after eighteen years. Peter wanted to stay and fight, but in this undignified fashion he was rushed out of the country never to return. And so: "From noon to noon he fell, from noon to dewy eve, a summer's day, and with the setting sun, dropt from the zenith, like a falling star."

Peter in England, pleaded to be allowed to parachute back into his native land and join the resistance movement gathering around the Serbian general, Draja Mihailovitch, but the Allied governments had other things to think about. Yugoslavia, losing the cohesion of monarchy, split into its traditional animosities. Croats under the German puppet, Anton Pavelitch, massacred 500,000 Serbs living in Croatia, in an orgy of hate that remains one of the most grisly atrocities of this century. When the Communist Tito emerged as a unifying leader, Peter's faint hopes of return were extinguished.

In 1944 Peter, aged twenty-one, married a Greek Princess, Alexandra, aged twenty-three. Alexandra's father, Alexander, had been King of Greece briefly and had died before she was born, after being bitten by a monkey. Peter was too young, knew nothing of life, and Alexandra, despite her greater years, was a child bride, a helpless product of a helpless royal society, often able to sense truth when she encountered it, but utterly unable to evaluate it.

Into a world with too much money this young King and Queen were thrown, and Peter, having lost his crown already, proceeded to lose his patrimony. He invested in a plastics factory and a shipping venture, figuring, not unreasonably, that even if one failed the other would probably succeed. Both failed. Crown gone, money gone, Peter next went on to lose all sense of reason. He ran wildly into debt. Once, in Paris, Alexandra had her entire wardrobe seized by the bailiffs for non-payments of debts. Peter sold everything he had, his jewels, his wedding presents, his royal Orders. He deserted Alexandra and his baby son, Alexander, became infatuated with an American girl. He and Alexandra found themselves blacklisted at hotels and in real estate offices where they sought apartments. From the depths of her woman's compassion for her husband, Alexandra summarised everything in a paragraph. "His life had been torn from its roots when he was eleven. As a child he had to struggle to grasp and control a situation that was too big, too complex and too cynical for experienced politicians to handle. As a young man he had immense wealth and power at his finger tips. Now, at twenty six, just when he would have been ready and at his best to manage the life to which he had been born and trained—he had nothing."

In 1953 Tito came to London, and Peter humiliated himself enough to ask the Prime Minister, Winston Churchill, to petition his national enemy for an allowance. Churchill did so, but Tito just laughed.

When Alexandra took a desperate though rather perfunctory slash at her wrists, Peter's madness lifted from him, and they were reunited. Peter wrote a good book about his life, and Alexandra wrote a better one about her's, and together they settled down to wrestle with the jigsaw of poverty, moving whenever things got too tough, back to the home of Alexandra's mother, Princess Aspasia, in Venice.

To-day Peter and Alexandra give to the many-sided European royal scene, a rare and sometimes enjoyable quality, that of buffoonery. Peter rushes hither and thither in pursuit of money. One moment he is busy writing a detective story, next he is buttonholing some Franco-American executive in the Carlton Hotel in Cannes to ask for a job on the Riviera.

"Do you think you could live on $200 a month like some of our other French employees?" asks one severely.

"Oh Lord," says Peter and disappears. He and Alexandra call Princess Aspasia in Venice, streaming exasperation in English, French and Italian to the telephone operators. Peter's face goes white. "What do you say?" he bellows into the telephone. "*Qu'est ce que c'est? I don't believe it!*" He turns desperately to his wife. "Your mother can't come to the telephone. She has just this second fallen off another tree and sprained her ankle. If I have told her once I've told her a dozen times to stop climbing trees."

All this can be, and is charming were it not that Peter's enthusiasms make him blunder time after time through the delicate mesh of what is and what is not admissible. Friends find Peter and Alexandra apartments and houses with the greatest of difficulty as their credit is so poor. They do not turn up to claim them. A friend offers to give a party in their honour to reciprocate all the hospitality they have accepted. Peter suggests that the money be better spent on a new car, and in the end gets neither party nor car.

For the many Yugoslav monarchists both within the country and in exile, the decline of King Peter as a national symbol is a sad one. In Communist Belgrade, at the end of the war, Tito organised "spontaneous" parades for partisans chanting the slogan, "*Hočemo Tito; nečemo Kralja*," meaning "We want Tito. We don't want the King." But Brigadier Fitzroy Mac-Lean, the British observer, heard others shouting "*Hočemo Kralja iako ne valja*," meaning, "We want the King even if he is no good."

If one sits at the bar of the Negresco in Nice one can laugh at Peter's antics. In the dank, ill-smelling avenues of Commu-

nist Belgrade laughter is not so easy. It is not fashionable today to feel admiration for the bourgeoisie, but in Belgrade and
Zagreb the bourgeoisie has fought Communism with the highest determination and courage. The villas in which they live
were built before the war with taste and confidence, are now
stark, unpainted ghosts, occupied but without life. Being pleasant and with a good view they were taken over first by the
Germans who emptied the cellars of wine, and then by the
Russians who burned the rare books for firewood. Afterwards
the Communist regime decreed that the houses be broken up
into flats to ease the housing shortage. Despite all the losses
the old families, those who had not disappeared or become
slumped in a coma of bitterness, hang on to their claims of
ownership, and they still live there in corners. With that instinct for self-preservation which makes them so detested by
left-wingers they refuse to be licked, and maintain some shreds
of an old way of life by sub-letting strictly to Western diplo-
mats. They would adhere fervently to a royal symbol if only
the royal symbol were worth a farthing, and one can see the
stake which Tito has in keeping Peter hungry and discredited.

As it is, one Kingly symbol remains to the conservative
Yugoslavs of Belgrade; not Peter, but another, the last real
royal relic still surviving behind the Iron Curtain, and the
man who by rights should be the King of Yugoslavia today,
the "mad" Prince George Karageorgevitch.


Every day he rides along the Dedinsky Boulevard on his
bicycle, his groceries hanging from the handlebars, a wrinkled,
untidy old man in his seventies, his blue eyes fixed ahead, his
white hair waving under his hat. If a pedestrian stops to
salute him—and many do—he ignores them and goes his way.
Understandably nervous of drawing attention to himself, he

lives at the centre of a tiny circle of friends, but he still attracts among the people of Belgrade a remarkable curiosity and loyalty, and when the barber and the taxi driver talk about "the Prince," there is no doubt who they are referring to.

George's life seems like something out of the dark ages. As a young soldier he was a violent libertine. His excesses at the Court of St. Petersburgh before World War I were so notorious that a minister was sent from Serbia to reason with him. George knocked him down. He took the wheel of the first car ever seen in Belgrade, seating his brother, Alexander, in the seat behind. As it gathered speed, he opened the door and leaped out, leaving the car to roar out of control. It cannoned off a tree, the branches cutting the Prince badly. Alexander, with great presence of mind and ignoring his injuries, tumbled into the front seat and finally pulled the car to a standstill in a ditch.

At the play and the opera Prince George would stamp and yell his comments from the royal box until he was barred from the theatre. Once in a restaurant he sent an aide to a table where foreigners were dining and told them to turn the other way as his Royal Highness did not like their faces. They happened to be an ambassadorial party and the Serbian Foreign Office had a hard time soothing offended diplomatic dignities.

In the first war George assumed a command of Serbian troops and during the Austrian bombardment of Belgrade swaggered under the Austrian guns challenging them to hit him. But in spite of the mitigating circumstances of his bravery the incident of the groom who had died after being kicked had finished George's career, and with the war ended, he was considered too dangerous to have at large. He was declared insane and locked away, although Serbian historians do not believe he was anything more than incurably wild. Mad or sane he remained—like the Count of Monte Cristo, jailed in the lonely Castle of Nish near the Tower of Skulls, subsisting almost entirely on eggs which he collected himself from hens in the yard—from the early twenties until the Nazi invasion of 1941. The Germans, who fondly believe they know how to use and lose foreign princes at will and cannot, in fact, do either, released George, but the Prince would have nothing to do with them.

The end of the second war found him in proud possession of a jeep which was then stolen from him by the Russians. George went underground, and only emerged after the Red troops had gone.

Some years ago he married an elderly Yugoslav lady and lives in part of a pleasant villa in Belgrade overlooking the Danube, the upper rooms of which are rented to a Western embassy family. He lives on a pension of 60,000 dinars a month, (about $90 at the free rate) granted him personally by Marshal Tito.

George is an old man, and his long sufferings have told on him. His only foreign language is French, which he speaks excitedly and with old-fashioned phrasing. He asks of life only that it leave him alone, and it is only when he is with his friends that he can relax and allow them to call him "Highness." He may have been mad, but unlike many saner Balkan monarchs he has kept his head.

The urge to be a King has not died just because we live in the twentieth century. General Trujillo would make himself King of the Dominican Republic tomorrow if he thought he could get away with it. Were other philosophies prevailing Tito would probably have crowned himself King Tito of Yugoslavia. Other philosophies did prevail in the Balkans in 1928 and Ahmed Zogu, a tribal chieftain of Moslem faith, simply proclaimed himself King Zog the First, and undoubtedly the Last.

To the degree that he can make his presence felt King Zog leaves no-one in doubt of his position. In the gardens of the Villa Saint Blaise, near Cannes, Zog's twenty-room kingdom, bodyguards patrol to safeguard him from invasion and a score of courtiers attend him to prevent him from feeling lonely. These address him as "Your Majesty," and "Chief of the Sons of the Eagle," and, on withdrawing, bow out backwards.

Zog does not have very much to do, and he has a lot of time on his hands. He receives, he says, regular reports from Albania, all assuring him that Communism is on the point of collapse there and that the people pray for his return. This one can well believe. Presumably they would expect him to bring back with him the nation's gold reserves with which he departed on Good Friday, 1939, the day on which the Italians invaded and took over the country.

Zog's wife, Queen Geraldine, is half American and of more interesting lineage than her royal husband. Her mother was Gladys Stewart of New York, her father, Count Apponyi who represented Hungary at the League of Nations until his death in 1933. Countess Apponyi subsequently married General Giraud of France.

Thanks to his foresight in departing with the nation's exchequer, Zog is one of the richest of the ex-Kings, and like many rich men he has an ideological objection to paying taxes. In 1953 he was sued for $2,914.50 in back taxes on his derelict Long Island estate by the Treasurer of Nassau County, New York. It was not the sum but the principal of the thing that hurt Zog and he protested. Zog has a genius for winning arguments with statements so unexpected that opposing strong points of logic and commonsense are overturned. He instructed his American lawyer to argue that as a King he should enjoy sovereign immunity from personal or real estate taxes. He also argued that the tax claim was a violation of international law and of treaties between Albania and the United States. The tax officers pointed out a few truths to him, and Zog paid up.

The following year the Egyptian authorities put a much bigger squeeze on him for "fraudulent tax evasion." His assets were frozen and he and Queen Geraldine were refused exit visas. In his Alexandria villa Zog fumed and chain-smoked. "I am kept a prisoner here," he said, "while the free world needs me to free Communist Albania."

To the tax officers he replied with dignity, "A King pays no taxes." And he was answered rather bluntly, "You are not a King. You are an ex-King. You are simple Ahmed Zogu and you owe us a lot of money. You have made huge profits from your import-export business in Egypt. We are not only going to tax you. We are going to fine you too."

Simple Ahmed Zogu! This was cruel and not altogether justified. There may be no place in the world to-day for the Chief of the Sons of the Eagle, but there was once. Born in 1895, he was the head of the Zogolli, one of the four ruling clans of the Mati district of Albania, the word "Zog" being Albanian for "bird." He was educated in Constantinople and served in the Austrian Army in the first World War. Albania, the most primitive country in Europe, had in these years progressed into a form of independence, and had even briefly joined the European family of monarchies. Early in 1914 interested Western powers had scoured Europe for a suitable King for Albania and had settled on an honest young Prussian officer called Prince Wilhelm zu Wied. The logic which singled out Wied has scarcely been exceeded, not even in later years in the councils of the United Nations. It was decided that a ruler of Albania should know something about the Balkans and young Wied's father's sister was Carmen Sylva, the poetry-writing wife of King Carol I of Rumania. That was considered enough. Being a soldier and a Protestant, Wied was also considered a promising arbiter for a country that was ten per cent Catholic, ninety per cent Moslem and one hundred per cent homicidally inclined. Wied was not so sure. He asked his uncle King Carol for his advice. "There's not much of a chance," said Carol "but you might give it a try."

Wied had been promised money by France and Italy, and arrived in Tirana, his capital. He found he had inherited a country without roads, sanitation or even the most primitive amenities. He was lost among an illiterate, Oriental and vendetta-wielding people speaking incomprehensible dialects. To make matters worse he had scarcely arrived when the first World War began and the money he had been promised was going in other directions. With a hearty *"Verdammt,"* Wied returned to Bavaria and was only occasionally heard from again until he died in Rumania at the end of World War II. He retained his claim to the Albanian throne, however, and is recognised, at least, by the *Almanach de Gotha*. His son, Victor, lives in Munich.

In this savage and chaotic land, Zog rose fast. He became Minister of the Interior in 1920, Minister of War in 1921 and Prime Minister in 1922 when he was only twenty-seven. By this time no fewer than six hundred blood feuds had been declared by various Albanian tribes against Zog. They almost nailed him in 1924 when an uprising forced him to take to his heels out of the country and into Yugoslavia with five hundred of his followers. The Yugoslavs lent him money and mercenaries and Zog returned to Albania at the head of three thousand men. He occupied Tirana and made himself dictator.

Constitutionally Albania was a Regency, ostensibly waiting

for Wilhelm zu Wied to come back. In 1926 Zog proclaimed the country a republic, and a couple of years later crowned himself King. Zog's reign was not one to be dismissed lightly. He was more liberal and less ruthless than his neighbour, King Alexander of Yugoslavia. He banned the time-honoured Albanian practice of polygamy. He had the various tribal dialects amalgamated into an Albanian language. He freed religion, improved education and transport. He reorganised the gendarmerie, calling in British officers for advice.

Meanwhile he had ungratefully abandoned his Yugoslav mentors and turned to Mussolini instead. In exchange for Italian loans he gave Italian business wide economic concessions and a military alliance. He remained unmarried. One legend has it that Zog, as a young man, fell in love with a girl called Miriana Zougdidi, whose father refused Zog's petition for marriage. The story goes that Zog, in a rage, swore that one day he would be King of Albania. He sent liegemen to abduct the girl but her father intercepted them, killed his daughter with his own dagger rather than permit her to marry Zog, and sent the girl's body to Zog as a present. Zog swore never to marry, and as an afterthought killed the father and the rest of the family.

Nevertheless, once he was King and having reached forty without marrying, he felt he needed an heir. He was too busy to seek a wife himself and put marriage brokers to work, but without success. One day he saw a photograph of the teen-age Princess Alexandra of Greece and sent his ambassador to the girl's mother, Princess Aspasia, with a proposal of marriage. It was done in some style. "My King," said the ambassador, "has heard that the lovely Princess has a passion for oranges. He begs me to inform you that now, at this moment, crates of the world's finest oranges are being shipped especially for her." It so happened that Alexandra was too young to marry and did not like oranges anyway, so the feeler came to nothing.

Then, in Milan, Zog was introduced to Geraldine, the young Countess Apponyi, "the white rose of Hungary," as one dazzled journalist called her. It is easy to see how attractive Zog looked to the cultured young American-Hungarian girl. He was lean and barbarically handsome with his red hair and pointed moustache. The very image of a warrior-King, he had about him the exciting smell of danger. They were married.

Geraldine, however, was not destined to get to know her new country well. An Italian vise was closing in on Albania. Italians controlled the whole economic life of the country. Some years earlier, in 1934, Zog had tried to struggle free of the Italians and had ordered his Italian advisers out of the country. Mussolini felt that a hint should be dropped and ordered the Italian fleet into Durazzo harbour. Zog crumpled. He knew a bell tolling when he heard one, and he made his plans. When the Italian army landed on April 7, 1939, Zog was ready for them. Geraldine had given birth to a son, Leka, two days before. She and her baby were hurried from their bed and packed, with Zog's five sisters and ten coffers of gold guarded by twelve faithful liegemen of Zog's old tribe, out of the country.

While the Italians were proclaiming Victor Emmanuel King of Albania, Zog was making a wide detour. Fearing the presence of the Italian fleet in the Mediterranean he travelled the long way through Rumania, Poland, Sweden and Norway, to France. The war found Zog brooding and bored in a forty-room mansion in Buckinghamshire, England, finding diversion by suing newspapers for libel. An appeal by eight members of the Albanian community in England (in fact they constituted the entire Albanian community in England) asked "on behalf of the country" that Zog give up the State treasury to help finance the partisans in the Albanian mountains. Zog sighed with sympathy. "All I saved from my fortune," he said sadly "was £30,000."

After the war, at the invitation of King Farouk, he went to live in Egypt, accompanied by 2,000 pieces of baggage. Calling on his next-door neighbour in Alexandria, "Count Pollenzo" he found—to their mutual horror—that the "Count" was actually his former conqueror and the usurper of the crown that Zog himself had usurped, ex-King Victor Emmanuel who shortly afterwards expired.

To-day Zog lives in the South of France in poor health, with his wife, sisters and dreams. He has a serious cardiac condition which has more or less removed him from the Riviera colony of Kings. He keeps talking about coming to the United States but does nothing about it. All he does is wishfully think, and this he does on his customary extravagant level of philosophy. "I believe," he says "that Communism is on the retreat, and Albania can lead the way." It is unfortunately by the Zogs and Peters of the world that newspaper readers measure monarchy in exile.

Middle European monarchy has a habit of caging within itself furies which fester generation after generation and finally burst, not on the assassin-kings, the royal "foxes," or the remakers of frontiers, but on the most hapless of their descendants. Charles of Austria, Michael of Rumania, Peter of Yugoslavia, were all smashed by disasters created for them by their elders. No story is sadder than the story of the baby Simeon, a pawn of Balkan politics, so ill-treated by fate that exile proved itself a mercy.

Simeon's paternal grandfather was the Tsar Ferdinand of

Bulgaria, who brought his country on to Germany's side during the first World War, abdicated in 1918 and lived in Germany beyond his time to 1948, by which time he was eighty-seven, and had seen his two sons die horribly and his grandson kicked off the throne. Simeon's maternal grandfather was the shrewd, sly, King Victor Emmanuel of Italy.

Everything happened to Simeon before he was nine, and nothing after. When he was twelve days old, his father, King Boris, showed him to his troops and made him a soldier in the Bulgarian army. In 1943, when Simeon was six, Boris followed the disastrous example of his father and declared war on the United States and Britain. In the same year Boris paid a call on Hitler, and shortly afterwards sickened and died. Nobody to-day can do more than guess at the solution to this mystery. A story circulated that Hitler had had him poisoned as a result of his refusal to declare war on the Russians. Boris himself seemed to suspect some such thing for as soon as he started to feel the pains he screamed, "I've been poisoned." In any event, Simeon was the new Tsar of the Bulgars, the country being officially directed by a Regency, headed by Boris's younger brother, Prince Cyril. Actually the country was held tightly in the grip of Germany and incapable of independent action.

By this time, Italy had quit the war and Bulgaria's Italian Queen Giovanna and half-Italian King were in considerable danger from the malevolent Hitler. Sure enough, Simeon had not been King more than a few days when a polite but ominous suggestion came from Hitler that he be made Simeon's guardian. With great courage Giovanna managed to smuggle the boy through Turkey into Syria for the rest of the war.

They returned to Sofia after the retreat of the Germans, but now the Communists were in power, an event which usually, once it happens, tends to perpetuate itself. A referendum was rigged, revealing that the Bulgars "overwhelmingly" rejected the monarchy, and Simeon was ordered to leave. He was lucky. Bulgaria is not only the most pro-Russian but also the most violent country in the Balkans, a country where the normal means of changing government is by assassination and execution. In true Bulgarian spirit the Communists shot all three Regents, including Prince Cyril, then sentenced and executed eight personal advisers to King Boris, two former Prime Ministers, twenty-two former cabinet ministers and sixty-eight former deputies.

Uncomprehending of this holocaust, little Simeon packed his toys and chattered about seeing his cousins and his grandfather in Egypt. Anxious to get the Royal Family out of the country and get on with the slaughter, the Bulgarian government promised compensation to the amount of $20,-000,000 for the loss of property, an obviously absurd sum, for the Bulgarian Royal Family at the best of times was about the poorest in Europe.

On September 16, 1946, they left with a loyal retinue of ten courtiers. Needless to say, they received not a penny from Bulgaria. Giovanna was reduced to applying to the International Refugee Organisation for relief as a displaced person. Year after year they stayed in Egypt in poverty, Simeon growing into a shy but normal boy. At one point his fancy took him to pour glasses of water from his hotel balcony on the heads of passers-by. He lost interest in this pastime after a French journalist took him by the scruff of the neck and chastised him.

Meanwhile Queen Giovanna sought a home. She asked the Italian government for asylum but her native country turned her down. The most they were prepared to do was grant Simeon a tourist visa. In 1950 the Bulgarian Government decided to regret not having shot Simeon too, and a plot for his assassination was uncovered by the Egyptian authorities, suggesting that the young King still retained sufficient loyalty in Bulgaria to worry the Communists.

In 1951 General Franco invited them to come to Spain and live. Franco had been taking pity on the plight of dispossessed monarchs, and his gesture was a turning point in the fortunes of the Bulgarian Royal Family. Giovanna, Simeon and their six retainers—four had disappeared en route—arrived in Madrid and were given a house, two cars, five Spanish servants, diplomatic status and full royal privileges. Subsequently, the large fortune left by Victor Emmanuel was freed and shared out, Giovanna receiving one seventh.

So Simeon, unlike poor Peter, has had his financial problems solved for him. Simeon is good-looking in the virile Balkan way, with the terseness that tends to come of the mingling of German and Italian blood. He dances well, shoots well and is a favourite of the Swedish Royal Family which includes four high-spirited princesses. For Simeon, the future looks tranquil enough, except for one thing, the royal burden that cannot be shaken off, the cross that he must bear for the rest of his life.

In June, 1955, the worn-out royal record went on to the gramophone and sounded through the horn. Simeon was then eighteen years old and, royally speaking, of age. A *Te Deum* was celebrated in Madrid, and a declaration, translated into uncertain English, circulated to the press. It stated that the Bulgarian constitution had never been legally abrogated and that it was "still in force to-day, as it expresses the unshaken will of the Bulgarian people towards the rights which they hold sacred. I am still invested," Simeon concluded "with the mission assigned me by Providence."

So unshaken, in fact, is the Bulgarian will that up to the time of writing it is the only Iron Curtain country, apart from

Albania, which has not made even the slightest show of resistance to the Communist regime. In most of the free countries the various Bulgarian National Committees in exile are anti-monarchist, but Bulgarian monarchist factions exist here and there. In the candle-lit Russian church in Buckingham Palace Road, London, an Orthodox bishop read Simeon's royal manifesto to assembled London Bulgars. For this solemn occasion the bishop wore a golden crown and purple robes. He offered prayers for the welfare of "His Majesty." Bulgarian monarchists had turned up in force for the ceremony. They numbered just thirty.

Not long ago Queen Giovanna told a journalist, "When a child has to leave his country, even if he is only one year of age, he will always remember it." The misfortune of Simeon is that this is just not so. The golden rain of the American women's magazines can never be for him. The young King has lived a fantastic life but it all happened before even the most plausible of ghost-writers could remember it for him.

# XIII

# *The Student Princes*

## A Blueprint for a New Monarchy

"It is our job to make this monarchy business work."
—Prince Philip of England.

*W*hat gift of God or nation do men like Philip of England, Bernhard, King Frederick of Denmark and Paul of Greece possess that the Zogs and Peters do not? Why do the Saxe-Coburg-Gothas and the Schleswig-Holstein-Sonderburg-Glucksburgs thrive while the Hohenzollerns and Savoys die? That is the great imponderable of monarchy. Why does it survive where it survives, and why has it succumbed so feebly where it seemed to be at its strongest? And, most important of all, what can an aspiring monarch do about it?

If the monarch is intelligent he will face the facts of his position squarely. This is harder than it sounds, because it is so easily avoided, and, if faced, can make some depressing reading. First of all, every monarch seeking power must deal with a country divided for him or against him, the issue at best being on a low priority level. On the basis of twentieth century experience it can be seen that few princes in an emergency can call on the aristocratic houses for any support other than moral or covertly financial. The fortunes of the old families are too precarious themselves for them to risk their lot with a prince who will probably sink anyway. If his is a Catholic country the prince is likely to have the support of the Church, but the record fails to show a single prince who has been successfully shored up by Rome. In a showdown the bourgeoisie will pray for him and should he succeed, will hang his portrait in their homes. But in the end all he will be able to bank on will be a few right-wing hooligans like the old *lazzaroni* of Naples or the *camelots du roi* of France, plus a handful of lack-lustre mercenaries commanded by renegade or Fascist officers.

The moral of this is never to make an issue of one's own position. Avoid any trial of strength. If a trial becomes inevitable, avoid it all the more assiduously. Leopold, for example, faced the issue squarely and honestly and put it to his people, who voted him back on to the throne which he proceeded to occupy effectively for all of forty-eight hours.

The honest prince does not let himself be fooled by the cheers of the multitude, although it is a seductive temptation. King George V of England, a most hard-headed sovereign, after he had been cheered vociferously in Dublin, never lost the sneaking suspicion that the Irish trouble was an artificial creation of the politicians. Oliver Cromwell said to Thomas Fairfax as they acknowledged the cheers of the people, "They'd turn out with the same enthusiasm to see us hanged."

The prince in exile does not daydream over the opiate of "reports" from his native land. The reports always come from royalists and speak of discontent, anarchy, imminent revolution and a pining for return to the monarchy. Republicans tend not to bother to give reports to ex-kings.

Face to face with such a catalogue of handicaps, it is difficult for a prince to know which way to turn. But this perplexity in itself has been turned to advantage. The prince no longer asks himself so much what he can do. Instead he asks himself what sort of person he ought to be. The desire to return is strong and with it a determination, commendable in itself, to be worthy of the task should the opportunity come. The result has been the emergence of a cult which I shall call— though I have never heard anyone else call it that—the cult of the super-Prince. It does not necessarily involve any plot or conspiracy. It does not need to. It comes to the young prince as automatically as patriotism. It is a cult towards an ideal royal personality, influencing by example, seeking no power but suggesting, nevertheless, that should power fall into its hands it could fall into none better.

The super-Prince is part soldier, part politician, something of a lover, all statesman, all man. The concept is not a new one. The Kaiser Wilhelm imagined himself consciously in the role of super-Prince, but fundamentally, in its modern form, it dates from after World War I and the ruin of the German nobility.

The cult is a German one and basically not only un-English but quite alien to English thinking. It has followed German princelings wherever royal fortune has taken them: to Greece, to Holland and to Great Britain. The first important experiment in the super-Prince ended in fiasco when Edward VIII decided that a love affair was more important than his Empire. All the emotional devotion, not only in the British Empire, but throughout the world, was concentrated on the Prince of Wales.

The Prince of Wales was not unaware of his role. His pride in his German blood, the pleasure he took in speaking German obviously stemmed from a feeling, perhaps inarticulate, that he was more than just a prince in Britain, but rather the repository and symbol of Anglo-German royalty. George V, if he ever thought of such heady stuff, would have had none of it. His well-known remark during World War I remains the most endearing definition of British monarchy in this century. When H. G. Wells attacked Britain's "uninspiring and alien court," the King replied furiously, "I may be uninspiring but I'll be damned if I'm an alien."

King George VI was as English as his brother was Germanic, and kept himself so. This was resented by European monarchists. Europe, acknowledging as it does the supremacy of the English Throne, distrusts a too-English court. It is significant that King George VI, so deeply loved by his people and so highly esteemed in the United States, was dismissed as a nobody in Europe where the true political heart of monarchy beats. Similarly today. When influential right-wing monarchists on the Continent of Europe think of the British monarchy they think of Philip. The Queen is too insular, too uncompromisingly English for their taste or their comfort. Philip they think, rightly or wrongly, is one of them.

The super-Prince is a state of mind. We have seen in earlier chapters that monarchy may not be so far from a return to power in some countries as one generally assumes. Should a change, either gradual or apocalyptic, in the structure and fortunes of the world, throw monarchy back into the European saddle, the prince must, morally, temperamentally and physically, be equipped to fulfil his destiny. He has the job of convincing his people that monarchy is the best form of constitution possible for them, and the requirements of his tutors are specific.

He should be physically strong and of a determined character. He should, if possible, be handsome, but centuries of breeding have usually made princes goodlooking. He should be brave and have participated ably in whatever war he may have fought. He should be either English, Danish or German or ideally a combination of the three. He must be democratic and sociable. There must be no locking of oneself in the ceremonial. Guided tours of factories are all very well, but the prince should know how things work and if they don't, be capable of grabbing a spanner and making them work himself. The giant King Paul of Greece does this sort of thing admirably. At a reconstruction project Paul seized a shovel and drew the cheers of admiring labourers by the vigour and skill with which he made the dirt fly.

The super-Prince takes food, tobacco and alcohol as they come, without becoming a victim of any of them. In love and sex he must be virile but discreet, and women must not become too important a factor in his life. Nor should he lean too closely to mysticism or the gentle arts. This would be regarded askance by his tutors. His passions must be for speed and sport, with not too much emphasis on golf. It is better if, at some formative period of his life, he has gone without money or worked seriously at a job.

He must be patriotic. This last is the greatest revolution in royal thinking which the available monarch must adjust himself to. The royal tradition always insisted that a King was a member of the international nobility, and a prince had to be ready to serve any nation which offered him a throne. Queen Victoria asked, when it was proposed that her grandsons Prince Albert Victor and Prince George should join the Royal Navy, "Will a nautical education not engender and encourage national prejudices and make them think that their own Country is superior to any other?" And she added, "A Prince, especially one who is some day to be its Ruler, should not be imbued with the prejudices and peculiarities of his own Country . . . Our greatest King, William III, and next to him . . . the Prince Consort, were *both* foreigners and this gave them a freedom from all national prejudices which is very important in Princes."

That fine old Bavarian nobleman, Count Albrecht Montgelas, declared that "the true royal tradition died on that day in 1917 when, for a mere war, King George V changed his name from Saxe-Coburg and Gotha to Windsor." It may be deplored but it is a fact that the cosmopolitanism of princes is dead: Kings fill other roles today. The jetsam of former noble houses lies on international society and the international set like a shoal of stranded jellyfish. The nearest they come to being recognisable as part of any state is in their tendency to possess American passports. Such a *déraciné* approach to life would be disastrous for any prince who still hopes for a throne.

It is easy to see how this general description fits not one but several princes of Europe: Prince Philip of England, Bernhard of the Netherlands, Paul of Greece to a lesser extent, and Englishmen like Lord Mountbatten, or Germans like Prince Ernst or even Prince Christian of Hanover.

Prince Bernhard grew up a poor princeling from the lesser German house of Lippe. As a young man he worked for I. G. Farben, the big German chemical combine, until he met and married Princess Juliana of the Netherlands. Once in a position of responsibility, he devoted himself to his work, mastering the quaint Dutch language, studying Dutch industrial and imperial problems. He became a zealously and passionately loyal Dutchman and a symbol of Dutch resistance to the Germans in World War II.

His escape is speed and danger. In the German invasion of 1940 he personally shot down a Dutch Nazi sniper. In 1945 he was reported drowned while taking underwater pictures near Curacao. His diving gear broke and trapped him and he barely made his way to the surface. In 1950 his doctors gave him only a few more years to live, as the result of complications from an earlier accident, a prognosis which happily proved pessimistic, although for a long time he carried the forecast around with him without telling his family. While the apparent sentence of death was still on him, he flew an F-86 jet bomber through the sound barrier. More recently he overturned his car at ninety miles an hour. Juliana, frankly alarmed by her husband's exploits, once gave him a photograph of herself and their four daughters, on which she had written: "Think of us too."

The Dutch are chronically allergic to the Germans and Bernhard has leaned so far over backwards to renounce his German past that he has almost become an Englishman. He comes to England as often as possible, dresses like an Englishman in a bowler hat and rolled-up umbrella, or else in the ubiquitous English week-end blazer and scuffed suede shoes. He talks like an Englishman, without necessarily thinking like an Englishman, or giving the impression of being an Englishman. There is about him something cold and authoritative that the Englishman with his more deprecating self-assurance does not possess. Bernhard has done a praiseworthy job under immense pressure both from within himself and outside, and only once, during the incident with his wife and the faith-healer in 1956, did he let indiscretion or weakness prejudice his hard-won position.

Philip was born in Greece, a German princeling, but grew up English under the protection of his grandmother, the Marchioness of Milford Haven, and his uncle, Lord Louis Mountbatten. He had a hard, loveless and almost penniless youth, his education carrying him aimlessly to England, France, Germany and Scotland. He became a professional sailor, saw the world and had a good war. After his marriage he filled out quickly from an awkward, unsure youth into a stern and dominating figure in English affairs. He has the same Germanic toughness that his friend Bernhard has but it is lightened by an English sense of humour that can always be appealed to. He works himself hard, to the point of irritation and breakdown, the loyalty he demands from his staff being exceeded only by the fanatical loyalty he gives in turn.

Nothing, perhaps, in the life of Prince Philip does him more credit than his absolute refusal to turn his back on his friend, Commander Michael Parker, when divorce threatened to end the career of that most loyal and cheerful of servants.

Philip's sport is polo, his drink beer, his car a fast Lagonda. While rightly jealous of his position and privileges he has never let them blind him to the responsibility of sharing his destiny with his fellow-Britons.

Lord Mountbatten has, by his birth, been limited in his opportunities to grow up with the masses, but he has compensated for this in several characteristic ways. As a sailor he mastered the complicated and unfashionable craft of wireless telegraphy and many sailors say to this day that Mountbatten is the best "sparks" in the Royal Navy. He had a long spell when he was reputed to be a Socialist, but he got over it. He has now reached his lifelong ambition of achieving his father's position as First Sea Lord.

The pattern of life followed by these men suggests strongly a unity of philosophy in those responsible for their education. That, of course, does not prove a cult. For evidence of the cult one must look elsewhere to several apparently unconnected events and incidents.

In 1956 the British courts unexpectedly upheld an old and half-forgotten statute which provides in effect that nearly every Protestant King, Queen, prince and princess in Europe is automatically entitled to British nationality.

The statute stems from 1705, when it was important to secure the Protestant succession on the death of Queen Anne, then forty years of age and with all her numerous children dead. Parliament ruled that if Anne died without issue the throne would go to her cousin, the Dowager Electress Sophia of Hanover. Just in case the Catholics should intervene with some new Papish plot, Parliament forthwith, and in haste, made the Electress a British citizen. It also stipulated that all the heirs of her body should be British citizens providing they were not Catholics. The principle was that those benefiting from the position of the Electress should be given the opportunity to come to England, settle down and learn to understand the ways of the country. Sophia only just missed being Queen herself. She died two months before the dropsical Anne, and her son became George I of England. The statute, having successfully served its purpose, was forgotten for the next 250 years.

By upholding the statute the courts granted British citizenship to nearly five hundred members of European royalty. The man who disinterred the statute, and the first to claim the blue passport of British respectability, was Prince Ernst of Hanover, brother of Queen Frederika, an interesting figure who would have been King of England today had the crown been entailed on the heirs male of Sophia instead of the heirs general. Ernst is a relative and an intimate friend of Philip's and Elizabeth's, and stays at Windsor on his frequent visits to England.

Ernst's move had unexpected repercussions. Some of the prouder German nobles were furious. Louis Ferdinand in particular, was horrified to the depths of his Prussian soul. "I am a German and I shall always be a German," he said. "I am also a European. One thing I am not is an Englishman." But other princes, especially those from Eastern Germany, quickly realised that this was a bandwagon sent them from heaven to climb. Shortly after the second World War the British and Polish Governments had set up a fund totalling

£5,465,000 to compensate British subjects for losses in Poland, including those areas of Eastern Germany annexed by Poland in 1945.

Eastern German nobles immediately used their British passports to press their claims. Prince Friedrich of Prussia, Louis Ferdinand's younger brother, put in a claim for half a million pounds' compensation for lost estates. This was legitimate enough. Friedrich was married to Lady Brigid Guinness, lived in England and was a British citizen from before the war. But Princess Magdalene, Louis Ferdinand's sister-in-law, claimed thousands for her Priskenau estates. The Saxe-Weimar-Eisenachs and the Saxe-Meiningens claimed more than half a million for estates around Breslau, and up to the time of writing still others are getting into the line for their British passports. It was a moving demonstration of the German princes' loyalty to the British crown.

Ernst's next act was even more interesting. Quietly and unobtrusively, he tried through his legal representation in England to have restored his family title of Duke of Cumberland which was suspended in 1917 during the first World War. Ernst's legal argument was intriguing. British titles were suspended from the Duke of Cumberland, the Duke of Brunswick and Viscount Taaffe (Baron of Ballymote) during the Great War as a punishment for adhering to the enemies of King George V. The fact that there might one day be a second war in which the German princes might adhere to the enemies of George V's descendants was not contemplated at the time. Ernst pointed out that he was a child in the first war, and what he did in the second was not legally relevant.

Ernst did his best to keep his petition secret but it came out and the British press was nasty about it. Ernst was advised to drop it for the time being and try again later.

Despite this setback, the British Court decision really meant that the private war that had been going on between the British and German nobility without pause since 1914 was at last at an end. There was to be a gradual moving together of the old family relations, fostered on one side by Ernst of Hanover and on the other by Philip of England. The German nobles have become Anglo-German nobles, as, until 1914, most of them considered themselves anyway. In practice it meant that Princess Alexandra of England, say, could probably, if she so desired, marry a European prince, which, a few years ago, would have been unthinkable to British public opinion.

None of this, apparently had anything to do with an unusual controversy which briefly stirred England in the summer of 1957. Donald Edgar of the London *Daily Express,* one of the most sensitive journalists in Britain, was on his way back from Germany where he had covered the wedding of Prince Philip's niece, Princess Margarita of Baden, and he stopped off at Salem, the school founded by Kurt Hahn, where Philip received an important part of his education. It did not occur to Edgar that there was any link between this institution and the recall of the old statute of 1705. Nevertheless, after looking over the school and the pupils Edgar was possessed of an eerie feeling. "At the end of the tour," he wrote, "I came to the conclusion that there is something crazy about Salem, although it is difficult to say why."

Kurt Hahn, in the first war, was secretary to Prince Max of Baden, the Kaiser's last Chancellor. After the Armistice, Hahn and the Prince surveyed the wreck of the German ruling classes side by side and in dismay. Hahn propounded an idea that he had been nurturing for some time. He sought to found a system of education, based on the philosophy of Plato, for the training of future leaders. Plato, in a not altogether dissimilar period during the decline of Ancient Greece, dreamed of a system for the education of leaders, leaving nothing to chance, creating so far as possible the ideal man, the "Guardian," possessed of a "philosophic disposition, high spirits, speed and strength."

So impressed was Prince Max that he gave him part of his family estate to use as a school. This was at Salem, in a Cistercian abbey which had been taken over by the Margraves of Baden, in rich green country near Lake Constance. One of Hahn's pupils was young Prince Philip of Greece. When Hahn ran into trouble with the Nazis he moved to Britain. So did Philip. What Hahn was looking for in Britain was a place, remote and hard, for the rigorous Spartan training in which he believed. He founded his school at Gordonstoun in the bleak north of Scotland. Today the Hahn system has spread around the world. A branch school was founded in 1949 at Anavryta, near Athens, by Queen Frederika, and Elizabeth and Philip visited it in the following year. Prince Constantine of Greece, heir to the throne, went there. Constantine's official title, by the way, is the Duke of Sparta. There are branches in Khartoum and in East Africa. It is linked to a system called Outward Bound Schools where carefully selected young men and girls are sent on short character-building courses.

The present author also visited Salem and while he disagreed with many of Edgar's views, he gained the impression that here, certainly, was a concept for a new type of boy—and girl—and this new breed is already recognizable in the modern prince. It is easy to see why Hitler closed the school down. Marks are given for such things as civic-mindedness, sense of justice, living habits, the ability to recall and record facts precisely, the ability to form a judgment of one's own and defend it in the face of opposition.

UNITED PRESS INTERNATIONAL

King Olav V of Norway (left) and his son, Crown Prince Harald.

WIDE WORLD PHOTOS

King Frederik and Queen Ingrid of Denmark while in England.

WIDE WORLD PHOTOS

Above, Queen Juliana of the Netherlands returns from the formal opening of the Dutch Parliament. With her is Prince Bernhard and their two youngest daughters, the Princesses Margriet and Marijke.

Right, Greete Hofmans, the Dutch faith healer involved in a rift between Holland's Queen Juliana and her husband, Prince Bernhard, which led to rumors in 1956 of the Queen's abdication.

UNITED PRESS INTERNATIONAL

Britain's Prince Charles on his ninth birthday.

Princess Margaret of England

Queen Elizabeth II and Prince Philip of England, in the Music Room at Buckingham Palace.

Monaco's royal family. Left to right are Princess Caroline, Prince Ranier, Princess Grace and on her lap, crown Prince Albert Alexander Louis Pierre.

Everything at Salem is based on *ehrlichkeit*, the honour system. Salem children do not cheat. No teacher sits in class during examinations. Punishments consist of long walks into the village or extra coal carrying, again without supervision.

The course at the schools is severe and every minute of the boys' and girls' working time is supervised. Someone asked Hahn the reason for the presence of forty or so girls in a school of about 170 boys. Hahn laughed and said, "Boys like to have girls around." In an account of the Hahn system however, it says that "the Spartans attached a great importance to the education of their future wives and the mothers of their children and we should do the same." In other words, Spartan girls for Spartan boys.

The school system is Platonist. The head of the school is the "Guardian," the guardians being the ruling caste in Plato's republic. He is assisted by twelve "helpers." Under them come the "colour bearers" who wear a stripe on their pullovers.

The attention paid to cultural pursuits is somewhat perfunctory. Plato—perhaps rightly—banished the poets from his republic. An American woman writer visiting Anavryta in Greece gave her impression of the school in *McCall's* Magazine. It is worth quoting, as a woman's point of view stripped of significances. "The Hahn system differs from American progressive schools . . . in that progressive schools consider the child as the centre of the universe with the family, school, community revolving round him. But in the Hahn system . . . the child is prepared to face life as it is. The school's purpose is to give boys from all walks of life an opportunity of training as a means of developing their own capacity to face hazards, difficulties, hardships and emergencies of all kinds."

The Hahn system scarcely bothers to deny that its aim is to produce leaders. Neither, for that matter, do Eton or Harrow. But Eton, as Edgar says, is an organic English growth developing over the course of centuries, not a conscious international training system for a brotherhood of leaders. No such idea could survive in the United States except by concealing its basic purpose.

It is stretching impressions a long way, however, to find anything sinister about Salem. Most people, including the present writer, would find it an admirable place to send children. The interest in Salem from the royal point of view is in a study of the names involved, and how they are interlocked by family and by family activity. The head-master at Salem is Prince Georg Wilhelm of Hanover, a shy, unaggressive man, who believes deeply in the school. His sister is Queen Frederika of Greece, founder of Anavryta. Georg's brother is Prince Ernst who inspired the recall of the 1705 statute, the man who would like to have his title of Duke of Cumberland restored to him. Ernst himself went to Salem. The owner of Salem is Berthold, Margraf of Baden, who is married to Theodora, sister of Prince Philip. Georg Wilhelm's wife is Princess Sophie, another sister of Prince Philip. It is an open secret that Philip would like Prince Charles to go to Gordonstoun. The advisers at the British Court have been under attack for a long time for the way in which they have allegedly hemmed in Queen Elizabeth with old-fashioned and moribund protocol. A prince needs sound advisers, from stock that comes of the land and the people, and not from an effete aristocracy. That surely is the value to the young prince of his fellow-students in the Salem system. Jimmy Orr, Philip's secretary, is a product of Gordonstoun, and so is Anthony Craxton, who produces Philip on television.

What all this means is that the most virile elements of the European royal families are combining to prepare for the future, whatever it may bring. There is nothing wrong with the idea so long as the Salem system does not, by its very virtues, overreach itself and impose an elite class in the courts of Europe. It would be an extraordinary achievement in itself if it could one day boast that two of the reigning monarchs of Europe, Charles III of Britain, and Constantine II of Greece, were products of the system. As it stands, it is responsible directly and indirectly for a newer, tougher type of prince who is infinitely more to be respected than the silly-ass prince of the twenties or the drone prince of present New York international society. Royal oddities will remain with us, as the next chapter shows but a type of prince has emerged and is emerging who means something positive and worth while to people who would not otherwise think twice about monarchy.

# XIV

# *Royal Round Up*

## The Ever-Hopefuls

"Take care not to be led astray . . . I am afraid you are living in that deceptive and intoxicating atmosphere which royalty tends to take with it into exile."
　　　　—Alexandre Dumas, Sr., to Queen Hortense, daughter of the Empress Josephine

*O*ut of the Iberian glare and off the mosaic pavements which burn through leather to the soles of the feet, one steps into a dark cave where shoe-shine boys sit side by side on a dirty floor among discarded shoes and empty tins of polish. At the far end there is a flight of worn wooden stairs pointing up into the darkness and flanked by walls of imitation tenement marble whorled in pencilled observations that somehow sound worse in Portuguese.

Two flights up, one presses a bell and two doors are opened at the same time, one by a housekeeper dressed in black who gesticulates and whispers in Portuguese, the other by a suspicious doorman who looks on in silence. Take either door and they lead to the same place, an unexpectedly elegant committee room decorated with oil paintings of Dom Carlos who was assassinated in 1908, and of Dom Duarte Nuno, the present Pretender, for whom Portuguese monarchists predict a much more glorious fate.

This is the headquarters of the *Causa Monarchica* of Portugal on Lisbon's Praça de Louis Camoes. Despite outward appearances it can be said that of all Pretenders to European thrones, Dom Duarte has the best chance of all. What has created the excitement is a speech which Dr. Oliveira Salazar, the dictator of Portugal, made on July 4, 1957. Couched, like all Salazar's pronunciations, in terms of circumlocutory scholarship, and without concessions to easy listening, Salazar gave notice that he was contemplating the idea of following his own long reign over Portugal with the restoration of the monarchy.

Salazar said, "The Government has done everything possible for the House of Braganza. . . to be placed on the high level of dignity which is meet for the direct descendants of the Kings of Portugal. It has acted in this way for two reasons: the justice owed to those who led the nation through eight centuries of history and the prudent view that there may come a time when the monarchical solution may become a national solution . . .Whether the House of Braganza is considered merely as the repository of a historical heritage or whether the possibility of future services to its and our homeland is borne in mind, it should be distant from a political leadership which might divide instead of unite the Portuguese people."

Clipped suddenly in the beam of good fortune Dom Duarte Nuno, living comfortably in exile until a few years ago, has been taken by surprise and considerably at a disadvantage. He is a small, courtly, pleasant man with receding sandy hair, blue eyes and a flat pink face. He was born at Seebenstein in Austria in September, 1907, and scarcely saw Portugal until he reached middle age. He speaks Portuguese with a strong Austrian accent, and, what is rare in the head of a royal House, he is a poor linguist, picking his way uncertainly through both French and English. To monarchists legitimacy of descent is more important than the man himself, but to Salazar, neither a monarchist nor a republican, the man is more important than the institution. Here trouble may lie.

Excellent a person though Dom Duarte is, the question

is, can the Portuguese, so long under Salazar's domination, turn to such a gentle figure for leadership when Salazar retires from the scene? Trying to guess what Salazar is thinking about is practically all that remains of politics in Portugal. Salazar may decide that Dom Duarte is an insufficiently vivid personality to resume the throne of the Braganzas. He probably wishes nostalgically that Dom Duarte had more of the splendid presence of Don Juan of Spain, or the easy-going charm of Umberto or the dash of the Count of Paris. Almost certainly Salazar is watching with care the progress made by Dom Duarte's three sons, Dom Duarte João,* the Prince of Beira, born in 1945, and the princes, Dom Miguel, born in 1946, and Dom Henrique, born in 1949. He will not act independently of Spain. Portugal and Spain are similar dictator-states except that Franco, the general, runs Spain as though it were an army and Salazar, the professor of economics, runs Portugal as though it were a boarding school. Most experts feel that if Salazar does restore the monarchy he will do it simultaneously with the resumption of the monarchy in Spain.

In any case Salazar is not letting Portuguese monarchists get too big for themselves. When they gave a party some time ago "in the name of His Royal Highness," Salazar quickly stopped it. He did not intend to have such grandiose declarations made in *his* Portugal. Dom Duarte avoids Lisbon and lives in the traditionally anti-Salazar stronghold of Oporto. His supporters are not politicians but aristocrats, and foolish aristocrats at that. Dom Duarte is no politician either, and is to a great extent at the mercy of his supporters. No man incapable of independent action is to be envied and a pawn in the hands of fools has his fate in a double hazard.

Nonetheless the soil is more fertile for monarchy in Portugal than in any other Catholic country, largely because the

* Pronounced the same and meaning the same as the French *Jean.*

Church, being less powerful, has also bred less anti-clerical-ism. Only the country's small middle class can be said to be republican; through all the other classes the desire to have a King back on the throne is unexpectedly strong. Queen Elizabeth and Prince Philip visited Portugal in 1957 and were rendered almost speechless by the tumult of their reception. Prince Philip, who must understand the nuances of cheering more acutely than most people, told a Portuguese acquaintance that he had never heard the kind of cheering he had heard in Lisbon. It seemed, he said, in different words, to be a sort of hunger.

Dom Duarte's wife, Princess Maria, is the sister of the Countess of Paris, (both of whom are Brazilians). They and the Brazilians from the other branch of the Orleans-Braganza family are closely interlocked. Brazil had an Emperor until 1889 and a popular one too, but only the very old in Brazil remember him, and few have any nostalgia for the monarchy. Nevertheless the family remains well represented in Brazilian society and provides the closest link between the international cousinship of European royalty and the New World. The Pretender, Dom Pedro, born in France in 1909, lives in Petropolis, near Sao Paulo, Brazil, with his wife, Princess Maria of Bavaria, and eight children. He speaks Portuguese with an ostentatiously French accent. All the Brazilian princes and princesses live in Brazil, but turn for their marriages to European royalty. Dom Pedro and Dom Duarte both find their relative, the Count of Paris, too exhausting for comfort, and relations between the Count and the others are, to put it mildly, curt.

The last attempt to create a new throne occurred as recently as 1941, after the flight of King Peter from Yugoslavia.

Croatia, under Anton Pavelitch, declared itself a monarchy and invited the Duke of Spoleto, brother of the Duke of Aosta and cousin of King Victor Emmanuel, to become King, and even gave him the title of Tomislav I. The Duke of Spoleto, a well-known sportsman before the war, and married to Princess Irene of Greece, sister of the Duchess of Kent, was too wise for that. He ignored the title completely and never went to Croatia. The monarchy was quickly forgotten in the bloodbath which followed when Croats massacred 500,000 Serbs. The Duke of Spoleto lived out his life in peace and died some years after the war.

The stillborn Kingdom of Croatia was the last attempt, so far, of a small ethnic group to turn back history and declare its right, through a monarchy, for recognition. Most of these groups have merged reluctantly into larger units, and from Moldavia to Wales national cultures grow fainter against the din of mass communication. But, while Europe may have run out of principalities and dukedoms, one can say with confidence that it will never run out of Pretenders.

The *Almanach de Gotha* runs to sixteen volumes. The brochure for *l'Annuaire de la Noblesse de France et d'Europe* lists among its contents, "THE SOVEREIGN HOUSES OF EUROPE — The PRINCELY and DUCAL HOUSES OF FRANCE (complete tabulation of living members)—The PRINCELY and DUCAL HOUSES OF EUROPE (listing the 550 living Princes and Dukes who are now the Chiefs of their Families, with the dates of creation of their Titles)—The 198 PRINCELY HOUSES of the RUSSIAN EMPIRE—The NOBLE FAMILIES of EUROPE—The TITLED and NOBLE HOUSES of the Kingdom of BELGIUM (tabulating the complete list of over 700 living Nobles who are the Chiefs of their Families in Belgium, with the date of creation of their nobility and their present address)—The BIRTHS, MARRIAGES AND DEATHS of the NOBILITY—The ORDERS of KNIGHTHOOD and CHIVALRY—The NATIONAL COUNCIL of the ITALIAN NOBILITY—The ANCIENT REPUBLIC OF SAN MARINO, etc., etc."

Most nobles who retain their estates and positions live quietly. The diversion is caused by the various royal bastards, the lunatic pretenders, token princes, casual claimants and snappers-up of unconsidered titles who will advocate their claims before anyone patient enough to listen.

For sheer ambition the record is held by a handsome young Milanese called Vittorio di Martine Valperga Lascaris, Prince of the Canavese. Lascaris collects all the Kingdoms available and quite a few which are not. He traces his royal line back 1,500 years, considers himself the descendant of one hundred emperors and claims the thrones of Turkey, Bulgaria, Jerusalem, Cyprus, Armenia and Britain. Later he added to his empire the thrones of Slovenia, Bosnia, Dalmatia, Toplitsa, Albania and Dardania (the Dardanelles). The closest he has come to recognition is from the Turks, who have barred him from their country.

A rival claimant to the Kingdoms of Byzantium is Prince Antonio de Curtis Griffo-Gagliardi, otherwise known as Toto, the Italian movie clown, and the most popular comic figure on the Italian screen. Toto declares he is the direct descendant of the Emperor Constantine, and he is not kidding. He has spent several thousands of dollars petitioning the Pope and the Government of Italy for recognition of his claim. The camp chair reserved for stars to sit on when they are working on the set is carefully marked, "Prince Antonio de Curtis." So is his stationery, and Toto becomes angry if acquaintances forget to address him as "Your Royal Highness."

The first son of King Carol by Zizi Lambrino lives in Paris. Until 1957, by which time he was thirty-four years old, he was called just Mircea Lambrino. He had fought a long battle in the French courts to have his identity established in the teeth of opposition from Carol himself, who claimed he had never heard of anyone called Lambrino. Mircea finally won by an ingenious device. He grew a moustache in exact imitation of Carol's and the judges agreed that he could be nobody but Carol's son. Royal recognition did not produce any money but it changed Mircea. He now styles himself Carol Prince Hohenzollern, and, like Toto, insists on being addressed with deference due to the majesty of his position.

He has never met his half-brother, ex-King Michael, and Michael is happy to keep it that way. Nor is there any likelihood that Lambrino will succeed where Michael failed, in wringing any of King Carol's fortune out of Mme. Lupescu. This fortune has been the subject of long litigation between Michael and Carol's widow, who lives luxuriously in Portugal and insists that no fortune exists. A considerable mystery surrounds the whole subject. Rumanian authorities have complained to the Portuguese that Carol departed with some priceless El Grecos which belong to the Rumanian cultural heritage and should be returned. As recently as 1953, before Carol's death, one El Greco was seen hanging in his ground-floor sitting room. But it has disappeared and officially nobody knows of the existence of any El Grecos at all. It is possible that Mme. Lupescu has sold them to the Portuguese Government in a deal which all parties must keep secret for the time being, Mme. Lupescu to protect her protestations of poverty and Portugal to avoid suit by the Rumanians.

The scorebook shows that a Catholic throne is secure in inverse proportion to the size of the state, the only Catholic monarchies remaining today being Belgium, Luxembourg, Liechtenstein and Monaco. Even the throne of Prince Rainier and Princess Grace of Monaco is not without its troubles. Until 1958 all the power of the tiny principality was in Rainier's hands, a circumstance which permitted him to draw almost half a million dollars a year in salary, or more than the Presidents either of France or the United States. A general election in January, 1958, in which 931 out of 1,216 electors voted, returned to power the Independent Party, which won eleven out of the eighteen seats, and pledged itself to curtail—"loyally"—Rainier's powers. Exactly a year later Rainier suspended the constitution and dismissed the Councillors. Nobody seemed to care very much.

Meanwhile a lady in Paris has a claim on the Principality. She is the Countess de Caumont la Force, Anne-Marie de Chabrillan.

In 1955 the Countess de Caumont la Force petitioned the French Government to study her case. Her move, unfortunately, was badly timed. The Government was busy with a dynastic crisis of somewhat greater moment, namely, what to do about Morocco which was perplexed by the possession of two Sultans. In the middle of the crisis the President of France, the Prime Minister and the Foreign Secretary were obliged to take time off to consider the Countess's petition, and their reply was lacking in French diplomatic courtesy. "The idea," they said, "of claiming the Prince of Monaco's throne could only occur to a person ignorant of all Monegasque problems."

The Royal Families of Europe have enjoyed themselves conjuring up witticisms concerning Rainier and Grace. The expression *"that wedding,"* with which all members of European royalty refer to the marriage, is originally attributed to Louis Ferdinand of Prussia. With calculated bad manners, most of them ignored invitations to the wedding. In fact the arrival of a beautiful Hollywood actress as the "Serene Highness" of Monaco, has been a success in every way. It obviously had to be that way in spite of the forecasts of the pessimists. A girl of Catholic faith and proper Philadelphia upbringing, even though she happened to be a film star, would clearly respond to a position of responsibility. The only question was which of the two personalities would prove the dominant, the personality of the cosmopolitan prince with a traditional attitude to marriage, women and fidelity, or the personality of an American girl with inborn ideas of equality and the unshakable conviction that wives are more equal than husbands. The result, justifying the worst fears of *Neues Abendland,* has been overwhelming victory for the American way of life.

From a white castle overlooking the Rhine, Prince Franz Josef II, now in his early fifties, runs the Principality of Liechtenstein as a monarchy that could be absolute if he chose to make it so, which he does not. He is a man of artistic taste with the Hapsburgian quality of aristocratic dreaminess which the Germans call *weltfremdheit.* His love of solitude is such that in a country which covers only 61 square miles only a handful of the 14,000 population have ever set eyes on him. To the peasant he is a mysterious figure, referred to respectfully as *"der Prinz,"* never by his name, and around his dining table sits as strange a band of expatriates as any ever collected by the attraction of low taxes. They range from Paul Gallico, the writer, to Count Bendern, the Principality's Diplomatic Counsellor, a former British soldier and Member of Parliament who became a naturalised Leichtensteiner and devotes his time to vegetarianism and the cosseting of lame birds.

Franz Joseph is a typical round-faced Hapsburg in appearance, and the long oblong face that made the Liechtensteins such a distinctive and handsome family, has, for the current generation at any rate, disappeared. Franz Josef has ruled Liechtenstein since 1938 and he is married to the former Countess Georgina (Gina) von Wilczek, whose family estates in Silesia were lost to the Poles in 1945.

The reign of the House of Liechtenstein began in 1719 when the two German provinces of Schellenburg and Vaduz were sold outright to Prince Hans Adam von Liechtenstein. From that day to this it has been a happy land, devoted unselfishly and unsleepingly to the cause of complete opportunism. By the law of the Holy Roman Empire it undertakes to supply eight soldiers to Austria in time of war, and there its international commitments end. Until 1918 it was closely linked with Austria, using Austrian currency and Austrian passports. The Princes attended the Austrian court and served in the Austrian Army. Liechtenstein sent fifty-eight soldiers to help Austria against Italy in 1866, and to the mild surprise of everyone, fifty-nine returned. On the collapse of Austro-Hungary, Liechtenstein sagaciously transferred itself to Switzerland and the Swiss monetary system. It permitted Swiss Protestantism to make inroads into the country's religious thinking, and when Hitler came to power no youth flocked to the swastika more fervently than the youth of Liechtenstein. Only when Hitler declared war and it was seen that good Nazis had to fight as well as shout did enthusiasm cool. Today Liechtenstein offers sanctuary to one thousand individuals and four thousand businesses which seek to escape the cruel persecution of taxation. Liechtenstein citizenship is officially not for sale, but the exchange of, say, $50,000 helps.

So well has the House of Liechtenstein emerged from the storms of European history that the Prince has been able to sustain a stupefying financial loss as a result of Communist expansion and still come up rich. Until 1948 when the Communists took over, Franz Josef was the largest land-owner in Czechoslovakia, with twenty-seven castles and 160,000 hectares of land. Although he has received nothing in compensation, he can still count himself a millionaire many times over, through investments and one of the world's great art collections which his family has been building up for more than a century. For one Leonardi da Vinci alone he has been offered £1,500,000 by an American art dealer. His collection also includes Botticelli, Rubens and van Dyck.

An heir, Prince Hans Adam, born in 1945, ensures the succession to the throne of this secure and amoral little land.

Another land incorrectly listed among the comic-opera countries of Europe is Luxembourg, which, however, is one of the top steel producers of the world and one of the richest countries in Europe. Luxembourg is a constitutional monarchy, ruled since 1919 by the Grand Duchess Charlotte and her consort, Prince Felix of Bourbon Parma, son of the prolific Robert of Bourbon Parma mentioned earlier.

Like George VI of England and King Baudoin of Belgium, Charlotte came to the throne unexpectedly and at a time when monarchy in the land was in a state of crisis. She was the second of six daughters born to a chronically son-less prince, the Grand Duke Wilhelm IV. When he died in 1912, the crown passed to Charlotte's elder sister, Marie-Adelaide, who was then eighteen, and who belongs to the long list of the really tragic princesses of history. A beautiful girl of strong will and with the piety that characterises the Braganzas, from whom she stemmed on her mother's side, she assumed the responsibility of the throne humbly, but without hesitation. In 1914 when she was twenty and the thoughts of a young princess normally turn to love and marriage, the war began, and

Luxembourg, which possessed no army, was invaded. Marie-Adelaide, on hearing the news, drove her motor car to face the German soldiers alone. When she saw the advance skirmishers she swung the car round to bar their path, and ordered them from her country. A chivalrous German officer turned the nose of the car and escorted her back to her palace.

During the four hard years of occupation Marie-Adelaide continued to run her country on German patronage and with a pro-German court. On one occasion she cabled the Kaiser Wilhelm that she was praying "every day" his armies would be successful and "bring back to Germany a heavy harvest of laurel."

These expressions doomed her in the eyes of her anti-German people, and although she stood side by side with General Pershing on the royal balcony when the American Army marched in to liberate the country, her days as a ruler were numbered. She was given no time for the war hysteria to settle or for the *enragés* of her own country, of France or of Belgium to simmer down. While mobs in Luxembourg shouted, "Down with Marie-Adelaide," and liberals discussed the possibilities of a republic united to France, the fate of Marie-Adelaide and Luxembourg was being settled at the Quai d'Orsay.

"Marie-Adelaide must go," the Luxembourg representative in Paris was told. "Charlotte is ineligible because she is engaged to Prince Felix, an Austrian officer. So is Antonia because she is engaged to Rupprecht of Bavaria. How about the third sister, Hilda?"

"She would never accept the throne, and the other two are minors."

"So it looks like a republic."

The Luxembourg delegate spoke for the monarchy. "Charlotte's fiancé is not really Austrian," he said cajolingly. "He is a Bourbon-Parma, a brother of the Empress Zita. Their brother Sixtus was the Allied spokesman when the Emperor Charles and Zita were seeking a separate peace for Austria."

"Oh all right. Charlotte, then."

With this chilly accolade Charlotte was accepted as the successor to Marie-Adelaide. She was tall and dignified, twenty-three years old, without the intense religious passion of her sister. The two sisters stood side by side at the oath-taking at Colmar Berg in January, 1919. Marie-Adelaide's face was impassive, but her younger sister broke down. "Poor Lotte," said Marie-Adelaide, embracing her. "Forgive me for having put such a heavy burden on you." Charlotte brushed away her tears and dismissed her ministers. Marie-Adelaide stood on one side and merely inclined her head slightly to each minister in turn as he withdrew.

Her health and spirit broken, Marie-Adelaide entered the convent of the Carmelites, the most rigorous of all the women's Orders, at Modena, in Italy. Her luxuriant hair was shaved off and she was admitted as a novice. But her state of health was too poor and she was released, drifting submissively to Munich where she entered the University to study medicine, still a girl and indistinguishable, with her books under her arm, from the other students. In 1924 she moved to Schloss Hohenberg in the Bavarian Highlands where her sister, Antonia, had married Crown Prince Rupprecht. There, at the age of thirty, she died.

Nine months after coming to the throne Charlotte married Felix, a ceremony which the French and Belgian governments pointedly ignored. Lightening the coldness, however, was a message of congratulation from King George V of England. Charlotte bowed before the inevitability of constitutional monarchy and allowed her right to the veto of bills to fall into disuse, although she did continue to name the fifteen members of the Council of State which serves as the Upper House of Luxembourg's legislature.

The Grand Duchess's success can be measured by the reaction of the people to the throne when, in the second World War, Luxembourg was overrun yet again by the Germans. The Royal Family escaped to the United States. Defying their occupiers, the Luxembourgers broadcast a naive but moving message which read, "Tell our Sovereign that we remain steadfast; tell her we thank God she is safe and guarding the flame of our independence on a national altar across the seas. Tell her we will not allow her foot to touch the ground when she returns with our liberty and happiness. Say that we will carry her on our shoulders from Rodange to Luxembourg."

The marriage of Charlotte and Felix has produced two sons and four daughters. Court protocol is unexpectedly rigid for such a tiny country and the deferences due to royalty are closely observed. At home in their feudal castle at Fischbach and at the Grand Ducal Palace in Luxembourg the family talk is mostly in German and French, although to keep in practice they sometimes slip into the national patois, *Letzeburgish*, which is a mixture of French, low German and, surprisingly, English.

An heir to the throne, Jean, was born in 1921, and grew up a pleasant-looking young man with a striking resemblance to his first cousin, Otto of Hapsburg (whose mother, the ex-Empress Zita, lives in Luxembourg).

In 1953 he married Princess Josephine-Charlotte, daughter of Leopold III, who, as a result, will one day become the sixth member of her family to occupy a throne. With her background this could well be a source of foreboding rather than enthusiasm, for the catalogue of her family disasters is an oppressive one: her mother killed in a car accident, her father forced to abdicate, her aunt, Queen Marie-José, forced from the throne of Italy, her uncle, Prince Charles, stepping down from the Regency of Belgium to become a bitter recluse, and Baudoin only just emerging from the valley of the shadow of a reign where every step had been beset with controversy. But although Luxembourg is flattened every time Europe fights a war, it is a lucky land. Josephine-Charlotte's accession to the throne one day, as the wife of Prince Jean, may mark the end of the infelicity which has followed the Belgian House for nearly a quarter of a century.

Of the Russian Royal Family, once the terror of the world, almost nothing remains. A few Romanoffs survived the holocaust of the Revolution, and are scattered through Europe and America, all hope and even interest long ago abandoned. To-day they do little more than point up a good Bolshevist moral that the one way to destroy all claims to a throne is to assassinate all the claimaints. Head of the House is the Grand Duke Vladimir Kirillovitch, great-grandson of the Tsar Alexander II and of Queen Victoria. Vladimir, born in 1917 in Finland, is married to a Russian princess, Leonida Georgievna Bagration, and lives in Madrid, a neighbour of Queen Giovanna of Bulgaria and King Simeon, all assisted by Franco who bestows favours on them just in case times change. Vladimir's elder sister, Kira, is married to Prince Louis Ferdinand of Prussia. Vladimir keeps up a front of optimism. His apartment is decorated to look like a piece of old St. Petersburgh, and within its confines he maintains a strict protocol. One might think that the remnants of this dynasty were too insignificant for the Russians to bother with, but Communists never forget or forgive. The sister of Vladimir and Kira, the Grand Duchess Maria Kirillovna, had married, in 1925,

Prince Karl zu Leiningen. Captured while serving in the Wehrmatch, Karl's family association was enough for the Russians, and he "died" in a prisoner-of-war camp a full year after the war ended, in 1946.

# XV

# *The Scandinavians*

## Austerity in Paradise

The King of Naples (Marshal Murat) at the close of Napoleon's Russian campaign: "It is no longer possible to serve a madman. There is no hope of success in his course. In all Europe there is not one Prince who still has faith in his treaties. I am sorry I rejected the proposals of the English. If I had not done that I should still be a great monarch, like the Emperor of Austria or the King of Prussia."

Marshal Davout: "The King of Prussia and the Emperor of Austria are princes by the grace of God, the age, and the acceptance of the people. But you, you are King only by the grace of Napoleon and your French blood. The only way you can keep your title is through Napoleon and by remaining faithful to France. Black ingratitude has made you blind. I swear I will denounce you to the Emperor."

cℳurat was executed in 1815. Of all the Kings and Princes scattered around Europe by Napoleon's triumphs, all but one fell when Napoleon fell. The exception was Marshal Bernadotte, one of the Emperor's more flamboyant, if hardly one of his best, generals. Bernadotte obligingly converted himself from Rome to the Lutheran Church and founded a new dynasty as Charles XIV of Sweden and Norway in 1818. His family is still on the throne of Sweden today, a tribute to the Scandinavian genius for survival.

In fact the past fifty years which have seen the fall of so many crowns and battered at even such powerful thrones as those of Britain and Holland, have witnessed the reverse trend in Scandinavia. Beginning this century of aggressive monarchism with two thrones, Scandinavia today has three, all well entrenched. By their very security they do not come directly within the context of this book, but they are considered briefly in order to determine what influence they exert on the state of monarchy.

Although Denmark suffered enemy occupation in the second World War and the Norwegian King, Haakon VII, was forced into a four-year exile, it is in the remaining monarchy, Sweden, its virginity unsoiled either by war or occupation, that the cracks appear most wide. Longevity, unexpected death and a recurring taste for morganatic marriage have thrown Swedish succession wildly out of kilter, creating problems that affect the whole family.

The cast of characters is a long one. The principal figures who affect the Swedish royal situation today are these:

KING OSCAR II (1829-1907) married Princess Sophie of Nassau.
*son and heir:*
KING GUSTAF V (1858-1950) married Princess Victoria of Baden.
*son and heir:*
KING GUSTAF VI ADOLF (1882-) married firstly, Princess Margaret of Connaught who died in 1920 and secondly, Lady Louise Mountbatten, the present Queen Louise of Sweden.

    *children (all to first wife):*

PRINCE GUSTAF ADOLF (born 1906—killed 1947) leaving widow, Princess Sybilla of Saxe-Coburg and Gotha and five children, Margaretha, Birgitta, Désirée, Anne-Marie and CARL GUSTAF (heir born 1946).

PRINCE SIGVARD (born 1907)

PRINCESS INGRID (born 1910) now Queen Ingrid of Denmark.

PRINCE BERTIL (born 1912)

PRINCE CARL JOHAN (born 1916)

From this simplified family tree it can be seen that Sweden in 1959 was in the curious position that the reigning King was 77 years old and the heir to the throne only thirteen. It would be difficult to say which of the two bore the heavier burden, King Gustaf VI Adolf who came to the throne in 1950 when he was sixty-seven—two years past the official Swedish retiring age—or the boy, Crown Prince Carl Gustaf, the Duke of Jämtland, who at twelve is of an age to see clearly and is sensitive enough to know that he can never expect to lead the normal life of youth and young manhood.

The two events which threw the usually harmonious progress of royal birth and death out of rhythm were firstly, the fantastic good health of King Gustaf V, born in 1858, who was still playing tennis in his eighties and lived until ninety-three, and secondly, the unexpected death in an air crash, in 1947, of his eldest grandson, Crown Prince Gustaf Adolf, when he was forty-one, leaving his German-born wife Sybilla with four mettlesome daughters and an infant son.

The death left the future a shattered glass in the hands of nearly every member of the family. It tore a terrible gap in the succession, and put a new strain not only on the nonagenarian King Gustaf V but also on his elderly son Crown Prince Gustaf Adolf, who could no longer rely for support in his duties on a mature and conscientious prince. The widow, Princess Sybilla, was left stranded, her personal hopes frustrated and dreams in ruins. A Saxe-Coburg-Gotha with all the ambitions of that family, Sybilla saw a throne vanish before her eyes. As the result of her husband's death she can expect nothing more than to make, one day, the uninspiring change from King's daughter-in-law to Queen's mother—not even Queen Mother at that.*

Which of the dead prince's three younger brothers would take on the royal role? The second son, Sigvard? He had, in 1930 staggered the family and lost his inheritance by marry-

---

* A subtle difference in title carrying an infinite difference in status. In order to be a Queen Mother one has first to be a Queen. The fact that she could never be called "Queen Mother" clouded in bitterness the last years of the Princess Victoria of Saxe-Coburg, the mother of Queen Victoria.

ing, in a London registry office, a pretty German of Bohemian habits called Erika Patzek. The marriage had quickly ended in divorce and Sigvard subsequently married a Danish noble-woman, Sonia-Helene Robbert, and had two children. Dynas-tically speaking, however, the damage was done. Bertil, the third son? He was himself contemplating a morganatic union with an Englishwoman. Carl Johan, the fourth and youngest? He had married a Stockholm gossip columnist, Kerstin Wick-mark. All three were involved in morganatic problems. Only one had not yet taken the decisive step.

So, whether he liked it or not the problem of succession was presented to the unmarried Bertil, a good-natured athletic man who was thirty-five years old when his brother died. Should anything happen to the infant Carl Gustaf he would be first in line for the throne of Sweden. Or, should King Gustaf VI Adolf die before the boy was eighteen years old, which is more likely, Bertil would become Regent. With a sense of responsibility and devotion which princes have not always shown in this century, he accepted the duties that had unexpectedly devolved on him. He was certainly no confirmed bachelor and would have liked to follow his heart where it led him, but as the marriage he would have wished was irrecon-cilable with his new position he put it behind him, and on the approach of fifty was still unmarried.

It is not surprising that the atmosphere in the royal palace at Stockholm is sometimes rather tense, or that Princess Margaretha's romance with the Englishman, Robin Douglas-Home should have produced such a violent reaction in the mother, Sybilla, who has been dealt by fate the worst cards of any woman of her position in Europe. She is a woman of rare beauty abruptly cut off from all contact with the events of the world. When her husband was killed she was left the appalling problem of bringing up four daughters and an infant son without a man in the house to help her. The King and Queen could be relied on only for grandparents' assistance which is, like the assistance of grandparents all over the world, over-indulgent and the kind that mothers appreciate least. She was united to the Royal Family neither by blood nor nationality, and she remained the German in the family, regarded without warmth either in the country or at home. She had, in short, a heartbreaking task for which the only conceivable reward would be to see her daughters marry well, particularly Margaretha, the eldest, whom Sybilla hoped would marry King Baudoin of Belgium. The appearance of the well-born, piano-playing Englishman was an understandable blow to the Princess. She had never loved the English, and an English mother-in-law had not changed her opinion of the race. With her various brothers-in-law she had also seen enough of morganatic entanglements not to wish to see it repeated in her own children. But the girls are all young and it seems that Princess Sybilla's troubles are only just beginning. The Swedish people are all on the side of love, and the Swedish family reflects the people's sense of the unconventional.

The humorous and civilised relationship that unites the Court and the people is indicated by an amusing exchange in London, in 1957, between the Marquess of Milford Haven and a Swedish business man.

The Swede asked Milford Haven politely, "Do you know Sweden?"

"Do I know Sweden!" Milford Haven exclaimed. "I am a Mountbatten. My aunt happens to be the Queen of Sweden, that's all."

The Swede was only momentarily silenced by this conversation-stopper, then rallying, he replied, "You must forgive me. It is only that Sweden is so democratic. Everybody there has a title."

When the Swedes accepted Bernadotte they took into the Royal Family new blood of an adventurous sort. Not in itself legitimate, it legitimised itself quickly by marrying successively into the German, British and finally Swedish Royal Families. Queen Victoria (1862-1930), a German, was a granddaughter of a Swedish princess of the ancient Swedish dynasty of Vasa. Still the romantic, *condottiére* strain of the Bernadottes dominated and was allowed full expression. When Prince Eugen told his parents, King Oscar II and Queen Sophia, at the end of the last century, that he wished to become a painter they gave their family approval on condition that he worked and did not play at it. Eugen did so and is considered one of the most distinguished landscape painters Sweden has produced. The present Prince Sigvard is one of the most outstanding designers in Europe. He designs pottery, interiors, and even yachts that figure highly in Sweden's export trade.

The present King Gustaf Adolf is an archaeologist of the first order and the Swedish Government, conscious of the contributions he has made to the subject, willingly allows him all the time he needs to pursue his interests.

The Swedish Royal Family has always kept pace with the people, or at least it did so until Princess Sybilla allowed her dismay over the Douglas-Home affair to get the better of her royal inscrutability. The Royal Family shops and dines in the city of Stockholm without escort. Asked once if he had a bodyguard, King Gustaf Adolf replied, chuckling, "Yes, seven million of them."

School education has been preferred to private education for the royal children and they have all been left free to follow their own particular interests. Princess Margaretha has studied domestic science, Birgitta drives her car every day to the Central Institute of Gymnastics in Stockholm where she both studies and teaches. Désirée, perhaps the loveliest of them all, is an excellent dress designer and designed and sewed the evening gown she wore at a Nobel Prize banquet. The youngest girl, Christina, specialises in plastic and interpretive dancing. Each is being given a chance to study abroad. For the Swedish princesses, as for princesses throughout Europe, the heavenly city is not Paris or Rome but London, where a built-in ready-made, younger-set royal society has been carefully created by the Princesses Margaret and Alexandra. It was through Princess Alexandra that Princess Margaretha met Robin Douglas-Home.

Through the years the Swedish Royal Family has been steadily democratising itself. Gustaf V, when he came to the throne in 1907, abolished the Coronation as an unnecessary decoration and expense. He admitted Social Democrats to the Cabinet for the first time. King Gustaf Adolf included women in the previously all-male preserve of the Honors List. Sweden being a welfare state where taxes are high and a show of egalitarianism obligatory, the Royal Family makes a great display of modesty and economy, but in fact it remains the most royal and the richest of the Scandinavian Houses. Unlike the Norwegians and the Danes, the Swedes still possess a hereditary aristocracy with titles. The royal forms are rigidly preserved within the court. Republican sentiment exists in the country but it is on the same good-humoured level as the rest of the Court-people relationship. One of the republican leaders, asked who he would elect as President if the monarchy were abolished, replied "Why, the King, who else?"

As long as there are republicans there must be a royal political issue, and in this respect Norway is even more favoured than Sweden, for here there are so few republicans that there are no monarchists. When all are black no one calls himself a Negro. The first decade of this century which witnessed savage royal assassinations like that of Dom Carlos of Portugal and his son, and King Alexander and Queen Draga of Serbia, witnessed also, in Norway, one of the most splendid royal incidents of the century, and one which showed what heights of authority and perspicacity a constitutional monarch may attain.

From 1814 to 1905, Norway had been united to Sweden under the Swedish King. Before that she had belonged to Denmark who had lost her by siding with France in the Napoleonic Wars. The political differences which led to the breakaway in 1905 are too long to be discussed here, except that briefly Norway wished to have a foreign policy of her own to protect the fortunes of her expanding merchant fleet. But as it was the King who was the connecting link of the union the conflict developed into a simple issue of royal power.

Norway, fearing the wrath of their more powerful neighbour, first asked Sweden for a Bernadotte prince to become King, but the Swedish hotheads were not appeased and in Gothenburg the Swedish Navy was ordered to get steam up. Oscar, heartbroken though he was, fought with all his energy against war hysteria. As a good King should, he spoke with the voice of moderation. He was determined that Norway would never become a Scandinavian Ireland and that Scandinavian would never fight Scandinavian under orders given in his name. But the situation was tense and Norwegian statesmen frightened.

The teeming royal studs of Britain and Germany were the obvious places to go King-hunting, but even then it was apparent that an Anglo-German fight was brewing and Norwegians wanted no part of it. Also they wanted a prince from closer to home, seeing that Norway was about to have the first King of its own since the death of Olaf V in 1387. They turned to Denmark where the name of an obscure prince, Carl, had been commended to them. Carl was only a vague image in their minds but he seemed acceptable. He was thirty-three, "a good age, not too young and not too old," the second son of Crown Prince Frederik, and married to an English girl, Princess Maud, daughter of Edward VII, and with a two-year-old son. In appearance Carl was impressive, standing nearly six feet six inches in his socks, a height which seemed even more towering when he stood with his wife who was barely five feet tall.

Carl made such a good impression during the interviews that one prominent Norwegian republican wrote to the Foreign Secretary, "We will achieve security and be better equipped for further enterprises through a dynasty . . . We two old republicans have therefore no choice but to do as Garibaldi did—'After having served the republic throughout his life he chose to serve the King.'"

But all sorts of problems were crowding in, the hesitations of Oscar II, the hostility of the Kaiser Wilhelm to Carl because of his English connections, and a sudden republican outburst from distinguished Norwegian citizens. Young Carl was taken aback by the clamor. Norwegian ministers hurried to Copenhagen to urge him to come at once, but he refused. King Edward VII, apprehensive for the fortunes of his son-in-law, cabled his envoy, "Urge Prince Carl to go to Norway as soon as possible or else a republic will be proclaimed." Carl refused to budge. He insisted that first he must have permission of his King, the 87-year-old Christian IX known as "the father, father-in-law and grandfather of Europe." The old King was agreeable but did not want to offend King Oscar. "No use waiting for Sweden," King Edward VII cabled frantically, but still Carl refused to move.

Desperate diplomacy swung the Kaiser Wilhelm to Carl's

side. King Oscar also prepared to accept the inevitable. Even now Carl would not go. He had been surprised by the republican noises coming from Norway. He was not reassured even when the two great republics, America and France, added their voices in persuading him to accept the throne, fearing for the fate of a small Norwegian republic at the hands of the monarchies.

Day followed day in deadlock; Norwegians, British and Swedes were in despair, and only Carl, knowing his own mind, remained firm. The Norwegians sent Fridtjof Nansen, the explorer and statesman, and the country's national hero to talk Carl round. He found Carl insisting on a plebiscite.

"I thought it would be easy to change his mind," Nansen confessed later in his diary, "but I was faced with a man who had carefully considered the matter from every angle and who replied keenly and dexterously to my objections."

"I do not wish to go against the will of the Norwegian people," Carl told him simply. "But I will not go to Norway as a party King. A King must stand above party politics. I will accept the throne only if it is a task worthy of becoming my life's work. This it will be only if I am wanted by the people and not by a party. Otherwise I would rather remain what I am—a Danish officer."

Nansen, impressed, replied, "What you say convinces me that you are the right man for Norway's throne." He then used the whole immense weight of his international prestige to dazzle Carl with an overwhelming piece of rhetoric. "I," said he pompously, "am speaking on behalf of the Government whose authority and popularity are greater than those of any other government since 1814. Your Majesty can be assured that all the men in the Government will fully support you. Furthermore Bjørnson, the great poet and patriot, the author of our National Anthem and our country's foremost spokesman, will support you with all the means in his power. You will run no risk in accepting the offer."

Carl was unimpressed. "Yes," he said, "That is what you say now. But in twenty years time Bjørnson will be dead and so will you. Then the Norwegians may come to me and say, 'What the devil are you doing here?' "

Carl had his way and the referendum gave him the thundering majority of 259,563 votes to 69,264. He had shown himself both wiser and firmer than eminent statesmen. He had also recognised the difference between stubbornness and the courage of one's convictions, which is one of the true marks of greatness. On November 18, 1905, Prince Carl of Denmark, the democratically elected King of Norway, declared, "With the consent of His Majesty the King, my honourable grandfather, I propose to accept my election . . . and I adopt the name of Haakon VII and give to my son the additional name of Olav. My wife and I pray that God will bless the Norwegian people. As long as we live we will dedicate our future to their honour and happiness."

Haakon and Maud learned to ski, and although the tiny Queen with her old-fashioned English clothes and habits was never able to "Norwegian-ise" herself as her husband did, she became the object of delight and affection among the Norwegian people. Their son Olav, who is 19th in line for the throne of England,* became one of Norway's top ten ski-

---

* First twenty in line, incidentally, are: (1) Prince Charles, (2) Princess Anne, (3) Princess Margaret, (4) Duke of Gloucester, (5) Prince William of Gloucester, (6) Prince Richard of Gloucester, (7) the Duke of Kent, (8) Prince Michael of Kent, (9) Princess Alexandra, (10) the Princess Royal, (11) Earl of Harewood, (12) Viscount Lascelles, (13) Hon. James Lascelles, (14) Hon. Robert Lascelles, (15) Hon. Gerald Lascelles, (16) Henry Lascelles, (17) Princess Arthur of Connaught, (18) Lord Carnegie, (19) King Olav, (20) Prince Harald of Norway.

jumpers, and as a yachtsman he won two gold medals in the 1924 Olympics. He married Princess Märtha, the daughter of Princess Ingeborg of Sweden, thus healing old national wounds, but the Norwegian Family still remains much closer to the British and Danish Royal Families than to the Swedes.

Successive Socialist governments have bitten into many royal prerogatives. The nobility has been abolished and titles nullified. With an aristocracy comprised largely of shipowners and rich bourgeoisie, the Royal Family tended to be left in lonely isolation, but Haakon never ceased to be the true symbol of his country, and it was given to him to have one more period as brilliant as on his accession.

When the Germans invaded Norway in April, 1940, Hitler gave top priority to the capture of the King. (Queen Maud having died in 1938). Haakon and his Government were pelted with Nazi bombs, as they escaped, all the way up the prickly spine of Norway. Once a machine gun bullet hit the ground between King Haakon and Crown Prince Olav as they lay together in a ditch. Some members of the Government, their nerve failing, felt they should accede to Hitler's demand that they turn the reins of Government over to the traitor, Vidkun Quisling. Grey-faced with weariness and anger, the King said that if this was done he would abdicate. By this announcement the weak were strengthened, and Norway continued a bulwark of democratic resistance. Throughout the war the sign H7 chalked on the walls was a sign of defiance to the Nazis.

The war started a new and bitter enmity between the royal Houses of Sweden and Norway. The Germans in their invasion of Norway were allowed by the Swedes to move freely over Swedish territory, an act which the Norwegians have never forgotten and for which the Swedes profess themselves duly ashamed. Haakon, moreover, was convinced that the man responsible for this sibling betrayal was old King Gustav who had been unswervingly pro-German throughout the war. When he returned, victorious, to Norway in 1945 King Haakon swore he would never set foot on Swedish soil while "that old scoundrel" was alive. He kept his word. He came to Sweden to attend King Gustav's funeral.

In 1957 King Haakon's great reign came to an end. He died at the age of 85. The succession, however, was secure and without crisis although Olav's elder daughter, Ragnhild, in 1953 had married a commoner in circumstances not dissimilar to the Townsend affair in England, and departed to South America. Her husband, Erling Svend Lorentzen, was the son of a shipowner, and as an officer in the Norwegian Army had had the task of looking after the two small princesses, Ragnhild and Astrid, during World War II. The marriage caused a minor flurry in Norway but Haakon put an immediate stop to controversy by recognising the match and permitting Ragnhild to keep her title. The second daughter, Astrid, a beautiful, serious and very much Anglicised girl, born in 1932, embarked on what can be termed a career of maidenhood. With her mother, Princess Märtha, dead since 1954, and her father, King Olav, unlikely to marry again, it fell to her to act both as first lady of Norway and also as big sister to her brother, Crown Prince Harald, heir to the throne. Harald, brought up in the Norwegian sporting tradition, is an expert skier, and on entering the Army rose to the most difficult rank in the service, that of sergeant. Not until Harald marries will Astrid consider herself also free to marry.

South, in Denmark the Royal Family have added another three to the plethora of young Nordic princesses. Margrethe,

Benedikte and Anne-Marie, the daughters born to King Frederik IX and Queen Ingrid, together with Sweden's four, Holland's four and Norway's two, make an unusual total of thirteen girls as against two boys in the same families; and of all the girls only one, Ragnhild is married so far.

Queen Ingrid is the daughter of King Gustaf Adolf of Sweden and his first wife Princess Margaret of Connaught, and she combines the vigorous, precise manner of an upper-class Englishwoman with the liberal confidence of the Swede. The Danish girls joke together with their mother in public and comment about one another to outsiders. When Margrethe, at a public function in 1957, trod on her mother's dress, the Queen turned, and in front of other people exclaimed to her awkward, big-boned daughter, "Good heavens, child! Watch where you are going!" A remark calculated to endear a sovereign to her subjects more than any number of speeches from the throne.

Margrethe was born on April 16, 1940, exactly a week after the Germans had overrun the country. Occupation posed different problems for Denmark than for other countries because the Nazis were in Copenhagen before the Danes knew how to act. King Christian X, then seventy years old, agreed that Denmark should accept occupation under protest, but relations between the two countries soon deteriorated. In 1942 Hitler decided that a birthday telegram he had received from the King was too cold and used it as an excuse to intensify the German oppression in Denmark. Meanwhile a second daughter, Benedikte, was born in 1944 to Frederik and Ingrid. The war ended and in 1946 a third child was born, Anne-Marie. King Christian died in 1947, his health broken by the sufferings of the war years. Frederik became King and Margrethe was acknowledged specifically by the Danish Government as heir to the throne in her own right. Margrethe was growing into a freckled happy girl, engaging rather than pretty, with a vivid, Nordic smile. It will be interesting in future years to compare the temper of the two reigning Queens of northern Europe, Margrethe of Denmark and Beatrix of Holland, the former a girl with an excellent sense of the amusing and absurd, the latter inheriting the pugnacity of her grandmother, Wilhelmina.

King Frederik has the versatility one associates with Scandinavian Kings. He is an accomplished musician and when he gets time off from his duties he often conducts Denmark's leading symphony orchestras. With the Danish State Radio Symphony Orchestra he has conducted Cesar Franck's symphony, Sibelius's second symphony, and Beethoven's E flat major concerto with Edwin Fischer as soloist. On the seventieth birthday of his father-in-law, King Gustav Adolf, he conducted the Swedish Court Orchestra in Stockholm. Frederik's naval training has left him with a memento rare in Kings, a chest and arms thick with tattoos.

All princes seem to be German to some degree or other, but equally it can be said that most princes, until the generation which has now reached middle age, were Germans trying to be Englishmen. An English manner of dressing and behaving, an acquiring of English tastes in living, combined with a Teutonic heaviness of accent has been, until now, the almost unvarying characteristic of the European sovereign and prince, and is reaching its final expression in men like Bernhard of Holland, Paul of Greece, Don Juan of Spain, and Frederik of Denmark. It had its faults, this type, but it had its virtues too. The next generation will see more nationalistically-trained Kings like Harald in Norway, Carl-Gustaf in Sweden and Constantine in Greece, Kings who will turn less to England or Germany for inspiration than to their own countries.

The passing of old ways of life is always sad to witness but the new breed of prince is likely to be better equipped to deal with the temper of the times than the traditional breed. A pressure exists on monarchy that has never been known before. A King's every thought is revealed in the popular press almost before he has time to think it. The more the emphasis is laid upon how "democratic" a Royal Family is in the newspapers the more isolated from life and the more dehumanised it seems to become in real life. Only six monarchs ago in England, King William IV could spit through the window of his carriage as he drove on state occasions; today it is considered indecorous for Queen Elizabeth to kiss her children in public after she returns to London Airport from long trips abroad.

In the search for a human balance the Scandinavians lead the way. They have abdicated many of their royal functions to successive welfare state governments but they have kept their thrones as living things. The Scandinavian Houses may not be so regal as the British House, but the fact must be faced that they are more dynamic monarchies. It would be a tragedy incalculable if the reign of Queen Elizabeth II which began in such a blaze of excitement should recede into utter unreality, and if Britain, the most civilised and urbane of all the world's democracies should set itself aside and mutely watch the institution that gives it grandeur slowly suffocate itself in its own stuffiness. The British monarchy is the hope of Kings and an appeal to some of the most noble instincts of the world. One does not need to be British to love it, and no betrayal of their national systems is involved for those foreigners who give it reverence. The British monarchy could learn much from Scandinavia, but has it done so? How the British monarchy stands today will be considered in the final chapter, with its sister monarchy, the Dutch. These two are the most powerful in the world and if they were to fail none of the others could succeed.

# XVI

## The Dutch and the British

### The Vital Thrones

They're changing guards at Buckingham Palace./Christopher Robin went down with Alice./"They've great big parties inside the grounds./I wouldn't be King for a hundred pounds."/Says Alice.

—A. A. Milne

*C*onstitutional monarchy, based as it is on advice, tradition, precedent, leaves a monarch very uncertain about making important decisions on his own. In 1956 the Dutch Royal Family ran headlong into a crisis that might have been avoided but wasn't, and found themselves trapped by scandal. They were then saved, not by their wisdom but by the wisdom of their subjects. Family and subjects united. They closed ranks against the outside world and together they willed the crisis to death.

Nothing took the newspapers more by surprise than the revelation, in the summer of 1956, that a faith healer had secured a position of influence at the Dutch court. Rasputins could be conjured up for Russia, but not for Protestant Holland with its deeply loved, motherly Queen and her sophisticated consort. The story dated from 1948, when Queen Juliana, then Princess Juliana, the mother of three daughters, Beatrix, Irene and Margriet, came down with German measles in the early weeks of her fourth pregnancy. She and her mother, Queen Wilhelmina, praying for a son and heir to end the succession of royal Queens, agreed to hope for the best, rather than interrupt the pregnancy as doctors advised. Juliana gave birth to a fourth daughter, Marijke, who was born blind in one eye and with limited vision in the other.

The world's specialists were called, but there was no improvement. As Marijke grew it appeared to outsiders that she could see better than her distracted parents imagined. A pleasing, funny girl, she had that plaintive charm that thick glasses always give to small children and she was adored by both her family and the Dutch people. She had a quick ear for music, something unheard of in the House of Orange-Nassau where it is said the Queen Wilhelmina could only recognise the Dutch National Anthem when she saw people rise to their feet. Marijke played the piano early and even began to compose her own tunes. Her personality was irresistible. On one occasion she bobbed down in a curtsey to President Coty who was visiting Holland.

*"Bonjour, Monsieur le President,"* she said.

*"Formidable,"* cried the President of France in delight. *"Tu parles francais un peu."*

*"Pas peu,"* piped Marijke indignantly. *"Beaucoup."* Disarming quirks of character which, however, in view of her affliction, hurt rather than gave joy to her parents.

Eventually, Prince Bernhard heard reports of a faith-healer, Greet Hofmans, a disciple of Gurdjieff, whose abilities had been tested by some of his personal friends. That Mlle. Hofmans claimed to be in personal contact with God should have given Bernhard pause, but his anxiety for his child was too great. Hofmans was admitted to the Court, where she promised to cure Marijke in a year. The year passed. Marijke's sight did not improve, but Greet Hofmans showed no disposition to leave. On the contrary, Queen Juliana had now fallen under her influence, and Queen Wilhelmina too, to the dismay of Mrs. Eleanor Roosevelt, a family friend, who came to visit. The Queen's ladies-in-waiting were also affected.

Bernhard, who had brought the healer to the Court in the first place, found himself being isolated. Unexpectedly, after two years, the story broke, and an incredible six months began for Holland. Enemies of Bernhard—as a German, a *Mof* by Dutch slang, he had more than a few—said that he himself had leaked the story to a British journalist in order to bring the crisis to a head. Juliana missed audiences with foreign dignitaries and took off to Sicily, where she was hounded by photographers. Bernhard went to America. They did not meet each other on their return. Things went from bad to worse, culminating in one of the Queen's advisers uttering fantastic allegations against Bernhard, accusing him of plotting to force Juliana from the throne and set Princess Beatrix in her place.

In this undignified name-calling one thing emerged as an example to the family—the dignity of the Dutch people. They were aghast at the revelations, and simply closed their minds to it. Foreign tourists questioning taxi drivers, barbers and concierges, those walking gazettes, were met with silence. In their homes the Dutch did not discuss it. Journalists arriving from all over the world were headed off and maliciously short-circuited. The Dutch newspapers reported as little as they could. Resentment arose among the Dutch against the British, who they suspected wanted to export a new abdication crisis to Holland for sensation purposes.

It would not have been uncharacteristic of sovereigns if the Dutch royal couple had not even noticed this agonised loyalty of their people. One recurring fault of sovereigns is a tendency to ingratitude. Alexander II of Russia, in a passion, called his subjects "cattle," although in fairness it must be said that later they did blow him to bits. History suggests that Kings do not always deserve the loyalty their people give them.

They are too quick to resentment, and do not see that even the most outrageous intrusions into their private life are usually the motivations of love and goodwill. *"On ne pardonne rien a ceux de notre rang,"* said Louis XIV of his subjects. The opposite is the case. Subjects want to excuse their sovereigns everything.

To their great credit Juliana and Bernhard did notice how well, and under what tension, their subjects were carrying themselves, and abruptly they killed the crisis dead. Greet Hofmans was curtly dismissed from the Court. They both appeared to realise that everybody had suffered from a crisis that had arisen out of the best intentions all around, themselves, their people, their children, and especially Marijke. Then they began to re-emerge in public. "Together again!" headlined the British and French press. The Dutch press pretended not to have noticed anything amiss in the first place.

A new approach was made to the little princess. Instead of being watched every moment of the day she was allowed to wander, taking her tumbles as they came. She became more self-reliant. She learned to ride a bicycle and soon she was cycling along public highways to school. The faith-healer was slowly forgotten. The breach was healed, or at least kept within the walls of Soestdijk Palace, and Holland climbed back on to her solid feet once more. It was a noble end to an ungracious story.

But it is Britain, the mightiest of the monarchies, that is also the most troubled. Abdication, broken hearts, unlucky associations and almost continuous controversy have dogged the British Crown for more than twenty years. Its popularity has not been impaired but there has been a subtle and not yet calculable sapping of authority.

Until 1957 the Royal Family could usually be guaranteed to keep the headlines black by their own activities, even when they were nothing more important than playing polo on Sundays or following field sports. In 1957 the controversy entered a different phase, when the Royal Family was attacked not for what they did themselves but for what two outside observers, for no immediate reason, were moved to say about them.

The first occurred when Lord Altrincham wrote an article called, "The Monarchy Today" in a magazine, the *National and English Review*, which he edited, the second when Malcolm Muggeridge, former editor of *Punch* wrote an article called, "Does England Really Need a Queen?" for the *Saturday Evening Post*. Both articles created sensations.

The first was an attack on the Queen herself, her way of speaking and dressing, her advisers and the allegedly narrow, stilted circle of her friends. Lord Altrincham wrote as a declared monarchist seeking to be constructive. He confessed to friends that he wrote the article bluntly because if he did not no one would have taken any notice. Publicity being his aim, he succeeded probably more than he anticipated. In the subsequent uproar he was, among other things, slapped by a stranger in the street after a broadcast and challenged to a duel by an Italian. Malcolm Muggeridge wrote a scholarly article on the British monarchy, but marred it with some phrases wide open to misinterpretation. He said, for example, that "duchesses" considered the Queen "dowdy, frumpish and banal." Muggeridge left the "duchesses" anonymous, but their ilk may have sounded familiar. "Duchesses" became something of a dirty word after the 1936 Abdication. The duchesses and others whose idol was Edward VIII, were prepared to find Mrs. Simpson "charming" until the Abdication, when they scrambled for cover and suddenly could not recall having ever met either. Presumably also the same duchesses would overlook the Queen's dowdiness, banality and frumpishness if she ever bothered to encourage them.

This and a few other comments were not really offensive when taken in Muggeridge's general context. Unfortunately for Muggeridge, his comments were ripped right out of context and bannered across the front pages.

There is little doubt that much of the attack on Muggeridge was personal. A brilliant, caustic, iconoclastic man, he seems consciously to have cultivated for his own humour the impression, quite an erroneous one, that he is a rather nasty person. Having chastised so many others during his career he could hardly complain if he took some punishment in return, nevertheless he could argue in this case that he had been grievously ill-used. He appealed to the British Press Council to study the article on its merits, and they decided against him in a deplorably biased summing-up. Muggeridge, who had often been forecast as the next editor of the *Times* found that his career, temporarily, had taken a dive because of an article which, as he said with understandable bitterness, almost nobody in Britain had read in its entirety.

Neither Altrincham nor Muggeridge said anything revolutionary. They merely demonstrated—both unconsciously—the existence of a new and ominous attitude to monarchy that has been growing not only in Britain but in every country where monarchy is a subject of interest.

This assumes that there are two laws of personal conduct, one to be applied to human beings, and one to monarchs. Neither critic seemed to consider even in passing that the Queen was a person at all. Lord Altrincham in criticising the Queen's manner, her way of speaking and her taste in clothes, said things no gentleman should say about a lady. Had the remarks been made about his own wife he would have knocked the offender down. Muggeridge in dismissing King George VI's broadcasts as "funereal," did not add that what made them funereal was a gathering ill-health and that the last broadcast was painfully pieced together a few words at a time over a period of days by a dying man.

"You will have to learn a lesson I learned many years ago," said Princess Aspasia of Greece to her daughter, the present ex-Queen Alexandra of Yugoslavia. "An important lesson for exiles. You must learn to live one day at a time. Tomorrow is always soon enough to think of tomorrow." This is the essence of the royal dilemma. Almost every chapter in this book has been a chronicle of tragedy. Not even the most confident monarch can be sure that the whole edifice of his life will not be swept away tomorrow. Royalty is an increasingly hazardous game played by generally honest people and handed down willy nilly to innocent children. The killing of a politician, whether by an assassin or by a firing squad, may be deprecated, but one can at least say that nobody asked him to be a politician in the first place. Kings and Queens run risks from the day they are born until the day they die. Their palaces and hunting lodges, jewels, cars and their thousand memories may be torn from them at any time. Their childhood is haunted by elders who whisper behind hands of assassination, exile, the possible dangers of in-breeding which monarchs even to-day seem only uncertainly to understand ("The he's-your-cousin objection," as ex-Queen Alexandra, that admirable chronicler of inarticulate royal thinking, expresses it.).

Almost every published collection of royal letters is a torrent of grief. Nine of the Romanovs who wept over the deathbed of the assassinated Tsar Alexander II in March, 1881, were themselves to die a similar death. Even to recall a single generation is to encounter an appalling series of disasters. Prince Philip's father, after imprisonment, died in empty and lonely exile, his mother remaining a religious recluse in Greece. Peter of Yugoslavia's father murdered. Don Juan's father dethroned and humiliated. Bernhard's mother persecuted by the Nazis, Baudoin's mother killed, his father and stepmother reviled. Only the Scandinavian houses have largely survived the tragedy of their southern cousins, because the wash of history has generally stopped at their doorsteps.

This should not, of course, be taken too far. Sovereigns like to be sovereigns. That is part of the charm of the system. The time monarchy looks unhealthiest is when sovereigns do not appear to enjoy their job, as in Belgium today or in Britain in 1936. It is manifestly clear that Queen Elizabeth thoroughly enjoys being Queen and it is right that it should be so. Most monarchs out of power fight furiously to get back, and waste away when they fail.

The chief complaint royal families have about their own everyday existence is the intrusion into their private life, but this is nothing new. The masses have always taken a vicarious interest in what their monarchs were doing. In France they pressed their noses against the windows of Versailles Palace to watch royal banquets and even *accouchements*. In London blows were exchanged frequently over the merits of Charles II's two mistresses, Louise de Keroualle, who was French and Catholic, and Nell Gwynn, who was English and Protestant. One time Nell Gwynn was almost mobbed by a furious crowd in Oxford who mistook her for her rival, until she called, "Pray, good people, be civil. I am the Protestant whore." The more decorous nineteenth century did not spare its monarchs. The Emperor Franz Joseph resented having to show "sparkling intelligence" in public but he had to because "all the

twaddle I talk appears in the press." And his opinion of journalists: "reptiles."

Queen Elizabeth is the first sovereign of the Saxe-Coburg-
Gotha-Hanover-Windsor line to have British blood, through
her mother. At the time of Coronation in 1953, the Empire
and most of the world gave itself over to a frenzy of devotion
and daydreaming. The most outrageous flattery, the most
wildly improbable forecasts of glory were hardly uttered before they became pale by statements which followed and surpassed them. It was, to put it mildly, enough to make the most
modest Queen's head spin.

The Empire may have deceived itself but Elizabeth did
not and it is she alone who is to be congratulated for it. No
amount of good advice from husband, courtiers or ministers
would have prevented Elizabeth from succumbing to the
tumult had her head been spinnable. Whether by lucid reasoning or some gift of temperament, she did not. She neither let
herself be carried away by it, which would have been easy, nor
did she try to live up to it, which would have been impossible.
She remained the person she was, kept the same circle of un-
ambitious friends, and in her spare time indulged her sporting
interests. As the Coronation marathon gradually closed, leaving Britain once again with such problems as a dwindling
Empire, inflation, declining influence and finally Suez, the rosy
talk about a "new Elizabethan era" was left on the scrapheap
with the paper hats and false noses. The Queen went her own
way, and the hangover began to twinge. The woman who was
to rekindle the flame of Britain's greatness in 1953 was the
same person that one of her critics found such a "pain in the
neck" in 1957.

It is true, on the other hand, that Queen Elizabeth does
not give the impression of authority that her father and
grandfather did. This is something almost indefinable.

Neither George V nor George VI had anything more than a cautionary influence on policy of any sort. It was merely the sense they gave that they were *there*.

Of the serious illness which King George V suffered in 1929, Sir Harold Nicolson wrote: "The people of Great Britain, faced with the possibility of the King's death, were startled by the realisation of how much each one cared. Men and women were surprised, not only by the intensity of their own feelings, but also the reflection of that intensity in others. It came as a revelation to many that here was no transitory wave of mass sentiment, but a personal anxiety shared by all. Rarely has an emotion been so intimate and so diffused."

The portrait of George VI which carries longest in the mind is that painted by Winston Churchill in a speech at Edinburgh in 1942, two years after the Blitz: "I have seen the King, gay, buoyant, and confident when the stones and rubble of Buckingham Palace lay newly scattered in heaps upon its lawn." One could have wished that George VI had been on the throne at the time of Suez, not that he could ever have prevailed against the hysterical advocates of the adventure but that his instinctive sense of moderation might at least have been heard; and his presence would have eased the pain of the aftermath.

Such events as a royal illness or a prince's marriage problems used to put a pall over the entire country. How the subjects of monarchies respond automatically to the monarchical instinct was shown by a significant incident concerning Sir Stafford Cripps shortly after World War II. Cripps was Chancellor of the Exchequer and perhaps the most dedicated Socialist in the whole of Clement Attlee's Cabinet. One might go further and say that if one scoured all Britain for a republican one might emerge with only Sir Stafford Cripps. As Chancellor one of the items he had to consider was a legacy of £20,000 left by the Hon. Mrs. Ronald Greville, the famous hostess, to Queen Victoria Eugenie of Spain, then living in Switzerland. The Queen, an Englishwoman, had applied for the legacy to be converted into Swiss francs so that she could buy a home for her declining years.

If any application invited derision from a good Socialist this one did. The war was scarcely over and the Treasury was hungry for foreign currency. Swiss francs were as eagerly sought and as jealously guarded as American dollars. The Labour Party bayed for expensive Socialist reforms, all at the expense of private property. But the appeal of a British princess for assistance to sustain her traditional royal obligations was too much for Stafford Cripps. For the moment Socialism could wait. He passed the application.

For Queen Elizabeth the unique chemistry of monarchy, the progressive accretion of wisdom that comes from continuing experience of governments, has not had time to work. She has had a harder education than her predecessors. In the first all-important twelve years of his reign, King George V knew only two Prime Ministers, Asquith and Lloyd George. By the time the twenties came, with Prime Ministers coming and going in rapid succession (or more precisely Baldwin and MacDonald backing and advancing in turn) the King was wise enough to make his experience felt. King George VI had four Prime Ministers in his reign of fifteen years, but twelve years were spent in association with two outstanding ones, Winston Churchill and Clement Attlee.

It is said that George VI, feeling he had not much longer to live, himself persuaded Attlee to dissolve the impotent Parliament of 1950 because he wished to leave a country in good working order to his daughter. The request and the acceptance does both men honour. In Queen Elizabeth's first seven years of reign she had three Prime Ministers: Sir Winston Churchill, Sir Anthony Eden, and Mr. Harold Mac-Millan.

The Churchill that served her for her first three years was an old Churchill and slower than at his best, but none the less inimitable. A young Queen served by the greatest states-man of his age, a hero of Omdurman and the Boer War, makes an almost unimaginable bridge between past and future. The twenty-first century may see the Queen hale at seventy-three years, and rash ministers still unborn may hear a Queen say, "Sir Winston Churchill told me . . ." and be transported back more than a century. It could be a sobering experience.

But can the British monarchy wait that long? It is obvious that a royal crisis of major proportions is about to descend on Britain within the next few years. Of this there can be no doubt. The panoply of British monarchy was conceived to symbolise the greatest Empire the world has ever known. It looks somewhat forlorn symbolising a second-rate power which almost bankrupted itself fighting an unsuccessful two-day war against Egyptians who had already been beaten by the Israelis anyway. Reality can be blinked at for only so long.

The Altrincham-Muggeridge articles were an indication that something has gone wrong since the proud days of 1953. What? One thing that has affected the authority of the British crown in recent years has been the all-out press attack on the Establishment, on the Church of England, on successive Arch-bishops of Canterbury, on individual members of the Court, and influential aristocrats like the Duke of Norfolk and the Marquess of Salisbury. The attitude of the Church towards divorce is derided as archaic, and never an Ascot goes by without funny remarks about the ban on divorced people in the Royal Enclosure. The Queen herself, who is head of the Church of England, is almost never mentioned in these attacks, but with each new criticism, the royal authority is made to look a little less dignified, the crown tilts more rakishly on the head.

A second reason is the timidity of those around the throne —and this is not restricted to Britain. The Holland crisis demonstrates that people will still rally round when its Royal Family is in trouble, yet monarchs themselves seem sometimes to have the impression that one false move in any direction will bring on them the fate of King Feisal of Iraq. The consequence is that while royalty is holding its ground it is not progressing. What we live with today is a Cheshire Cat monarchy, consisting of a bright smile surrounded by nothing, a frightened, timorous, monarchy hoping not to be noticed so that the death sentence may be delayed; and which may hope for no better epitaph than:

> It is the curse of our proud dynasty,
> To move half-heartedly, stop half way,
> And adopt half measures hesitatingly.

Royal advisers—not without reason—fear to make a bold move because experience has shown that the wrong move has often meant—literally—death. They erroneously identify vigorous monarchy with absolute monarchy. But there are many functions for Kings beyond simple ceremonial, a vast area from which they have unnecessarily abdicated.

To take just one example there have been many suggestions that the Queen Mother Elizabeth be appointed Governor-General of Canada. It may be a good idea or a bad one, but it is worth thinking about. If Canada loves the Crown as much as it keeps saying it does then Mr. Vincent Massey, the Governor General is no substitute. Once more timidity prevails. One can safely wager that the idea has never been seriously discussed at the required levels, not because it is undesirable or necessarily impractical but because the Queen's advisers would never dare to bring the matter up. The issue belongs in the wasteland of lethargy and inertia to which all royal issues are consigned. "Let well alone," is now the royal motto.

And lastly, but not least in the decline of English monarchy since the accession of Elizabeth seems to be the distrust which the Mountbatten family continues to inspire among certain sections of the British nobility. The Queen's consort, constitutionally, can take no part in the sovereign's function. In the present case it means that the most dynamic member of the Royal Family, the one person who has experienced poverty, war and tragedy, and who is temperamentally suited for bringing the monarchy closer to the British people, is tied and silenced. That would be true even if the Duke of Edinburgh were not a Mountbatten but he is, and he seems to carry an air about him that makes the Queen's advisers jump like rabbits at his approach. He is too tough, too assured for the comfort of more deprecating courtiers. The decision to send Prince Charles to normal British schools is considered by the experts to be a Mountbatten victory over the more decorous elements in British court life who would prefer Charles to follow the rigid, lonely, traditional palace education of his ancestors.

But the present equilibrium can go on for only so long. If the Queen's standing is not so high as it was at the time of her accession the fault lies not with the Queen but with a Britain whose decline has been more rapid than anyone expected. The Queen is prevented by her sex, years, upbringing and isolated position from making the Monarchy a personal thing to her subjects, as her father and grandfather did. The Prince of Wales is too young to carry the emotional capital which the Commonwealth has sunk into the British Royal Family. Some orientation of royal responsibility towards the

Duke of Edinburgh may sooner or later become necessary unless the British Crown is to lose all sense of modern reality. The Queen is the symbol of British glory, but the Duke is the personification of a sports-playing, weekend-motoring, movie-going Britain of more modest aspirations. As it is, things may already have gone too far.

A small incident which occurred in the British press, in the summer of 1958, may mean nothing or it may mean a great deal. On Saturday, July 26, the Queen created Prince Charles Prince of Wales. The announcement was made at the end of the Empire Games meeting at Cardiff and was greeted with jubilation by 36,000 Welshmen in the audience. Next day the story was bannered across the front pages of every Sunday newspaper but one. The exception was the London *Sunday Pictorial* which many—perhaps most—observers consider the Sunday paper with the surest sense of British public opinion, particularly working-class opinion. The *Pictorial* decided that the British people could not care less that Charles was Prince of Wales, buried the story on an inside page and gave the lead to a story about atomic bombs. Perhaps they are right, and if they are it is a sad day for British monarchy.

An institution can no more stay immobile and unchanging than a human being can. It must wax or wane, progress or regress. The first requirement of all European monarchy is that it lose its chronic defeat complex and concentrate on its more dynamic members and its more dynamic ideas, the Salem idea, for example, for the creation of the modern prince. Monarchy can disappear from the earth in the next ten years. On the other hand, in the same period the monarchies of Europe could almost double themselves. Portugal, Spain, even France, even Austria, could find themselves with Kings and a corresponding guarantee of political stability.

Monarchy is not just a state of mind or a sentiment. It is a living organism dating from the very sources and responding to the earliest yearnings of history, and if it is not nurtured it will wither away. If Philip, Otto, the Count of Paris, Ernst August and the rest, are keeping the idea alive it is so that they may be ready for a future that cannot yet be foreseen, for an opportunity which, if it comes at all, can come once only and fleetingly, and must be seized if princes are not to become as dead as the Doges:

> Strange clouded fragments of an ancient glory,
> Late lingerers of the community divine,
> (Breathing) of that far world wherefrom they came,
> Lost halls of heaven and Olympian air.